✳ The American Establishment and Other Reports,
Opinions, and Speculations

* RICHARD H. ROVERE

The American Establishment
and Other Reports, Opinions, and
Speculations

 GREENWOOD PRESS, PUBLISHERS
WESTPORT, CONNECTICUT

Library of Congress Cataloging in Publication Data

Rovere, Richard Halworth, 1915-
    The American establishment, and other reports,
opinions, and speculations.

    Reprint of the 1st ed. published by Harcourt, Brace &
World, New York.
    1. United States--Politics and government--1945-
--Addresses, essays, lectures.   I.   Title.
[E743.R68 1980]   973.92   80-22247
ISBN 0-313-22646-6 (lib. bdg.)

This is a reprint of the First Edition.

Reprinted with the permission of Harcourt Brace Jovanovich, Inc.

Reprinted in 1980 by Greenwood Press,
A division of Congressional Information Service, Inc.
88 Post Road West, Westport, Connecticut 06881

Printed in the United States of America

10 9 8 7 6 5 4 3 2 1

For Mark

THE FIRST SECTION of this book exhausts its author's knowledge of the subject treated therein. Those who wish to know more about the Establishment are advised to buy the New York *Times* and read between the lines. They may also consult their friendly local F.B.I. agent and the House Committee on Un-American Activities.

Peter J. McGuinness, of Greenpoint, Brooklyn, died in 1948. He was a peerless leader, and Brooklyn's Assistant Commissioner of Borough Works, to the end.

The pieces on Truman and Dewey in 1948, Newbold Morris in 1952, the "kept witnesses" in 1955, and Ezra Pound in 1957 appear exactly as they were when first published. They are unchanged because they seemed to me to have some documentary interest that would be lessened by revision.

As for the rest of the book: in general, I have regarded republication as a second knock by opportunity. I have cut, I have amplified, I have rewritten. I have even fused articles done at different times for different publications. In such cases, the date used is that of the later, or latest, publication.

The appreciation of George Orwell is taken from *The Orwell Reader*, published by Harcourt, Brace and Company in 1956. "The Kept Witnesses" was originally prepared as a report for the Fund for the Republic. All the rest were commissioned by magazines. My thanks for permission to use them here go to the proprietors of *The American Scholar, Confluence, Esquire, Harper's, The New Republic, The New Yorker, The Progressive, The Reporter,* and the *Spectator* of London. Approximately half were written in the first instance for *The New Yorker,* whose editor, William Shawn, has counseled me wisely and with unfailing kindness for eighteen years.

Technical and literary consultants on this project were F. W. Dupee, Margaret Marshall, Frederick Q. Shafer, and Gore Vidal. Assistant production managers were Ann Rovere and Julianna Ruhland. Special effects by Eleanor Rovere and Elizabeth Rovere.

R.H.R.

New York
February 1962

✳ Contents

4 Judgments Reserved

PART ONE

THE AMERICAN ESTABLISHMENT

* The American Establishment *

To understand the United States today, it is
necessary to know something about the Establishment.
Most citizens don't realize it exists. Yet the
Establishment makes its influence felt from the
President's Cabinet to the professional life of a
young college teacher who wants a foundation
grant. It affects the nation's policies in almost
every area.—*The News & Courier*, CHARLESTON, S. C.
October 18, 1961

IT IS NOW, of course, conceded by most fair-minded and objective
authorities that there is an Establishment in America—a more or
less closed and self-sustaining institution that holds a preponder-
ance of power in our more or less open society. Naturally, Establishment leaders pooh-pooh the whole idea; they deny the Existence of the Establishment, disclaim any connection of their own
with it, and insist that they are merely citizens exercising citizens'
rights and responsibilities. They often maintain that the real
power is held by some other real or imagined force—the voters,
the Congress, Madison Avenue, Comsymps, the rich, the poor, and
so forth. This is an ancient strategy; men of power have always
known how to use it. "Wouldst thou enjoy first rank?" St. John

* Some of this material originally appeared in *The American Scholar*
("Notes on the Establishment in America," Vol. 30, No. 4, Autumn 1961,
pp. 489-495). Many readers professed to be puzzled by my approach. Some
even asked if I intended my work to be taken seriously. I found their
questions disheartening and, I might as well add, more than a bit offensive.
They cast doubt not only on my own integrity but on that of the distinguished journal which had the courage to publish my findings. *The
American Scholar* is, after all, an official publication of the United Chapters
of Phi Beta Kappa. Its editors, of whom I am one, would certainly not be
parties to a hoax.

3

Chrysostom wrote. "Then cede it to another." * The *News &
Courier* is absolutely right.

Conceptions of the Establishment, to be sure, differ widely,
just as do conceptions of the Church, the State, and other important institutions. Hilary Masters, a leading member of the
Dutchess County school of sociologists, defined it in a recent
lecture† as "the legitimate Mafia."‡ To William F. Buckley, Jr.,

* *Homilies*, c. 388.

† Before the Edgewater Institute, Barrytown, N.Y., July 4, 1961. *Vide
Proceedings*, 1961, pp. 37-51. Also see Masters' first-rate monograph *Establishment Watering Places*, Shekomeko Press, 1957.

‡ It was the figure of speech, not the actual analogy, that seemed so striking
and appropriate. Actually, the analogy was not actual—and doubtless was
not intended to be regarded as such. The Establishment exists; the Mafia
does not exist. Modern scholarship has pretty well destroyed the myth of the
Mafia. *Vide* "The Myth of the Mafia," in *The End of Ideology*, by Daniel Bell,
The Free Press, Glencoe, Illinois, 1960. Bell cites a report by Serrell Hillman,
a highly reputable journalist who went all over the country to find out if
there really was a Mafia at work. He checked in at the Federal Bureau of
Investigation and asked the top men there if they believed in the Mafia.
They said they did not. Chicago Crime Commission—same story. Hillman
could not check with the Central Intelligence Agency because it is forbidden
by statute to intervene in domestic affairs. But he did talk with innumerable
police officials, criminal lawyers, criminals, private detectives, and the like
—none of whom could put him on the trail of the Mafia. He was eventually
forced to the conclusion that the only people who believed in it were (1)
Senator Estes Kefauver, of Tennessee; (2) Hearst crime reporters; and (3) the
Treasury Department's Bureau of Narcotics. Senator Kefauver once described
the Mafia in concrete terms. "The Mafia," he said, "is the cement that helps
to bind the Costello-Adonis-Lansky syndicate of New York and the Ac-
cardo-Guzik-Fischetti syndicate of Chicago." This sounds good but isn't. Note
that tricky word "helps." Besides, it is unproved that there is any cement.
If I may interject a purely personal note here, I may say that I have done a
bit of work on my own. One day in the summer of 1960, I was on an airplane (United Airlines, Flight 420) and learned that the Hon. Frank S.
Hogan, District Attorney of New York County, was a fellow passenger. The
air was turbulent, and seat belts had to be fastened, so I could not approach
the famous prosecutor myself. I asked a stewardess if she would deliver a
note to Mr. Hogan. She said she would be delighted. My note read: "Dear
Mr. District Attorney: Is there a Mafia?" His reply was prompt and categori-
cal. "No, Virginia, there is not," he wrote. Still and all, I think that Masters'
phrase caught the spirit of the thing admirably. Dante's *Inferno* was a
product of the imagination, but it has helped many men to approach the
reality of beauty and even the beauty of reality. The Establishment really
is the cement that binds the Rockefeller-Gill-Sulzberger syndicate in New
York to the Stevenson-Field-Sandburg syndicate in Chicago. In the interests
of precision, Masters might have made a slight qualification of the adjective
"legitimate." There are a few places where the Establishment cannot function legally. But of that, more later.

and his collaborators on the *National Review,* it is almost inter-changeable with the "Liberal Machine," which turns out the "Liberal Line." Their Establishment includes just about everyone in the country except themselves* and the great hidden, enlight-ened majority of voters who would, if only they were given the chance, put a non-Establishment man in the White House and have John Kenneth Galbraith recalled from India or left there and relieved of his passport. Galbraith, himself a pioneer in the field of Establishment studies, sees the Establishment as a rather small group of highly placed and influential men who embody the best of the Conventional Wisdom and can be trusted with sub-stantial grants of power by any responsible group in the coun-try. The perfect Establishment type, in his view, would be the Republican called to service in a Democratic administration (*e.g.,* the present Secretary of the Treasury, Douglas Dillon) or the vice versa. "They are the *pivotal* people," he observed in one of his earlier studies. (Italics his.) That was before his appoint-ment as the Establishment's man in New Delhi. (He is not a member of his own Establishment, however, for he could not hope to be held over in a Republican administration.)

The fact that experts disagree on exactly what the Establish-ment is and how it works does not mean that they are talking about different things or about something that does not exist. Experts disagree about the Kingdom of God. This is not an argument against its existence; plainly the Kingdom of God is many things. Differences of opinion over the meaning of "justice" have given rise to one of the most honored professions in the world. One dogmatic Marxist may quarrel with another over the proper "role of the proletariat" and even about who should and who should not be counted as belonging to the "bourgeoisie." This does not make a fiction or a meaningless abstraction of

* It is characteristic of most thinkers and writers on the subject to define the Establishment in such a way as to keep themselves outside it and even victimized by it. Werner von Fromm has suggested that they all tend toward a mild paranoia, and what little clinical evidence there is tends to support him. The one exception known to me is François Grund, a French economist of conservative leanings, who has applied to the Establishment Burke's phrases for the nobility—"an ornament of the civil order . . . the Corinthian capital of . . . society." Both Von Fromm's and Grund's observations are to be found in the 1961 Edgewater *Proceedings.*

either the proletariat or the bourgeoisie. The Establishment can be thought of in many different ways, all of them empirically valid in one or another frame of reference. Masters, Buckley, Galbraith, and Corradini* look upon the Establishment from quite different points of view—which grow in the main out of their differing disciplines—but they would have no difficulty in agreeing that Douglas Dillon is true blue or that, say, Senator Thomas J. Dodd, of Connecticut, is on the outside looking in— disapprovingly, in his case. Despite their differences of emphasis and approach, none of them would have many reservations about the *News & Courier*'s definition:

The Establishment is a general term for those people in finance, business, and the professions, largely from the Northeast, who hold the principal measure of power and influence in this country irrespective of what administration occupies the White House. . . . [It is] a working alliance of the near-socialist professor and the internationalist Eastern banker calling for a bland bi-partisan approach to national politics.†

For my own part, I think the definition is a pretty good one. I would cavil a bit at the notion that "the Establishment is a general term" etc. It is a good deal more than a collective noun, as I shall make clear. Moreover, there is a slight ambiguity in the phrase "principal measure of power." Too many journalists, awed by their observations of the Establishment at work, leap to the conclusion that its power is not only great but invariably decisive. This is by no means the case. There are powerful anti-Establishment forces at work, and frequently they prevail. It seems to me perfectly clear, for example, that the Establishment has never found a way of controlling Congress.‡ Indeed, there

* H. E. Corradini, author of *Patterns of Authority in American Society* (Gainesville Press, 1958). Corradini, an anthropologist, draws a striking parallel between the American Establishment and the Ydenneks, an inter-tribal council that still functions in Canada.

† The newspaper's anti-Establishment bias is plain enough, as is the editorialist's sense of exclusion. "Southerners have no place in the Establishment," he writes, "except for a domesticated handful who have turned their backs on regional beliefs." For "regional beliefs" read Senator J. Strom Thurmond and Governor Orval Faubus.

‡ From time to time, it has managed to hold a balance of power in the Senate, but it has never done even this much in the House. *The Congressional Monthly* for January 1962, surveying the entire performance of the first

are times when Congress appears to be nothing more or less than
a conspiracy to louse up the plans of the Establishment. Whatever
the Establishment wants, it often seems, Congress mulishly op-
poses.

Nor has the Establishment ever made much headway in such
fields as advertising, television, or motion pictures. The basic
orientation of the leaders in all these fields is anti-Establishment,
and what Establishment strength exists is concentrated mainly
on the lower levels—in advertising, the copy writers; in television,
certain of the news departments (most notably at Columbia
Broadcasting); and in the motion pictures, a few writers and ac-
tors. Still, Establishment strength in these areas is generally unim-
pressive. In Hollywood, to take a simple example, ICMPAFPWJ,
the Independent Committee of the Motion Picture Arts for
Freedom and Peace With Justice, an Establishment front, held a
fund-raising meeting in the Beverly-Wilshire Hotel on November 20, 1961. Only twenty-eight persons attended, and the take
for the evening, after eloquent pleas for support from Paul
Newman and Joanne Woodward, was $3,067.50. (Of this amount,
$2,900 was in the form of pledges, only about fifteen per cent of
which, in all likelihood, were actually redeemable. On the very
same evening, at the Beverly Hilton, the National Foundation
for Amoebic Dysentery raised more than five times as much, all
in cash or checks of that date, from three times as many people.)

The Establishment does not control everything, but its influence is pervasive, and it succeeds far more often than its antag-
onists in fixing the major goals of American society. Though it
does not, as I have noted, come anywhere close to controlling
Congress, Congress is everlastingly *reacting* to it. Within the
next couple of years, for example, Congress will spend a good
part of its time fighting the Establishment program for a great
revision of American trade practices and for eventual American
association with the European Common Market. This whole

session of the Eighty-seventh Congress, found that only nineteen members
of the House had Establishment voting records of better than eighty per
cent. Of the nineteen, who accounted for less than five per cent of the total
membership, twelve were Democrats, seven were Republicans. Fourteen were
from the Eastern seaboard, two from California, and one each from Oregon,
Louisiana, and Minnesota.

scheme was cooked up at a three-day meeting of the Executive Committee at the Sheraton-Park in Washington immediately after President Kennedy's inauguration on January 20, 1961.* The odds are heavily against the Establishment winning this battle in 1962 or even in 1963. The important thing, though, is that the Establishment has taken the initiative and put its great antagonist on the defensive. Practically everyone is agreed that in time the victory, even in this difficult matter, will go to the Establishment.

The Establishment is not, of course, at any level a membership organization in the sense that it collects dues, issues cards, or holds meetings openly under its own auspices. It is a coalition of forces, the leaders of which form the top directorate, or Executive Committee—referred to sometimes as "Central." At the lower levels, organization is quite loose, almost primitive in some cases, and this is one of the facts that explains the differences in definition among experts. In the upper reaches, though, certain divisions have achieved a high degree of organization. For instance, the directors of the Council on Foreign Relations make up a sort of Presidium for that part of the Establishment that guides our destiny as a nation.† (The unimpeachable source, a dissident Executive Committee member who leaked the story about the Common Market decision, said that the Gist Subcommittee appointed to work on the Common Market matter had only two members not drawn from the Council.) The presidents and

---

* The meeting had been called not for this purpose alone, but to review the state of the world generally at the start of the new President's term. The question of American intervention in Cuba, for example, was discussed at length and, eventually, tabled because the Committee members were so divided among themselves. A resolution was passed urging President Kennedy to meet with Nikita Khrushchev "at an early date with a view to determining whether any basis for negotiations to reduce tensions presently exists." The Common Market matter came up when Roscoe Gist reported that George Ball, Under Secretary of State for Economic Affairs and himself a Committee member, wished to pressure the United Kingdom into joining the Common Market and looked to a day when we, too, might belong. By a vote of 23-5, with two abstentions, he was authorized to go ahead.

† The President, of course, has Constitutional responsibility for foreign affairs, and I am not suggesting that any recent President has abdicated to the CFR. But policy and strategy are worked out in the Council and reach the President by way of the State Department, which, of course, is largely staffed and always directed by Council members.

senior professors of the great Eastern universities frequently constitute themselves as *ad hoc* Establishment committees. Now and then, the Executive Committee regroups as an Establishment front for some particular end. In the summer of 1961, as a case in point, when anti-Establishment forces in Congress and elsewhere threatened the President's foreign-aid program, the Establishment, at the request of the White House, hastily formed the Citizens' Committee for International Development and managed to bull through a good deal of what the President wanted. The Establishment has always favored foreign aid. It is, in fact, a matter on which Establishment discipline may be invoked.

Summing up the situation at the present moment, it can, I think, be said that the Establishment maintains effective control over the Executive and Judicial branches of government; that it dominates most of American education and intellectual life; that it has very nearly unchallenged power in deciding what is and what is not respectable opinion in this country. Its authority is enormous in organized religion (Roman Catholics* and fundamentalist Protestants to one side), in science, and, indeed, in all the learned professions except medicine. It is absolutely unrivaled in the great new world created by the philanthropic foundations —a fact which goes most of the way toward explaining why so little is known about the Establishment and its workings. Not one thin dime of Rockefeller, Carnegie, or Ford money has been spent to further Establishment studies.†

* It should be noted, though, that it is becoming influential in Catholic journalism. A content survey of twelve leading Catholic periodicals showed thirty-eight per cent of the text to be Establishment-inspired.

† The situation approaches scandal at times. The foundations and universities have subsidized a number of first-rate Establishment scholars. Daniel Bell, H. E. Corradini, Alfred Kazin, and Mary McCarthy have received Guggenheim Fellowships and other such benefactions, but always for something other than Establishment studies. A few universities—Florida, Southern Methodist, Ramona, Virginia Military Institute, and Michigan State—have done what little they could to help out, and so have a few of the less well-heeled foundations. But there is a general lockout in the richer and better-known institutions. Some have even gone so far as to encourage what might be called "red-herring scholarship"—efforts to prove that something other than the Establishment dominates the country. A notorious example is C. Wright Mills' *The Power Elite* (Oxford University Press, 1956). It was subsidized by the Huntington Hartford Foundation, Columbia University's Social Science

If it were not for the occasional formation of public committees such as the Citizens' Committee for International Development, Establishment scholars would have a difficult time learning who the key figures are. Committee rosters serve Establishmentologists in the same way that May Day photographs of the reviewing stand above Lenin's tomb serve the Kremlinologists. By close analysis of them, by checking one list of names against another, it is possible to keep tabs quite accurately on the Executive Committee. A working principle agreed upon by Establishment scholars is this: If in the course of a year a man's name turns up fourteen times in paid advertisements in, or collective letters to, the New York *Times,* the official Establishment daily, it is about fourteen to one that he is a member of the Executive Committee. (I refer, naturally, to advertisements and letters pleading Establishment causes.) There are, to be sure, exceptions. Sometimes a popular athlete or movie actor will, innocently or otherwise, allow himself and his name to be exploited by the Establishment. He might turn up twenty times a year and still have no real status in the institution. But that is an exception. The rule is as stated above.

One important difference between the American Establishment and the party hierarchy in Russia is that the Establishment chairman is definitely *not* the man in the center of the picture or the one whose name is out of alphabetical order in the listings. The secret is astonishingly well kept. Some people, to be sure, have argued that when, as happens most of the time, the Establishment has a man of its own in the White House, he automatically becomes chairman—just as he automatically becomes commander in chief of the armed forces. I am quite certain that this is not the case. For one thing, the Establishment rarely puts one of its tried and trusted leaders in the White House. Dwight Eisenhower and John F. Kennedy have both served the Establishment and been served by it, but neither is or ever was a member of the innermost circle. Both, indeed, were admitted with some reluc-

Research Council, and Brandeis University. Even the parent body, the British Establishment, got into the act through the Oxford University Press, which, Mills admits, went "far beyond the office of publisher in helping me get on with this."

tance on the part of senior members, and Eisenhower's standing has at times been most insecure.

I am not sure who the chairman of the Establishment is today, although I would not be altogether surprised to learn that he is Dean Rusk. By a thrust of sheer intuition, though, I did get the name of the 1958 chairman and was rather proud of myself for doing so. In that year, I discovered that J. K. Galbraith had for some time been surreptitiously at work in Establishment studies, and he told me that he had found out who was running the thing. He tested me by challenging me to guess the man's name. I thought hard for a while and was on the point of naming Arthur Hays Sulzberger, of the New York *Times,* when suddenly the right name sprang to my lips. "John J. McCloy," I exclaimed. "Chairman of the Board of the Chase Manhattan Bank; once a partner in Cadwalader, Wickersham & Taft, and also in Cravath, de Gersdorff, Swaine & Wood, as well as, of course, Milbank, Tweed, Hope, Hadley & McCloy; former United States High Commissioner in Germany; former President of the World Bank; liberal Republican; chairman of the Ford Foundation and chairman—my God, how could I have hesitated—of the Council on Foreign Relations; Episcopalian." "That's the one," Galbraith said. He congratulated me for having guessed what it had taken him so much patient research to discover.

The Establishment is not monolithic in structure or inflexible in doctrine. There is an Establishment "line," but adherence is compulsory only on certain central issues, such as foreign aid. On economic affairs, for example, several views are tolerated. The accepted range is from about as far left as, say, Walter Reuther to about as far right as, say, Dwight Eisenhower. A man cannot be for *less* welfarism than Eisenhower, and to be farther left than Reuther is considered bad taste.* Racial equality is another

---

* Setting the limitations on the left is not much of a problem nowadays, for the left has been inching toward the center at the rate of about seven inches per year; the only extreme positions in this epoch are on the right, and these are inadmissible. It is interesting to consider the change that has come over the Establishment in the last twenty years. In their views on government intervention and related questions, Wendell Willkie in the early forties and Dwight Eisenhower in the early sixties seemed peas from

matter on which the Establishment forbids dissent. Opposition to integration is a cause for expulsion, or at least suspension for not less than a year, unless it is mere "token" opposition. The only *white* Southern members of the Establishment in anything like good standing are reconstructed Southerners or Southerners the Establishment has reason to believe would be reconstructed if political circumstances would allow it. Take Senator J. William Fulbright, of Arkansas. He is a pillar of the Establishment even though he votes with the unenlightened on racial matters. The Council on Foreign Relations gave him an "A-1" rating when he was up for chairman of the Senate Foreign Relations Committee.* The Executive Committee accepts him because it assumes his heart is in the right place. He is, after all, a former Rhodes scholar and a university president. Moreover, the Fulbright scholarships have provided an enormous subsidy for Establishment intellectuals.

The Establishment has lately been having a most difficult time with those of its members—clergy, scientists, and academicians, in the main—who have joined the Committee for a Sane Nuclear Policy. The Executive Committee—in particular that powerful "hard-line" faction led by Dean Acheson and Roscoe Gist—has no use at all for this organization and would deal very sharply with its supporters if they did not include so many people who incorporate most of the Establishment virtues. Exactly what stand it will take remains to be seen.

In nonpolitical affairs, great doctrinal latitude is not only tolerated but encouraged. In religion, the Establishment is rigorously disestablishmentarian. Separatism is another matter on which discipline may be invoked.† Like a city-wide ticket, in

---

the same pod. But Willkie in his time was regarded as an economic liberal, whereas Eisenhower in ours is clearly a conservative. It has been estimated that by 1968, views such as Eisenhower's will be considered excessively rightist—as Barry Goldwater's are today—and will not be tolerated.

* It exercised the veto power, though, when he was proposed as Secretary of State. It wanted Dean Rusk to get the job, and used Fulbright's record on racial questions as an argument against Fulbright's candidacy.

† "The Establishment," the Reverend F. Q. Shafer said, in the first of his 1961 Geist Lectures at Brownlee Seminary, "takes the view that religion is a matter of conscience and has no place in politics or in education. It evidently sees no contradiction between this and its endlessly repeated dictum that politics and education must always be informed by conscience."

New York, the Executive Committee is carefully balanced religiously as well as racially. (The only important difference is that several places are kept for nonbelievers.) The only proscribed views are the noisier ones. Though he now and then gets an audience in the White House, Billy Graham is *persona non grata* in Establishment circles. Bishop Fulton J. Sheen is regarded as a Catholic Billy Graham and is similarly a pariah.

Reinhold Niebuhr is the official Establishment theologian, and Bishop Angus Dun is the chaplain.

In matters of public policy, it may be said that those principles and policies that have the editorial support of the New York *Times* are at the core of Establishment doctrine. And those irregularities and eccentricities that receive sympathetic *consideration* in the *Times* (not only on the editorial page but in the Sunday Magazine and the Book Review) are within the range of Establishment doctrinal tolerance.

It is essential to an understanding of the Establishment to recognize its essentially *national* characteristics. *The whole of its power is greater than the sum of its parts.* Its leading figures have national and international reputations but very often are persons of only slight influence or standing in the cities and states from which they come. Former Chairman McCloy, for example, cuts a lot of ice in Washington, Geneva, Paris, London, Rio de Janeiro, Bonn, Moscow, and Tokyo, but practically none in Manhattan. In Albany, he is almost unknown. The relative weakness of the Establishment in the states undoubtedly helps to explain the shellackings it repeatedly gets in Congress. Statewide—or one might say, statewise—it is often torn by a kind of factionalism that seldom afflicts its national and international operations. In New York, for example, Averell Harriman and Nelson Rockefeller have often found themselves locked in combat like Grant and Lee; in Washington, they are Alphonse and Gaston. And so it goes.

A state-by-state canvass of Establishment strengths and weaknesses was conducted by Perry Associates, a St. Louis firm, in 1959. Some of the highlights follow:

THE AMERICAN ESTABLISHMENT

In three states—Texas, Oklahoma, and North Dakota—the Establishment is virtually outlawed. There are no restrictive or repressive measures on the statute books, but there is persistent harassment by police and other officials. The American Civil Liberties Union had expressed some interest in arranging a test case, but no suitable one was found. Despite constant police surveillance, there is considerable underground Establishment activity in the Dallas area and in San Antonio.

The Indiana authorities are openly hostile to the Establishment, and there has been continuing agitation for a law requiring Establishment agents to register with the Attorney General and be fingerprinted. It is hard to see what would be accomplished by this, for the Perry people could find no trace of Establishment activity anywhere in Indiana, except at Indiana University, in Bloomington. The faculty people there are state employees anyway and can quite easily be dealt with. In neither Nebraska nor Idaho could *any* Establishment influence be found. There were only the faintest traces in Wyoming, New Hampshire, Utah, and Florida.

Florida was the one Southern state in which Establishment forces seemed exceedingly weak. Elsewhere, it was learned, nearly all those who described themselves as "moderates" were actually connected with the Establishment.

The big centers are, as one might expect, the states with large cities and large electoral votes: New York, California, Illinois, Pennsylvania, Ohio, and Massachusetts. A rather surprising case, though, was Kansas, which ranked ahead of New Jersey and Maryland.

For some reason, Establishment studies have attracted few historians. Most of the work thus far has been undertaken by journalists, economists, sociologists, and psychologists. In consequence, very little has been done to uncover the origins of the Establishment. One British historian, Keith E. D. Smith-Kyle, maintains, in *America in the Round* (Polter & Polter, Ltd., London, 1956), that "the American pretense to equality was, to speak bluntly, given the lie by the formation in the early days of the Republic of the sort of 'command' group similar in most

respects to what Britons nowadays speak of as 'the Establishment.' By 1847, when the Century Association was founded in
New York, power had been consolidated in a handful of hands.
From then on, whenever there was a 'laying on of hands,' the
blood in those extremities was the very blood that had coursed
through those that had molded the clay of life in the so-called
Federal period."

It is plain that Smith-Kyle is trying to say, in a roundabout
British way, that a hereditary aristocracy runs the show here. He
is as wrongheaded in this matter as he is in most others.* American students, though they number few trained historians† among
them and none of a celebrity that compares with Smith-Kyle's,
subscribe almost unanimously to the proposition that the Establishment came into being at a far later date—to be exact, as well
as neat, at the turn of the century. They see the institution form-
ing during the administration of Theodore Roosevelt, who by
common consent was the first Establishment President—and in a
way the last.‡ The Founding Fathers of today's group zeroed
in on T. R. as if they had caught him in a perfect bombsight.
Consider them all, a few of them still alive, all of them within
living memory: Henry L. Stimson, William Allen White,
Nicholas Murray Butler, Robert Frost, Albert Beveridge, Abraham Hummel, Joseph Choate, William Travers Jerome, Jacob
Riis, Charles Evans Hughes, Felix Frankfurter, Ida M. Tarbell,
Joseph Pulitzer, Martin Provensen, Lincoln Steffens, Benson
Frost, Learned Hand, W. Adolphe Roberts, Jane Addams,
Nelson W. Aldrich, Eleanor Alice Burgess, John Hay, John Ray,

---

* *Vide* his revolting apology for Munich, *The Noble Experiment* (Heineken,
London, 1939), and his blatantly Stalinist *The Bear and the Jug* (Bafer &
Bafer, 1949).

† Arthur Schlesinger, Jr., has done fairly decent work in the past (*vide
The General and the President*, with Richard H. Rovere) but his judgments
are suspect because of his own connections with the Establishment.

‡ This is a rather fine point. Since Roosevelt's time, every President except Harding and Truman has taken office with full Establishment approval.
So far as can be determined, though, no one has ever gone directly from the
Executive Committee to the office of Chief Executive. Woodrow Wilson is
sometimes cited as an exception, but it is dubious in the extreme that he
was one. Charles Evans Hughes, his 1916 opponent, was an Executive Committee man.

John Jay Chapman, Van Wyck Brooks, Carl Schurz, Hamlin Garland, Oscar Straus, Winthrop Chanler, James R. Bourne, Whitelaw Reid, and Gifford Pinchot.*
There, plainly, was the first Executive Committee!

Some uninformed publicists confuse the Establishment with the Organization. The two could not be more different. The Establishment Man and the Organization Man could not be more different, or more at odds. The Establishment uses the Organization from time to time, as a ruling group must in an industrial and commercial society. But it devoutly hopes that in time the Organization will wither away. The Organization would like to overthrow the Establishment. It had a near success when it ran its 1960 chairman, Richard M. Nixon, for President of the United States.

The New York *Times* has no close rival as an Establishment daily. Technological advance is making it possible for the *Times* to become a national newspaper. This development should add immeasurably to the growth of the institution's powers.

Most Establishment personnel get at least one newspaper besides the *Times,* in order to keep up with Walter Lippmann and Joseph Alsop. Papers that carry both these columnists are in good standing with the Establishment and get a lot of advertising that way.

There are some specialized magazines but none of general circulation that can be described as official or semiofficial organs. I have pondered long over the case of *Time* and have concluded that it has no real place in the Establishment. It goes too far in attacking Establishment positions and it has treated many Establishment members with extreme discourtesy and at times with vulgarity. The Establishment fears *Time,* of course, and it now and then shows cravenness in its attempts to appease it by putting Henry Luce on some commission or other (on freedom of the press, national goals, and so forth), or by giving his wife some

---

* I am indebted for this list to F. W. Dupee's illuminating study "The Suckleys of Wildercliff and the Origins of the Establishment," No. IV in the *Occasional Papers* published by the Mid-Hudson Historical Society. Mr. Dupee is professor of English at Columbia University and perhaps the country's leading authority on Henry James.

political job. But the Luce publications generally must be considered as outside the Establishment.

Now that control of *Newsweek* has passed to Philip L. Graham, publisher of the Washington *Post*, it may be that the Establishment will adopt it as an official weekly.

U.S. News & World Report is widely read but held in low regard.

Foreign Affairs has, within its field, the authority of *Pravda* and *Izvestia*.

Harper's, the *Atlantic*, and the *New Yorker* all have Establishment clienteles but none can be regarded as official. The *Saturday Review* was once heavily patronized but no longer is. The *New Republic* is coming up. The *Nation* has long since gone down. A few of the younger Establishment intellectuals read *Partisan Review*, but the more sophisticated ones regard it as stuffy and prefer *The Noble Savage*, edited by Saul Bellow and issued at irregular intervals by the World Publishing Company.

As Thomas R. Waring, the noted Southern journalist, has pointed out, "The significance of the Establishment can be discovered by finding out who is *not* a member." No one has yet compiled a complete list of nonmembers, but the following names may help significance-seekers to get their bearings. These people are known to be nonmembers:

The Honorable Lyndon B. Johnson, Vice-President of the United States.

Frank McGehee, director, Nation-Indignation Convention.

The Honorable Richard M. Nixon, former Vice-President of the United States.

E. B. Germany, Board Chairman, Lone Star Steel.

The Honorable John Nance Garner, former Vice-President of the United States.

Cus d'Amato, prominent New York sportsman and manager of Floyd Patterson, heavyweight champion of the world.

J. Edgar Hoover, Director, Federal Bureau of Investigation.

General of the Army Douglas MacArthur.

Allen Ginsberg, poet.

The Honorable James A. Farley, former Chairman, Democratic National Committee.

Gus Hall, general secretary, National Committee, Communist Party, U.S.A.

Fowler Harbison, President, Ramona College.

James Hoffa, President, International Brotherhood of Teamsters.

Hetherington Wells, Chairman of the Board, Consolidated Hydraulics, Inc.

Spruille Braden, diplomatist. (Here is a curious case indeed. Ambassador Braden has held many leading positions in the Establishment and is even now a member of the Council on Foreign Relations. But he is also a member of the Council of the John Birch Society. He was read out of the Establishment on April 14, 1960, before his John Birch connections were known.)

Sherman Adams, formerly the assistant to the President of the United States.

Edgar Queeny, President, Monsanto Chemical Corporation.

Charles Goren, bridge expert.

Charles A. Lindbergh, aviator.

Stanton Evans, editor, Indianapolis *News*.

The Honorable John McCormack, Speaker, House of Representatives.

Archbishop Theodotus, Holy Orthodox Church in America.

The Reverend Norman Vincent Peale, pastor, Fifth Avenue Presbyterian Church and author of *The Power of Positive Thinking*.

Cyrus M. Eaton, industrialist and philanthropist.

The Honorable Everett McKinley Dirksen, United States Senator from Illinois and Senate minority leader.

Dr. Edward Teller, nuclear physicist, often known as "Father of the Hydrogen Bomb."

Conrad Hilton, hotel executive.

The Honorable Thomas Hughes, Governor of New Jersey.

Michael J. Quill, President, Transport Workers Union.

Morris Fishbein, M.D., editor and official, American Medical Association.

George Sokolsky, syndicated columnist.
Duke Snider, outfielder, Los Angeles Dodgers.
John L. Lewis, President, United Mine Workers of America.
Carleton Putnam, writer, former Chairman of the Board,
  Delta Air Lines.

The Establishment has in its top councils some people who
appear to the unsophisticated to be oppositionists. For example,
Norman Thomas, the Socialist leader; Norman Mailer, the self-
styled "hipster" novelist; and Norman Podhoretz, the firebrand
editor of *Commentary*, all enjoy close relations with leading
figures on the Executive Committee. The Reverend Martin
Luther King has been proposed for membership on the Executive
Committee. In 1957, a planning committee met for two days at
the Royalton Hotel in New York and reported that "we need informed, constructive criticism fully as much as we need support"
and urged the recruitment of "people who will take a long, cold
look at our policies and procedures and candidly advise us of any
weaknesses they see. We recommend that in the cases of people
playing this indispensable role of 'devil's advocate,' all discipline
be suspended."

It is interesting to observe the workings of the Establishment
in Presidential politics. As I have pointed out, it rarely fails to
get one of its members, or at least one of its allies, into the White
House. In fact, it generally is able to see to it that both nominees
are men acceptable to it. It is never quite powerful enough,
though, to control a nominating convention or actually to dictate
nominations. National conventions represent regional interests
much as Congress does, and there is always a good deal of
unarticulated but nonetheless powerful anti-Establishment sentiment at the quadrennial gatherings of both Republicans and
Democrats. Nevertheless, the great unwashed who man the
delegations understand—almost intuitively, it seems—that they
cannot win without the Establishment, and the more responsible
among them have the foresight to realize that even if they did
win they could not run the country without assistance from the
Executive Committee. Over the years, a deal has been worked out

that is almost an operating rule of American politics. I am indebted to the novelist Margaret Creal for this concise formulation of it:

"When an Establishment man is nominated for the Presidency by either party, the Vice-Presidential candidate must be drawn from outside the Establishment. When, as has occasionally happened, the Establishment is denied the Presidential nomination, it must be given the Vice-Presidential nomination."

The system has worked almost perfectly for the last thirty years. In that time, the only non-Establishment man in the White House has been Harry Truman, and he had been Franklin Roosevelt's non-Establishment Vice-President. Putting Henry Wallace aside as a pretty far-out case and not counting Alben Barkley (a Vice-President's Vice-President), the Vice-Presidents have all been non-Establishment: John Nance Garner, Harry Truman, Richard Nixon, and Lyndon Johnson.

Now observe what happens when the Establishment has to yield first place, as it had to do at the Republican convention in 1960. Richard Nixon, a non-Establishment Vice-President, simply could not be denied the Presidential nomination. So the Establishment Republicans demanded and of course obtained Henry Cabot Lodge. There was a similar case in 1936, when the Republicans went outside the Establishment to nominate Alf Landon for first place. The Vice-Presidential candidate was Colonel Frank Knox, the publisher of the Chicago *Daily News*, a Lippmann-Alsop paper, and later Roosevelt's Secretary of War. Four years later, the Establishment nominated Wendell Willkie on the Republican ticket and agreed to Charles McNary, distinctly non-Establishment. In 1944, it was Dewey (Establishment) and Bricker (Non). The Establishment was particularly powerful in 1948 and not only got Dewey again but Earl Warren. In 1952, the usual deal was made in both parties: Eisenhower versus Stevenson (Establishment) and Nixon and Sparkman (Non). Same thing in 1956, with Estes Kefauver in for Sparkman.

The Russians have caught on to the existence of the Establishment and understand some of its workings quite well. Nikita

Khrushchev showed himself to be no slouch when he told Walter Lippmann, last spring, that President Kennedy was controlled by Nelson Rockefeller. Many people regarded this as depressing evidence of the grip of old-school Marxism on Khrushchev's mind. They thought he was mistaking a faded symbol of industrial and mercantile power for the real wielder of authority under People's Capitalism. He was doing nothing of the sort. He was facing the facts of Establishment life. Not as a Standard Oil heir but as an Establishment agent, Nelson Rockefeller had forced the Republicans to rewrite their platform so that it conformed very closely to Chester Bowles' Democratic platform and provided for a vigorous anti-Communist defense program. Where did the central ideas of both platforms originate? In—where else?—the studies made by the Rockefeller Panel for the Rockefeller Brothers Fund and published as *Prospects for America*. Who was on the Rockefeller Panel? Here are just a few of the names, left and right:

Dean Rusk	Lucius D. Clay
Chester Bowles	Arthur F. Burns
Jacob Potofsky	Henry R. Luce*
Henry Kissinger	Oveta Culp Hobby
Anna Rosenberg	David Sarnoff

And when Kennedy became President, from what foundation did he get his Secretary of State? The Rockefeller Foundation, of course.

* The outsider inside. I once asked an authority on the parent body, the British Establishment, how he accounted for the sudden eminence of Barbara Ward. He explained that every Establishment agency (the B.B.C. directors, for example) had to have at least one woman and one Roman Catholic. Miss Ward was a neat package deal.

PART TWO

MATTERS MAINLY OF FACT

✶ The Big Hello

1 9 4 6

PETER J. MC GUINNESS, a big, tough, happy, red-faced Irishman who for the past twenty-two years has been the Democratic leader of the working-class section of Brooklyn called Greenpoint, is the first citizen of that grimy community and the last of New York's old-time district bosses. "I'm the boss of Greenpoint," he often says. "What I say there goes." McGuinness, who is fifty-eight, was Greenpoint's alderman from 1920 to 1931 and has been its Democratic state committeeman since 1924. He has been before its voters more than thirty times in primary and general elections. Each time he has done better than the time before. For the past few years, no one has bothered to run against him.

McGuinness is so well known in Greenpoint that he has no need to use his surname on campaign literature. "Peter for Sheriff"; "Peter for State Committeeman," his Greenpoint posters say. A flyer used in a recent campaign read:

> **VOTE FOR PETER**
> It's no wonder that everyone likes him.
> Peter is the only Politician
> in the Forty-eight States
> who devotes All his time to the People.

Sometimes he is spoken of as "The McGuinness." To many Greenpointers, his name is synonymous with statesmanship in general. A stock feature story for the *Weekly Star,* a community newspaper, tells of the schoolboy or first voter asked to name the mayor, the governor, or the President and answering "Peter J. McGuinness" or "The McGuinness." McGuinness is not only Greenpoint's political leader but its social leader and its arbiter of taste. The main social event of the year is Annual McGuinness Night, a black-tie affair that is held in the Labor Lyceum the first Saturday after Lent and causes a considerable upswing in the tuxedo-rental business. Another occasion of note is the Monster McGuinness Theatre Party, held in the late fall at Loew's Meserole, and still others are Ye Olde McGuinnesse Farme Barne Dance Nighte, a harvest celebration, and the Mc-Guinness Cotton Blossom Showboat Night, a midsummer cruise on a chartered river boat. Possibly the greatest tribute to Mc-Guinness's standing in Greenpoint is the flowering of the lyric spirit he has inspired. It may well be that more poetry has been written about him than about anyone in American politics since Abraham Lincoln. An example, from the *Weekly Star*, is an epic ballad of twenty-three verses by Maurice Dee, which begins

> There's a man in our town whom you all know well,
> A few things about him I'm now going to tell
> He's tall, broad, and handsome, with a smile that has won us
>   You can easily guess he is Peter McGuinness

and goes on to recite some stirring events in McGuinness's history, such as

> When we heard that the coolies were after our job
> And our daily bread they were trying to rob
> Then we needed a leader we were sure would be with us,
>   Then our old pal came forward, Peter McGuinness

ending on a note of near-despair over the difficulties of dealing with so grand a theme in so poor a form:

> Oh, I could go on writing till this pencil wore down
> About the ways he is loved in this town.
> But the thing we prize most is the fact he is with us
>   Our tall, broad, and handsome Peter McGinness.

At a time when people in general tend to be cynical about politicians and their motives, such standing as McGuinness enjoys in Greenpoint is not easily won or maintained. He has achieved it because he works hard and delights in his work. He tends his vineyard by day and by night. He is probably the only politician in the city who still follows the old custom of holding court on a street corner and greeting passers-by by name. Every Saturday evening and Sunday afternoon, in seasonable weather, he props his enormous body against a lamppost at the corner of Manhattan and Norman Avenues, Greenpoint's main intersection, and invites strollers to stop and chat with him. "That's when I give me people the big hello," he says. He enjoys giving people the big hello, just as he enjoys everything else about politics. He likes making speeches; marching in parades; attending weddings, christenings, confirmations, and funerals; and running Kiddies' Day outings. He says that the most memorable moment of his life came in the closing moments of the 1936 Democratic National Convention, in Philadelphia, when James A. Farley asked him to read, over a national radio hookup, the resolution thanking the networks for their coverage. "Bejesus," he says, "I stood up there on the platform with the Vice-President of the United States of America, Honorable John Nance Garner, behind me, and senators, and cabinet members, and governors from the states that are Democratic, and I talked to the whole goddam United States. Me nerves were all jumping. I was cold all over. I'm telling you, you could see the sweat roll down me back. Right then, me whole life passed before me eyes."

McGuinness can think of few pleasanter ways to spend an evening than to sit behind his bare and battered desk in the clubhouse of the Greenpoint People's Regular Democratic Organization accepting "contracts," the politician's word for favors he agrees to fulfill, from his constituents. "I get one hell of a kick out of that," he says. "Sometimes I even do favors for people in Jersey." A New York district politician who concerns himself with the welfare of the great unwashed on the Hudson's west bank is breaking new ground in human brotherhood, but McGuinness's high regard for his fellow man extends even beyond New Jersey. One Christmas he put an advertisement in the Brooklyn newspapers saying:

PETER J. MC GUINNESS
Democratic State Committeeman
Fifteenth Assembly District
and
Deputy Commissioner of Borough Works
Borough of Brooklyn
Extends Cordial Holiday Greetings
to the World

He thinks highly of the Jewish celebration of Yom Kippur, the Day of Atonement on which the pious are supposed to make some charitable gesture toward their enemies. When he first heard of Yom Kippur, he sent a memorandum to the Jewish members of his club instructing them to "do some nice favors for Republicans and Socialists." McGuinness is a Roman Catholic, but his favorite divine, until the man's death a few years ago, was the Protestant evangelist Tom Noonan, who was known as the Bishop of Chinatown and who ran what was perhaps the best-known Bowery mission before the war. McGuinness admired Noonan because Noonan had hit on the idea of doing favors over the airwaves. Noonan had a Sunday revival program on one of the local stations, and at the end of each program he would plead with his listeners to give old clothing, shoes, eyeglass frames, medicines, tinned food, and the like to his Bowery and Chinatown missioners. "That was one hell of an idea," McGuinness says. "I never knew anyone who done so much for the human race of people." McGuinness is probably the only man who ever ran for sheriff on a program of making life more agreeable for the prisoners under his care. In 1935, when he sought the shrievalty in Kings County, he assured the voters that the prisoners in the county jail would be happy and well fed if he were elected. "Under me, they'll get better meenus," he said in every speech. He was elected, and on his first day in office he gave a New Year's party in the jail. He issued orders that hot drinks be passed around before bedtime, that beef stew be served no less than twice a week, and that carrots be served at least every other day. This last innovation made all the papers. McGuinness, who has a sure instinct for publicity, had called in the reporters and announced it himself. "Carrots is eye food," he said. "Mother of God, I figure we want them to be able to see the straight and narrow when we spring them."

McGuinness is always in high spirits. Sometimes he finds it impossible to contain his exuberance. On such occasions, he begins by bouncing up and down in his chair; then he whistles a few bars of jolly music, flicks some imaginary dust from the shoulders of his coat with his finger tips, and rises to do a few jig steps. "Jeez, I'm feeling spiffy today," he says when this mood is upon him. "Don't mind me, pals. It's just me nature to whistle." Once he whistled and jigged in the midst of a solemn speech by a fellow Alderman. He was asked if the interruption was a protest of any sort. "Bejesus, no," he said. "You know me, pals—the soul of music. I even got a band on me hat." He calls everyone "pal," even people he has never met and is talking to on the telephone for the first time. His good nature has endeared him not only to the voters of Greenpoint and Brooklyn but to just about all the working politicians in town. In the places they most often gather—City Hall, Foley Square, and the Borough Hall section of Brooklyn—no one else is so popular. For more than two decades now, no social gathering of officeholders has been considered a success unless McGuinness has attended and done some unusual things with the English language. Before his feet began to bother him a few years ago, he often led contingents of city officials in the St. Patrick's Day parade, which he now watches from a place of honor in the reviewing stand. Since 1921, he has been master of ceremonies at the annual outing of city fathers and city-news reporters at Traver's Island, Whitestone Landing, or wherever. He is chairman of the Association of Past Aldermen of the City of New York and an official of a half-dozen other organizations in which politicians gather to honor themselves.

Among politicians, one good index of a man's standing is the frequency with which he is asked to be an honorary pallbearer. McGuinness is in greater demand for this service than anyone else in the city. He must sometimes decide which of two or more distinguished corpses he will escort to the grave on a given morning. The roster of those who have enjoyed his company, at funerals and elsewhere, over the years is long and impressive. Those on it have included Alfred E. Smith, Franklin D. Roosevelt, James A. Farley, Edward J. Flynn, William O'Dwyer, James A. Walker, and such reformers as Fiorello La Guardia, Newbold Morris, Herbert Lehman, Samuel Seabury, and Robert Moses. The late B. Charney Vladeck, a Socialist alderman from the lower East Side and a man who generally classed Democratic officeholders with sweatshop proprietors and exploiters of child labor, was one of his warmest admirers. "That Irisher!" Vladeck used to say. "Sometimes he makes me wish I was a Democrat."

McGuinness cultivates his friendships in many ways. He won Vladeck's favor by giving Democratic sponsorship to a number of Socialist resolutions. "Many's the time," he says, "I used to say, 'Cheeny, old pal, if you got something you really want to get through this here board, give it to me, and I'll make it Irish for you. I figure what the hell, if something was good enough for Cheeny, it was good enough for the other aldermen. Cheeny give me a lot of contracts to put through, and all the Democrats thought they were mine and voted for them." McGuinness is by no means innocent of the uses of flattery. Some of it is a bit on the sly side, as a typical and self-explanatory piece of his correspondence shows:

BOROUGH OF BROOKLYN
DEPARTMENT OF BOROUGH WORKS

Hon. Newbold Morris, President
Office of the President of the Council
City Hall, New York

Dear Pal Newbold,

I am in receipt of your splendid letter, and feeling as I do it was most welcome. I was just speaking of you to Judge MacCrate and Judge Lockwood, and we were discussing what a fine fellow you are.

I consider you my very dearest pal, and the way you accept some of my friends who have had occasion to request favors and have been advised by them of the wonderful reception they get from you.

Newbold, old pal, no words can express my proper feelings and thoughts about you, and while the sun is shining on the Great Irish, the sun will shine on us two, while we are enjoying that splendid luncheon at the Yale Club and basking in our wonderful friendship.

Your pal,
Pete
PETER J. MC GUINNESS

Newbold Morris is the city's ranking Republican and by far its most ardent evangel of municipal reform. He finds McGuinness irresistible and frequently has him to the Yale Club. McGuinness, for his part, gets along well with the reform administration headed by La Guardia and Morris. "The Little Flower is a most splendid gentleman," he said once in a speech in Greenpoint. "Under him, we know the poor people of this city will be looked after, irregardless of what may befall. What he done he done honest and he done good." Unlike many other Democrats, though, McGuinness never felt the need to turn his back on Jimmy Walker. When Walker returned pretty much in disgrace from Paris in 1932, McGuinness met him at a Brooklyn pier, threw his arms around him, and said, in the presence of the press, "Jimmy darling, me old pal, stay in Brooklyn if they won't give you a job over there. I'm sheriff here, and you can be me first deputy, me dear old pork chop."

To reciprocate the affection that other men in public life have shown for him, McGuinness honors them by voting them in as members of the Grand Benevolent Order of Pork Chops, a fraternal organization of large but uncounted membership, all of it elected by him. Whenever he meets a member, he says, "Hello there, me old pork chop!" He founded the G.B.O.P.C. twenty years ago, when he was an alderman. "It's just a kind of a humorous thing I thought up," he says reluctantly, when pressed for an explanation. "What the hell, I had to have *something* to call me best pals. I call them pork chops because all the old aldermen loved eating pork chops." The G.B.O.P.C. has held only one formal meeting. That was in 1931, upon the occasion of McGuinness's retirement from the Board of Aldermen. The Board adjourned its regular meeting, and after several nonmembers had been admitted to the chamber, reconvened as the Pork Chops. There were many testimonials to McGuinness, and he was presented with a gold watch, a chain, and a charm that he describes as "a gold statue of a pork chop." The Grand Master of the G.B.O.P.C. is Isidor Frank, a wholesale butcher who gives Democratic district leaders generous discounts on the turkeys and chickens they distribute to the poor at Thanksgiving and Christmas.

McGuinness is an anachronism. His approach to politics was

outdated before he was born. His language went out along with cops in jardiniere hats. His face seems improbable in the mid-twentieth century. Newspaper cartoonists say they can get a perfect caricature of the old-time boss by drawing the contemporary McGuinness true to life, which in fact seems larger than life. Nast and Keppler, they maintain, never created anything half so plausible as McGuinness. He stands just under six feet and weighs about 230 pounds, which is forty pounds less than he weighed three years ago, when his physician ordered him to reduce. He has a massive head, clear blue eyes, and a complexion a shade or two off ripe tomato. His hair is pure white yet still plentiful. He parts it neatly in the middle and scallops it daintily over his forehead in the roach style affected by bartenders fifty years ago. His nose and chin are huge, granitic affairs that jut far out from their moorings in the face and then tilt sharply upward. The face, all in all, seems the work of a sculptor of large and noble intentions but either imprecise or cunningly ambiguous execution. McGuinness can look as benign as Old King Cole or Kriss Kringle in a nursery book or as hostile and belligerent as Roughie McToughie, the generic hard guy. He dramatizes his belligerence much as he dramatizes his spiffy moods. He clenches his immense fists, crouches forward in his seat, and starts jabbing sharply at an imaginary antagonist. "You louse-bound bastard, you," he says to the shadow he is boxing. "Who you think you're talking to? Huh?" Before he was elected alderman for the first time, in 1919, he had spent fourteen years as a teamster, a lumberyard worker, and a boss stevedore, and had earned money on the side as a professional boxer, a distance runner, and a bouncer in the barroom of a Hudson River steamer. In those pursuits, he developed a hard, agile body which has taken on weight without becoming slovenly. McGuinness does not look fat. He looks beefy, powerful, massive, and stately. He carries his body and his head erect. His walk is slow, lordly, and rather ponderously graceful. Unlike the politicians of the era to which he seems to belong, he is anything but flashy in dress. He favors gray tweed suits, white shirts, quietly patterned blue ties, and gray felt hats. He wears black high-top shoes and white cotton socks. He owns no stickpins, and while he values the statue of

a pork chop, he seldom wears it. He does not need the trappings
of regality, for he is regal in bearing. His only ring is a solid
gold one, set with a garnet, which was given to him thirty-five
years ago by his wife, Margaret, a handsome woman of propor-
tions almost as heroic as his own. He speaks of her, as a rule, as
"the old Champeen." They have one son, George, an Internal
Revenue agent, who is thirty-five and bigger than either of them.
The members of McGuinness's club once raised a thousand dollars
and bought him a ring with an enormous sparkler, but although
they had bought the largest band the jeweler stocked, it would
not fit on any of his fingers, which are as big around as pick
handles. "Bless us, but it don't even go on the pinky," he said in
his speech at the presentation ceremony, trying to make the
best of an awkward situation. He could have had it enlarged but
did not do so. The possession of it is an embarrassment to him.
He keeps the ring at home and has spent several years debating
the propriety of having the stone set in a ring for Mrs. McGuinness. "Maybe I should sell it and buy a nice pool table for the
club," he says.

McGuinness has a silver tongue and loves to work it. In his
twelve years on the Board of Aldermen, he missed only two
meetings. He made a speech at almost every one he attended,
generally a long speech. "There's nothing I liked like giving a
hot spiel," he says. "I guess me pals are glad I don't do that
any more. I was getting to be a gasbag." Years of windjammer
oratory have had a curious effect on him, not unlike the effect
of too many blows to the head on a fighter. He is speech-drunk.
Just as an old pug will come out swinging at the sound of a
dinner bell, so McGuinness will break into a speech at the
mention of George Washington, Pope Pius XII, Franklin D.
Roosevelt, or any other name that is hallowed in his kind of
politics. Sometimes he will declaim merely to fill in a gap in
conversation. One wintry afternoon, not long ago, he was talking
with several friends when someone came in out of the cold,
rubbed his hands together, and observed that it was a good day
for a cup of hot soup. Everyone nodded or mumbled agreement.
Then, since that subject seemed pretty well covered, an uneasy
silence followed. Before it had gone too far, McGuinness broke

it with close to ten minutes of rhetoric on soup, the theme being
that the malaise of our times might be due in large measure to
the lack of the nourishing, character-building soup brewed by
American womanhood in braver, happier days. His conversational voice is low and rather scratchy because of the wear and
tear it has had over the years. Often, when he is trying to drive
home a point, he speaks in a hoarse, confidential whisper, as
though he were talking in church. Before an audience, however,
his tones are clear and resonant and have a volume comparable
to that of the late Joe Humphries, the fight announcer who could
fill Madison Square Garden without the use of any mechanical
devices. The strength of his larynx muscles, like the strength of
all his other muscles, is the subject of tall tales in Greenpoint. In
one of them, as reported in the *Weekly Star*, McGuinness was
speaking over WNYC, the municipal station, when the trans-
mitter suddenly lost all its power: "Peter raised his voice slightly
and came in strong and clear in Greenpoint."

McGuinness is one of the most successful pork-barrel raiders
in the city. He has got Greenpoint many millions of dollars'
worth of playgrounds and public baths, one of the two largest
swimming pools in the city, a first-rate dispensary, a nurses' home,
a new high school, and an incinerator. These are largely the
fruits of eloquence. One of his most notable achievements was
keeping a ferry running for thirteen years after it had ceased
paying for itself. For a half-century, this ferry service to East
Twenty-third Street provided Greenpoint with its only direct
communication with Manhattan. Chiefly because most people
who now live in Greenpoint work in its factories, the ferry's
patronage declined to a point at which it was no longer used
enough to justify its operation. Nevertheless, McGuinness was
determined that it should be continued for the few who did
commute on it and for those who rode it on summer evenings to
keep cool. Every year he appeared before the Board of Estimate
to appeal for its continuance and every year he was successful.
Once, addressing himself to Jimmy Walker, who as mayor
presided over the Board meetings and cast three of the Board's
eight votes, he concluded a long speech by saying, "Please don't

take away the old ferry, Mr. Mayor. It would be like separating an old couple that has been together for years to divorce Manhattan and Greenpoint. There would be tears of sorrow in the eyes of the old ferryboats as there would be tears in the eyes of the people of Greenpoint if them splendid old boats were put to rot in some dry dock or sold at public auction. Tell me, Mr. Mayor, now tell me, that you will love them old ferryboats in December as you did in May." (Walker was the author of a maudlin song entitled "Will You Love Me in December as You Did in May.") "I do love them, Peter, and I love you. You're my favorite alderman," Walker said. The ferries kept running.

The next year McGuinness came up with the intelligence that the boats were valuable relics; they had, he claimed to have learned, been used as Union troop transports on the Mississippi in the Civil War. Abraham Lincoln, he said, "would turn over in the sod" if the ferries were discontinued and destroyed. (McGuinness is still fighting the Civil War, in which his mother's father, Major James Fee, was killed. He dislikes the South. "I don't like that Jim Crow they got," he says, "and I don't like their goddam white crow no better.") Another year he said that the ferries would be the only means of escape from Greenpoint, in the main a community of frame buildings, in the event of fire. "Listen, pal," he told Mayor John P. O'Brien, "if somebody set fire to Greenpoint and them old boats weren't there, we'd all be roasted alive." The ferries ran.

In 1933, a year in which appeals to sentiment and history were largely unavailing, the service was at last suspended. The melancholy event was noted in the *Weekly Star* by Anon:

THE OLD FERRY

Ay, tear her tattered ensign down
For fifty years it's flown
And many a heart in Greenpoint
Will raise a heartfelt moan.
Upon her decks on many a morn
The crowds have rushed to work,
To reach Manhattan's dingy isle
In fog or rain or murk.

Her pilot oft has gripped the wheel
To breast the river's tide,
While Pete McGuinness, glad, looked on
It was his greatest pride.
On many a summer's evening
It took the kids in tow,
The little ones of Greenpoint
Who had no place else to go.

O better that her aged hulk
Should ne'er be seen again
Brave Peter fought to save it
But all alas in vain.

Drydock her somewhere down the stream
And strip her to the keel.
You can't imagine anyhow
How sad the people feel.

McGuinness knows the uses of irony as well as of sentiment. Once, in the late twenties, his leadership was briefly threatened by the appearance of a brash young attorney who argued that a forward-looking community should have as its leader a person of culture and refinement, such as himself. The Higher Learning was enjoying immense prestige at the time, and the newcomer was impressing a good many Democratic voters with his Brooklyn Law School vocabulary. McGuinness, whose only diploma was acquired when he finished the eighth grade at Public School Number 31, disposed of the interloper with a strategy that is still a favorite with connoisseurs. The young man challenged him to a debate, and McGuinness accepted. After the challenger had finished his erudite presentation, McGuinness, who had not yet been invited to the Yale Club, rose and glared down at the audience of shirt-sleeved laborers and housewives in Hoover aprons. Then he bellowed, "All of yez that went to Yales or Cornells raise your right hands." Not a hand went up. There was some tittering in the audience. "The Yales and Cornells can vote for him," he said. "The rest of yez vote for me." They did.

McGuinness is a working politician. As a rule, he is content to leave questions of theory to the theoreticians. He also has a strong sense of jurisdictional propriety and comments only rarely on national and international issues. He is an interested observer of the passing show, though, and he now and then applies his busy mind to matters of high policy. He watched the rise of Hitler with deepening anxiety, and he believes that the Greenpoint People's Regular Democratic Organization was the first political club in the country to pass an anti-Hitler resolution. He could be right. It took the form of a telegram to President von Hindenburg early in 1933 advising him to yield no further powers to Hitler and to take steps to assure his personal security. McGuinness says that his reading of the news from Germany had convinced him that Hitler was personally plotting the assassination of Hindenburg, and claims to be certain that Hindenburg's death in 1934 was at Hitler's hand. "I knew all along what that one was up to," he says. "I'll go to me own grave knowing he killed the old gentleman." Not long ago, he took a stand against the appointment of Jesse Jones as chairman of the Reconstruction Finance Corporation. "I got it figured out why they want *him*," he said. "He's a rich cheapskate. He'd never let go of any of the money. God bless us, we don't want a piker in a job like that." All during the North African phase of the late war, he disapproved of our collaboration with General Henri Giraud, whom he held personally responsible for the misfortune that befell General Mark Clark when, at the secret conference before the invasion, he lost his trousers and the $18,000 they contained. "I'm down on that crowd," he says. "That was a hell of a thing, them letting that happen. Any decent leader, when he gets someone like General Clark coming into his district, the least he can do is make sure no one rolls him while he's there." In another recent foray into national affairs, McGuinness aligned himself with those favoring the release from prison of Earl Browder, the Communist leader. "I say let him out," McGuinness told an inquiring reporter a while back. "There's lots worse than him. He's got a very good job with the Communists."

Like most district leaders, McGuinness has managed to keep himself on the public payroll most of the time. In addition to being an alderman, he has been sheriff of Kings County and county register, and at present he is assistant commissioner of Borough Works in Brooklyn. In one sense, his current job is a comedown, since it pays only $7,900 a year. The shrievalty paid $15,000 and the register's job paid $12,000. The offices of county sheriff and county register, however, were abolished three years ago on the ground that they served no useful purpose. On the very day in 1941 that the voters of Kings County elected McGuinness their county register, the voters of New York State adopted a constitutional amendment doing away with the office. McGuinness had to take his present job, an appointive one, as the next-best thing. He assumed it in 1944, upon the death of the incumbent. "I don't mind the money part," he says. "I don't drink nor gamble none, and me and the old Champeen got to go easy on potatoes." As for his responsibilities, he enjoys them because they are so few in number. "I like this here work pretty good. It don't keep me tied down none," he told a friend not long ago. The Department of Borough Works is charged with the maintenance of streets, sewers, and public buildings. It is run by civil engineers, and most of its employees are engineers and laborers. McGuinness does not pretend to be an expert on public works, although having once worked in a lumberyard, he considers himself something of an authority on the Coney Island boardwalk and inspects it often. "I trample it now and then to make sure it ain't rotten," he says. He has an office in the Borough Hall, and he spends two or three hours a day in it, but most of that time is spent working on his contracts. He has no qualms of conscience whatever about holding a job that involves little work. He feels that his real service to society is the one he performs as a political leader in Greenpoint, and he regards his being on the municipal payroll merely as a technical device to give him the money to carry on. It is a public subsidy for an enterprise of public utility. "The thing of it is," he says thoughtfully, "you got to make jobs like this so a political man can get his work done. If I was still in a lumberyard or if I was in a factory, I wouldn't have time to run Greenpoint." The Citizens Union disapproves of him and of his attitude and feels that he has no right to be at the public trough. "The record clearly indicates that he is not qualified for any public office," it declares each time he seeks one. McGuinness does not take this seriously. "They mean I ain't a Republican," he says. "Bejesus, that's right." Robert Moses, a sometime

Republican who does have the approval of the Citizens Union and one who has given a lot of thought to such matters, sides with McGuinness. "It's absurd," he says, "to expect a man like Peter to be an administrator. Peter is a leader and one of the best in the city. Call him a boss if you want—I don't care. I've known him and worked with him for twenty years, and whenever I've needed to know anything about Greenpoint, I've got more practical help and co-operation from Peter than I could ever have got from a hundred social workers, sociologists, city planners, poll takers, and all the rest of that trash. No matter what you say about them, men like Peter have held New York's neighborhood together, and if the reformers ever succeed in driving them out, take my word for it, this city is going to fall apart into racial and religious mobs. If you ask me, that's happening right now."

McGuinness may spend only a few hours a day at his Borough Hall office, but his working hours can be long and arduous. He is up by seven, and by eight has started on a long round of errands. Some days he travels mostly by foot, bus, subway, and trolley; other days he is chauffeured around in one of the automobiles at the disposal of the Borough President. He may stop in a doctor's office or a hospital to arrange for the care of an ailing constituent, attend one or two funerals, pay his respects to a bereaved family, argue with some constituent's landlord about heating problems or unpaid rent, run down a loose-footed husband and try to persuade him to return to his lawful wife, arrange with the head of a city bureau to shift an employee from night to day work, and call upon several public agencies to clear up various problems of widows' and veterans' pensions, Social Security, Workmen's Compensation, service allotments, old-age insurance, or any of the other government business that brings the poor so much closer to politicians than the well-to-do. He also visits a good many courts and police stations on his tour, and the possibility exists that he now and then tampers with justice. He is reluctant to say very much about his transactions with officers of the courts and of the law; he considers that his function is at least related to that of an attorney, and he feels that he must keep his clients' confidences inviolate. "I never talk about me people's troubles," he says. "But you know how it is. You're walking along the street, and somebody you don't even know bunks into you. So you give him the back of your hand, and he comes back for more. One of that kind—you know. You give him another, and he's back again. You belt him good, and then some goddam patrolman busts in and takes the two of yez down to the station. *He* don't know who started it, so it's drunk and disorderly, the two of yez. What the hell are you going to do? All the nerves in your body are jumping. Your pulse is trobbing hard. You're cold all over. You're thinking you ain't got a friend in the world. Then it comes to you. 'I'll call Peter McGuinness,' you say to yourself. 'He'll get me out of this.' Bejesus, I got to give you a hand on a proposition like that." Not all of his interventions are on behalf of drunks or occasional street-brawlers. Though he does not care to discuss it much, he is willing to give a hand on more serious propositions. When pressed to explain his point of view, he will do so. "Murder, rape, and robbery with a gun—them I never touch," he said recently. "But something like housebreaking—what the hell, the first couple times don't prove there's anything wrong with a boy."

Once every week or two, McGuinness spends a whole day in Greenpoint, covering his district on foot. He checks on such matters of public interest as garbage collection, playground administration, compliance with the tenement laws, the efficiency of the Fire and Police Departments, and the condition of the pavements. If he sees or hears of anything wrong—a stopped-up sewer, a hole in the pavement, or traffic on a play street—he gets in touch with the appropriate authorities. Often he works with his nose. Greenpoint is today the most heavily industrialized part of the city, and among its products are soap, varnish, gasoline, and other things whose manufacture is malodorous. One of McGuinness's many boasts is that he has made Greenpoint smell better. He has forced factory owners to install devices that eliminate objectionable smells and smoke, and he is constantly sniffing for new evidences of polluted air. As soon as he detects an unpleasant odor on the wind, he calls the manager of the offending plant and threatens to hail him into court for violating a whole series of city ordinances.

The close watch McGuinness has kept on Greenpoint has produced some unexpected dividends. During the 1936 Presidential campaign, Franklin D. Roosevelt spoke in Greenpoint. Before he was introduced, he confided in McGuinness that he was troubled by the *Literary Digest* straw vote, in which Governor Alfred M. Landon, the Republican candidate, was well in the lead. "That was one of me very biggest moments," McGuinness says. "I told him, I said, 'Mr. President, don't you go giving it another thought. I got that goddam fake figured out.'" The President asked McGuinness what he meant. McGuinness explained that he had recently assigned three reliable members of the Greenpoint People's Regular Democratic Organization to spy on the city incinerator in the district. Some constituents who lived near the incinerator had complained that horses were being cremated there. They were certain they had detected the stink of burning horseflesh. The McGuinness followers spent three nights hiding in some bushes near the plant to see if horses were being cremated there, and they discovered that every night, after the Sanitation Department trucks had dumped their loads, some men they knew to be Republican party workers were coming in and buying up stacks of paper. Closer snooping showed that they were collecting discarded *Literary Digest* ballots. "Mr. President," McGuinness said to Roosevelt, "the people of Brooklyn get them fake ballots, and they trun them right out. The Republicans go to the incinerator and buy them for a nickel a piece. That's why Landon's ahead." Roosevelt laughed. Later in the campaign, he sent word to McGuinness, through Jim Farley, that he was no longer worrying about the straw vote. "He thanked me for relieving his brain," McGuinness says. "Bejesus, you feel good when you do a thing like that."

McGuinness gets to Borough Hall at about noon each day. He stays there until two-thirty or three, checking up on his contracts, welcoming constituents who find it more convenient to see him there than at the Clubhouse, and passing the time of day with old friends. Early in the afternoon, he goes across the street to the press room in the Supreme Court Building, where he spends an hour or so catching up on political gossip, general news, and sitting in on the all-day rummy game there. These visits often yield a feature story for the next day's papers. Over the years, McGuinness has made the papers more often than public figures of far higher rank, for his attitudes and his language, even when bowdlerized slightly, are almost always somewhere off the beaten political track. He leaves for Greenpoint not later than five, dines at home with Mrs. McGuinness, and then walks to the Greenpoint People's Regular Democratic Organization, a three-story frame building just around the corner from his own house, which is very much like it. His desk is in a corner of a large, gloomy room decorated with some blown-up, tinted portraits of McGuinness with his arms around Jimmy Walker; a faded pennant bearing the name and likeness of Franklin D. Roosevelt; and a huge picture of McGuinness as a brawny young dock walloper. He sits down at his desk ready for whatever the evening will bring. Constituents start arriving shortly after six and wait their turn in straight-backed chairs in a room adjoining his office. These chairs, aside from a couple of small, plain tables, and McGuinness's desk, chair, and safe are the only furnishings on the main floor of the club. McGuinness, who admires a touch of color in his surroundings, would like his clubhouse to be cheerier, but he says it would be foolish for the Organization to spend much money on furniture or decorations. "The fellows that come in here," he says, "get to talking about baseball and things like that, and you never know what's going to happen, especially on a Saturday night. We keep the girls' room upstairs fixed up real nice, but down here it wouldn't pay." The club telephone is kept in a padlocked squirrel cage, which McGuinness has to unlock every time the phone rings.

McGuinness stays in the club until twelve thirty or one. He may see anywhere from a dozen to a hundred people before ten o'clock, but not many show up after that. Still, he feels that he should stay. "You never know when there'll be a late struggler," he explains. At about nine, some friends arrive and set up a rummy game, in which he takes a hand whenever he can. Most of his clients want the kind of routine favors he has done for others earlier in the day. The services he offers make him a combined attorney, job broker, accountant, and social worker. He also, now and then, serves as a domestic-relations court. "It's one of the greatest happinesses in me life," he likes to say, "to think of all the husbands and wives I've kept together." His matrimonial advice to husbands consists almost entirely of variations on one theme: "The old girl is always best." "When it's the missus who's beefing," he says, "I give her the old song—A Good Man Is Hard to Find."

McGuinness was born in Greenpoint on June 29, 1888. His father was a brass polisher, and there were thirteen children in the family besides Peter James, who was the third to be born. The family was not poor. The elder McGuinness owned his own home, and when he died, twenty years ago, he left an estate of about $20,000, none of which went to Peter, because, he says, his father was ashamed of having a politician in the family. He had wanted Peter to follow in his footsteps as a brass polisher. "To the old gentleman," McGuinness says, "there was no job in the world as good as brass polishing. I never seen it that way." McGuinness's career in politics began when he was eight years old and became a junior ward heeler for State Senator Pat McCarren, then the boss of Greenpoint and for many years the boss of all Brooklyn. From the time he was five or six, he had worked at odd jobs in the neighborhood. He ran errands for storekeepers, carried growlers of beer for workingmen, and sold the eggs of some hens he kept in the back yard. On weekends he served as the standard-bearer for a marching society known as the Rinky Dinks. "The Rinks were a lot of young fellows around the Point," he says. "All of them was keeping company with girls, and the girls marched with them. Nobody wanted to leave his young lady friend to carry the flag, so they hired me to do it." By the time he was ten, McGuinness was well known throughout Greenpoint. "I was pals with the whole town," he says. "When I wasn't working or in school, I used to sit in the gutter on Greenpoint Avenue, the corner of Norman. That way I got to know everybody because everybody came by there. People would come along and say, 'Bejesus, there's Petey McGuinness in the gutter. Hello, Petey me boy, what are you doing today?' I'd say, 'Oh, I'm fine, thank you, Mr. Flaherty. I was just sitting in the gutter here because it's so nice and sunny. How are you today,

Mr. Flaherty? And Mrs. Flaherty?' Even in them days, I was out there giving them the big hello." One of McCarren's men, taking note of McGuinness's politeness and of his good standing in the community, took him on as a doorbell ringer. On Election Day in 1896, McGuinness made a dollar for getting out thirty or forty votes for Bryan and Free Silver. Each election and primary day he did the same thing, and between elections he was a chore boy for the local Democratic organization, the Jefferson Club. "I knew I liked that kind of work the best," he said. "I was always a great one for anything that had to do with people."

When he was fourteen and had completed the eighth grade at P. S. 31, McGuinness left school, and though he continued to live in Greenpoint and to work in the local Democratic machine, he ferried to work every day in Manhattan. He was an office boy for R. H. Hoe & Company, the printing-press manufacturers; then a runner on the Bowery, delivering Thomas J. Plunkitt's Cele-brated Cigars to the Chatham Club, Steve Brodie's, McGurk's Suicide Hall, and other well-known resorts of the period. Every-thing about McGuinness's speech and appearance suggests the old Bowery, but he never considered himself a Bowery Boy. "There was some splendid people on the Bowery in them days," he says, "such as Chuck Connors and Big Tim Sullivan, but I never thought too much of the place. I'm a neighborhood man myself, and the Bowery wasn't really what you'd call a neighbor-hood. It wasn't so tough as they say, neither. Right now Green-point is tougher than the Bowery ever was, and it's a decent place, too." Later, when he grew old enough for man's work, he became a teamster for S. Brinckerhoff Hay & Feed, and worked evenings keeping order in the saloon of a Hudson River steamboat. He was also, for a time, a promising young middleweight. He won thir-teen of his fifteen fights and drew two. He left the ring partly because he could not see how it could contribute to his political advancement and partly because, much as he enjoys fighting for fun and honor, he is not the sort to punch people for money. He says that he likes a job in which he can feel that he is serving his fellows, and he sometimes classifies the various political offices he has held according to the opportunities they have offered for social usefulness. Thus, he did not enjoy being sheriff of Kings County nearly as much as he liked being an alderman. "Being a sheriff and arresting people isn't a very loving thing," he says. "When you sum it all up, I'd say that alderman was about the most loving job I ever had."

On the whole, McGuinness is sorry he did not get more schooling. He believes in education. He particularly favors the liberal arts and for many years fought for the building of a high school in Greenpoint. "It's a shameful crime," he once told the Board of Estimate, "that the greatest mercantile center this side of the Mississippi should have no high school for its young ones. Woe be to him or they who will stand in the way of onward progress of the boys and girls of Greenpoint." In time he won, but the victory was not as sweet as it might have been, for the handsome school that was built turned out to be the Automotive Trades High School. He regarded this as an affront, and undemocratic. He seems to feel that the assumption behind it was that since Greenpoint is a working-class district, it can breed nothing but mechanics. "The crumbs thought they put something over on us," he says. "I'm going to get me another high school in here before I'm through, and this time we're going to get an educational school." In one way, though, he considers it fortunate that his own schooling ended when it did. He had his heart set on a political career, and education might have helped. But he wanted to become a district boss as soon as possible and to spend no more time than necessary in the service of some other boss. By making a name for himself, as he did in his early twenties, outside the regular machine, he was able to become a full-fledged leader at thirty-six; he feels that if he had gone to high school or college, he might have been tempted to take a political job immediately upon graduation and then wait his turn for the leadership in the hierarchy of the Jefferson Club, which, like most hierarchies, was rigidly based on seniority. In that case, he might have spent the better part of his life as a timeserver in a municipal office or perhaps in the state legislature or Congress. No thought appalls him more. Like most politicians of his generation, McGuinness considers Congressmen members of an inferior class. To him, the local bosses who pick the legislators and tell them what to do are the elite of politics, and Congressmen are men, to give them the benefit of the doubt, who, unable to make the grade as leaders themselves, must serve as legislative errand boys to the bosses. He cannot understand the tendency, comparatively recent in this city, of political bosses to take Congressional nominations for themselves. "I'd never be such a sap as to send meself to Washington," he says, and "believe me, I'm glad I was never in a fix where anyone else could send me. I'm asking you, if a man's a leader in New York, what the hell business has he got being in Washington?"

Long before McGuinness became political boss of Greenpoint, he was boss of its water front. In 1908, when he was twenty, he gave up his career on the Bowery and started as a lumber handler and stevedore in the John C. Orr Lumber Yard in Greenpoint. He was soon a rising figure in Lumber Handlers' Local 955 of the International Longshoremen's Association and in time was known throughout the section as the toughest of all the dock wallopers. "You could just about say," an associate of those days recalls, "that Peter was the king of this here water front right down to the Navy Yard and even Irishtown and Brooklyn Bridge. He could work better than anyone, and he could lick anyone." Early in his career, he had a chance to bring himself dramatically to the attention of his fellow longshoremen. He caught a pair of crooked union delegates in the act of splitting up the swag. "It was at a meeting of the local in Germania Hall," he recalls. "I was in the Gents' Room. I was sitting down. These two delegates come in and start talking. They don't know no one is there. I'm a son of a bitch, they're divvying up one hundred thirty-two bucks they just took in dues. The sweat's running down me back. I pull up me pants and go for them. I flang one of them through a glass panel door and knocked the other cold. Then I marched them into the room where the Lumber Handlers was. Me and a friend made them empty their pockets on the table. They come up with a hundred and fifty. I made a motion we teach them a lesson by using the other eighteen for beer and bologna sandwiches for the whole local. Me friend seconded it, and it passed unanimous." Before the meeting was adjourned for the beer and sandwiches, there was a purge of the Local 955 leadership, and McGuinness got the first of several promotions.

He says that his fight with the delegates was one of the very few serious fights he ever had. "We had fights almost every day," he says, "but they were just for fun. Besides, you had to do that to become boss in them days. The others figured that if they could lick me they could be boss theirselves. Most of the time we'd fight at lunch hour or after work. Everybody'd stand around and watch. After the fights I'd practice me oratory. I'd stand on a pile of lumber and give them all a hot spiel on something—Irish liberty or George Washington, something like that. Me friends would say, 'Bejesus, Peter, you're improving every day. Pretty soon we'll be after sending you to the Board of Aldermen.'"

McGuinness greatly enjoyed the ten years he spent working in the lumberyard, and he regards lumber handling as one of the pleasantest occupations he knows. "Working in a lumberyard is like being in a health resort all year long," he says. "You're out there in God's good air all the day long, and from the smell of the different woods, you might as well be in a forest. And another thing—you're in with the most splendid people. I never knew a higher-class type men than lumber handlers." Not long ago, he told a group of reporters in the Supreme Court press room that he wished to make a suggestion on peacetime military training. "If they was to leave this conscription thing up to me," he said, "I'd have the boys putting in a couple of years in lumberyards. It builds up every muscle in your body. Lumber handlers are the toughest men on earth. Bejesus, if the Russians or somebody knew they'd be up against lumber handlers, they wouldn't start no trouble."

Today McGuinness is a pillar of the Brooklyn Democracy and will tolerate no irregularity. In his youth he was a seditionist. In 1919, the boss of Greenpoint was James A. McQuade, who enjoyed a brief celebrity during the Seabury investigation, when he explained his bank deposits of more than a half-million dollars by saying that he had borrowed the money to feed "the thirty-three starving McQuades." McQuade was a short, squat, and essentially drab Irishman who spent most of his time at the race tracks and in the saloons of Greenpoint, places that McGuinness never patronized. McGuinness was frank and naturally exuberant; McQuade was inclined to be sly and lugubrious.

Nevertheless, McQuade was a reasonably popular leader and was powerfully entrenched. When McGuinness was getting his start in politics, he knew that if he accepted patronage from McQuade, he could not become boss himself until McQuade retired or died, and at the moment either event seemed remote. He therefore undertook to overthrow McQuade, a job that took him six years and was regarded by those who watched it as a masterpiece of insurrection.

At the beginning of the war between the McQuade and McGuinness forces, Greenpoint was a discontented neighborhood. In the late nineteenth century, it had been a happy and reasonably prosperous community—more, in fact, a town than a section of a city. (McGuinness and many of its citizens claim that it was the inspiration for "There'll Be a Hot Time in the Old Town Tonight." It appears to be a fact that Theodore A. Metz wrote the music while drinking beer in a saloon on Meserole Avenue, but Joseph Hayden's lyric is generally assumed to refer to St. Louis, and it sounds a good deal more St. Louisian than Greenpointian. The atmosphere on Meserole Avenue, however, may have helped Metz in contriving the sprightly lilt of the music.) Its citizens, mainly Irish, worked in the lumber and ship yards along the water front. It was an important shipbuilding center. The *Monitor*, the odd little "cheese box on a raft" that defeated the *Merrimac* in Hampton Roads in 1862, was built there, and in its honor the principal hotel had been named the Yankee Cheesebox. Most of its buildings were row houses, owned by the people who lived in them, and there was ample open space. Salt water could be seen from almost anywhere, for the site was literally a "green point" in the waters of New York Harbor. On the west was the East River; on the north and east was Newtown Creek, a salty inlet that is shaped like a scythe, and on the south another salty inlet that has since been mostly filled in. But at the start of the new century, Greenpoint began to change, both physically and economically. New York had grown up all around it, so that it was no longer a village but almost the exact geographical center of Greater New York. Its water front was too valuable to stay in the hands of minor industries. The sprawling ship and lumber yards were replaced by factories and oil refineries, and they brought about an influx of low-wage immigrants, who in turn caused congestion. A hedge of smokestacks rose along the water front, shutting off the view and pouring out upon the residential section clouds of soot, smoke, and smells. Property values fell. People who could afford to leave Greenpoint did so. Few investors could be found to finance the replacement or improvement of old property. The city was reluctant to do much to benefit a residential community that was degenerating so fast. One of Greenpoint's poets, a woman of insight, wrote in a local paper:

> Daily neighbors move to other sections
> Where buildings rise in process of erection
> Where bridges close and cars are ever moving
> Where roads and all conditions are improving.
>
> Yet, dear Greenpoint, noble town of fame
> Year after year e'er remains the same
> Through lack of unity to make a stand
> To fight for the improvements we demand.
>
> Oh, those on high who watch mere mortals act
> Send us a fighter strong, clean, and intact,
> That we may save our fair town from decay
> And from the chains of unrest break away.

McGuinness began his attack on the McQuade machine by blaming it for Greenpoint's plight and by becoming the "fighter strong, clean, and intact," for whom the poet—Julia V. Conlon, who was to join him as his first district coleader—had called. The press was his first forum. Every time he learned of a new grievance in the community, he wrote a letter to one of the local newspapers blaming McQuade and his organization. He held McQuade responsible for Greenpoint's lack of playgrounds and schools, for the deplorable condition of its pavements, for the smokes and smells from the factories, for the garbage in Newtown Creek, for gypsy encampments, and for the fact that livestock was being herded through the streets of Greenpoint to the abattoirs of Long Island City. His letters revealed the mastery of a concrete and vivid prose style. "These animals," he wrote of the cattle in passage to slaughter, "knock over baby carriages with babies in them, and they knock down Greenpoint mothers, and the bulls kick them and knock them down, running into store windows and kicking them and breaking them. Why does Greenpoint have to put up with this? What's our dude leader Jim McQuade and his Alderman and his Assemblyman doing to stop these beasts?" Other neighborhoods, he complained, were getting public baths and showers, but Greenpoint, which was short on domestic plumbing, was not. "What's the matter with Park Avenue Jim McQuade?" he demanded to know. "Don't he think his own people are good enough to have baths and showers? What we need around here is fighting leaders. Why shouldn't Greenpoint be right up there with Flatbush and places like that?" McGuinness also attacked John McCooey, the boss of Kings County and a mighty eminence in New York thirty years ago, who supported McQuade against the rebel McGuinness. Like all good politicians, McGuinness pretended to be scornful of politicians in general and presented himself merely as a long-suffering private citizen who had been driven to action by corruption, abuse, sloth, and official insolence. "I have to laugh," he wrote to the editor of the *Weekly Star,* "when I think of these big bluffs of politicians coming into this district around election time, getting on the platform and telling the people what they will give them, and when elected you will never see the old blowhards again. If you ask me, all this is Mr. McCooey's work. Now, I say, let Mr. McCooey and his officeholders refuse us these improvements, and we'll show them what Greenpoint can do. Who is this McCooey, anyway? Does anyone ever see him around Greenpoint? Our motto here should be—Greenpointers work for Greenpoint."

In 1918, McGuinness felt that the iron was hot enough for striking. He announced that he would run against McQuade's alderman, William McGarry, in the next year's Democratic primary. When the Jefferson Club, for which he had worked since childhood, barred him and his followers, then mostly his fellow lumbermen, he defiantly organized what he called the Open Air Democratic Club and held meetings on street corners. He ran small ads in the *Weekly Star:* "The Man of the Hour. Who Is He? Peter J. McGuinness." "Vote for the Man Who Will

Bring Patronage to the District—Peter J. McGuinness." One
display ad read:

GET ON THE LAUGH WAGON
Laugh.
The best tonic in the World is Happiness.
Laughter induces happiness,
and happiness is the theme of our existence.
McGuinness for Alderman

He continued to write letters to the editor, and he made himself
good copy. Innumerable items appeared in the *Weekly Star*.
"When you see Greenpoint's fighting candidate for Alderman,
Peter McGuinness, ask Peter why he don't eat macaroni. He's
got some answer." Or: "Jim McQuade had better watch out.
Peter McGuinness was down at the Du Tel Pleasure Club the
other night, and the boys say the Stormy Petrel of the North End
is really on the war path." He organized the Peter J. McGuinness
Greenpoint People's Regular Democratic Organization, the Peter
J. McGuinness Greenpoint Patriotic League, and the Peter J.
McGuinness Charity and Welfare Association. The first of these,
from whose title his own name was docked when he succeeded to
the district leadership, still exists. The others were wartime
organizations. McGuinness claimed that McQuade was not doing
enough to boost the morale of Greenpoint's soldiers. He ordered
his followers to canvass the neighborhood for money to buy
presents for the men going off to war. Naturally, this was a
popular cause. In that war, the drafted men entrained for camp
in public. Whenever a batch of Greenpoint boys left, they were
given a send-off by McGuinness and his partisans, carrying the
banners of all three McGuinness organizations, and by the Full
Military Brass Band of Professor William J. Connolly, a musician who was, and still is, one of McGuinness's most important
political allies. Each draftee was presented by McGuinness with a
bon voyage package containing food, cigarettes, soap, razor
blades, and an inspirational leaflet by the candidate for alderman.
The soldiers continued to receive presents in camp and overseas,
and when they returned most of them joined the Greenpoint

Labor Veterans League, Peter J. McGuinness, Hon. President. One local boy who claimed to be the first soldier from Greenpoint to reach German soil wrote home a letter that was prominently displayed in the *Weekly Star:*

I was thinking [he wrote] of Greenpoint through every minute of it. . . . In the last few months I've seen a lot of Greenpoint boys over here. . . . I find that most of the boys feel about the way I do. They think that Peter J. McGuinness is doing very good work for Greenpoint. We sure hope he keeps it up and that Greenpoint appreciates him.

It all paid off handsomely. McGuinness defeated the McQuade incumbent in the primaries and was easily elected in November. He worked as a stevedore until a couple of hours before he took the oath of office.

McGuinness stayed an alderman until 1931, and for those dozen years he was unquestionably the most celebrated member of the Board. He makes the newspapers quite a bit nowadays, but the volume of his publicity now that he is in Borough Hall does not compare with what he got when he was in City Hall. During the twenties, he was the subject of almost as many feature stories as Daddy Browning, Admiral Richard E. Byrd, and Dr. John Roach Straton. A comment by McGuinness on Prohibition, the New Woman, or the war debts—frequently accompanied by a picture of the Alderman striking an aggressive pose alongside MacMonnies' statue of Civic Virtue in City Hall Park—was almost a regular department in the afternoon papers. He liked to give out statements defending New Yorkers against bluenose attacks on their city. His favorite adversary was the Board of Temperance, Prohibition, and Public Morals of the Methodist Episcopal Church. McGuinness answered its every charge. When it accused New Yorkers of general immorality, he replied, "New York is the cleanest city on earth. You can't find a more moral race of people anywhere." When New York's theaters were under attack, he said, "The theatres of New York are great educational institutions. Some people would be happy if Broadway was a pasture. The hell with them. I'm for the Great White Way." When New York language was said to be profane and obscene, McGuinness was irate. "There's no more profanity here than in Peapatch. New Yorkers may swear a lot on their impulses, but they never swear from the heart." To the complaint that New York women exposed too much of themselves, McGuinness replied, "New York has the healthiest air in the country. What if the girls do go in for few clothes. The good air gets to their bodies and makes them healthier. Look at Adam and Eve. They weren't all bundled up. Think how many descendants they had. Good night, there's no harm in women wearing few clothes." There was recurrent controversy over his favorite piece of statuary, Civic Virtue, and he was always in the thick of it. He did not find its nudity offensive, but he once, with some reporters, slipped a pair of red drawers on it. "Now he's decent, I hope everybody'll stop knocking him," he said. When it was moved to Foley Square, he took the floor in the Board of Aldermen and said, "It is noteworthy that the Municipal Art Commission placed that immortal piece of art, Civic Virtue, in such a heavenly retreat like Foley Square. I doff my hat to the Municipal Art Commission and may it have long health and pleasant dreams and may the sunshine always rest on its brow." For a while, he girded his enormous stomach with a belt whose large silver buckle had "Civic Virtue" engraved upon it.

The papers also followed his doings in Greenpoint. They particularly favored his wars on gypsies and coolies. Greenpoint was plagued with gypsy encampments during the twenties, and once a local box factory used for its work force a contingent of Chinese laborers who came in vans under cover of night and slept, some three hundred of them, inside the factory. McGuinness had the law put a stop to this. The gypsies he went after himself. Whenever they moved in, he and a group of his club members would go to their camp and bellow, "Get out—all of yez." As a rule, they would follow his instructions, and he would issue a victory proclamation. "I hereby declare Greenpoint to be free from Gypsies. There is nobody here now but Democrats and some Republicans." But they kept coming back. "I will not permit any gypsy troupes to settle in my district," he said. "They frighten children, intimidate grownups, and steal at every opportunity. They are a menace to the garden spot of the universe."

Once, after a successful drive against the gypsies in Greenpoint, he invited their leaders to make peace with him and join him in one of his current enthusiasms—a demonstration against Prohibition that was to be known as Jimmy Walker's Beer Parade. The gypsies were pleased to join, and McGuinness strutted happily at the head of their band. "They steal a lot, but bejesus they're musically inclined," he said.

New York contributed no more valiant or resourceful battler than McGuinness to the war against the Eighteenth Amendment. He probably made more attempts to find a legal way around Prohibition than any other legislator in the country. "America does not want to be a dry country," he told his fellow aldermen. "New York will never be arid. Let us keep the parched desert in the torrid countries and permit New York and her sister states to be peopled by real humans." No epidemic of grippe or head colds could strike the city without McGuinness putting before the Board a resolution petitioning Congress to "so amend the Prohibition Law as to allow the sale of spirit liquors for the benefit of the sick." "It's a criminal shame," McGuinness, himself a teetotaler, said, "to allow whiskey to lie idle while people are lying at death's door who could be saved by it." He worked Greenpoint up to such a fury that it voted eighty to one for repeal—the solidest vote, he said, and probably correctly, in the country. He got the name of Doughty Street in Greenpoint changed to Ruppert Place, in honor of the brewing family.

McGuinness's most admired speech before the Board of Aldermen was delivered upon the occasion of Mrs. Ruth Preatt's resignation from the Board following her election to Congress. He delivered a testimonial on behalf of his fellow aldermen, which ended:

Ruth, all we have to say is that when you go down to Washington you want to take along that beautiful fur coat that your dear husband gave you. You want to take that coat to Washington, Ruth, because it's very, very cold down there. Washington may be further South than New York City, but the people there are cold as ice. They don't love one another the way people here do. Why you know yourself, Ruth, that here in the Board of Aldermen of the City of New York there isn't a single man who if you were cold and unhappy couldn't put his arms around you and hug you and make you feel good. But you'll never in your life find such loving hearts in Washington. I know, Ruthie darling, because I been there and in the coldness down there I nearly froze meself to death. So you'll sure need that coat, Ruthie me darling.

McGuinness was an early supporter of Franklin D. Roosevelt. He likes to think of himself as one of the architects of the New Deal. He asserts his claim by pointing to a series of resolutions, sponsored by him in 1922, which gave what he calls the "per dime" employees of the city paid holidays and sick leave. These measures, which are, of course, negations of the idea of per diem employment, were, he believes, forerunners of such legislation as the National Fair Labor Standards Act and the National Labor Relations Act. "When you look back on it," he says, "you can see I was working on a lot of them humane matters meself twenty-five years ago."

An example of his resourcefulness comparable to his saving of the Greenpoint ferry was his campaign for farm gardens for the children of Greenpoint. During World War I, a good deal of gardening was done in the city parks, parts of which were plowed up and parceled out to amateur vegetable growers. McGuinness found that the Greenpoint children enjoyed working in the gardens, and when the war was over he persuaded the city administration to let them continue. After a few years, however, when his skill at legislative maneuver was getting Greenpoint far more than its share of appropriations for improvement, the Board of Estimate began to rebel. To keep the gardens, McGuinness was in time forced to employ his large talent for guile. One year he got his garden funds from a reluctant Board by announcing that, to show how much the children benefited from the gardens, he was going to bring six hundred of them to City Hall for a Board of Estimate meeting. "I knew that would scare the bejesus out of them," he said. He told a Board secretary that he had chartered several buses to bring them over. "They'll need a lot of room, God bless them," he said, "because I want them to have their little rakes and shovels and hoes to show how much they love tilting the soil." The prospect of six hundred youngsters thus armed produced immediate assurance from Mayor John F. Hylan that he would vote for the appropriation.

The following year, McGuinness got the appropriation by nominating Mayor Hylan for President of the United States. He says that he argued for an hour before the Board and saw that he was losing. "The sweat run down me back," he recalls. "All me nerves was jumping. I could just see them kids when I had to tell them there would be no gardens. Then it just come to me. It burst right into me brain. I made it up as I went along." He said:

Mr. Mayor, in the history of our glorious country, there have been two great Presidents. One was the Honorable George Washington, who led the nation to freedom, and the other was the Honorable Abraham Lincoln, who freed the poor slaves in 1865. Ever since 1865, a pair of old black shoes have been standing beside the President's desk in the White House. Those shoes are old and worn, but they stay there in the White House because they know that the man who used to walk around in them was loved in the hearts of the poor people of America. And he loved the poor people too, Mr. Mayor. He was the man that said that God must have loved the poor people because he made so many of them. Now when they laid Abraham Lincoln away, those shoes came walking back to the White House and got themselves beside his desk, and they've been waiting there ever since for a man who loves the poor people as much as he did to come and fill them. Today, Mr. Mayor, the City of New York is going to fill those shoes with one of its own, John Francis Hylan, who in his splendid wisdom in voting for these farm gardens is bringing happiness into the hearts of the little ones of Greenpoint and is showing his people, and the great Democratic Party which has always fought for the poor people that he loves them too. John Francis Hylan will be the next President of the United States.

Hylan cast his three votes for the appropriations. The next morning's papers ran stories headlined "Hylan for President Move Started by Local Democratic Leader." When reporters called on McGuinness, he ducked most of their questions. "Hylan's a splendid man," he said, "one of the highest-type men in the country today." When he was finally pinned down, however, he said, "What the hell, pals, I don't mind giving out a few nominations if it will help Greenpoint."

After he was elected alderman, McGuinness let four years pass before he challenged McQuade for the district leadership. In 1924, he took the leadership away from McQuade in a primary and told McQuade he had better close up the Jefferson Club and join the McGuinness Club. McQuade declined. Backed by McCooey and the county machine, McQuade tried to regain the leadership in 1926 and 1928. He lost his county backing in 1928 but tried again in 1930 and 1932. The war was bitter and hard fought. The two clubs were across the street from one another, and night after autumn night the rival leaders would address their followers from their clubhouse steps. The crowds spilled into the middle of the street, and there were frequent border incidents. "Bejesus, I don't like to think how many busted noses there must have been," McGuinness says. "And shiners—there must have been ten thousand." And sometimes McGuinness had so many Greenpointers parading that there were none left to watch and be impressed. McGuinness parades were generally held to celebrate a triumph in wheedling improvements from the city. "Almost every time we'd get a new lamppost, we'd have ourselves a parade," he recalls. Since the improvements were for the benefit of the entire community, everybody marched, even McQuade and the handful of Republicans in Greenpoint. McGuinness's club members were always first in the line of march—just behind Professor Connolly's band. Sometimes they rode horseback. McGuinness used to borrow dray horses from the John C. Orr lumberyard. "The parades was at night," he says, "and the horses wasn't working then, so we thought it would be nice to have them in the parades." McGuinness often led the parades mounted on a white truck horse and wearing a ten-gallon hat. The greatest parade of all was held to celebrate the opening of the swimming pool, and the list of participating organizations as reported in the *Weekly Star* tells a good deal about McGuinness and Greenpoint:

Rodeo of St. Cecilia's RC Church   *Greenpoint Patriotic League*
Black Post 1818, Veterans of   *The Boys from Bourkes*
   Foreign Wars   *Merry Pals Social Club*
Happy Boys Social Club   *Du Tel Pleasure Club*

International Longshoremen's Association

Italian-American Democratic Club

Soldiers and Sailors Kin

The Boys from Lindsay's

RKO Greenpoint Theatre

Chums' Pleasure Club

Melody Boys Social Club

Greenpoint YMCA

St. Catherine of Siena's Boys Band

Polish Legion

Greenpoint Property Owner's Association

Alpha Republican Club

Slovak Citizen's Club

Lexington Council, Knights of Columbus

Diamond Athletic League

Greenpoint Chamber of Commerce

The Aggressive Democrats

Bugs Athletic Club

Knights of St. Anthony

Greenpoint Merchants' Association

Loew's Meserole Theatre

Businessmen of Greenpoint

Hospital Visitation Post 241

Greenpoint YWCA

The King Bees of Greenpoint

Along with the parades, McGuinness arranged a good many clambakes and kiddies' outings as well as such annual events as Ye Olde McGuinnesse Farme Barne Dance Nighte (Professor William F. Connolly's Hayseede Orchestree! Prizes for Most Realistic Rube! Most Fetchinge Farmerette! Youngest Bald-headed Man!). Most of these parties were designed mainly to promote good will in the district, but they were also "rackets" (the word once had a reasonably innocent connotation—meaning nothing more than a fund-raising party run by politicians) to pay off campaign expenses. Part of the money went for some of the most cryptic propaganda in political history. McGuinness believes less in the placards which most candidates put up in store windows and on fences than in throwaways the size of calling cards. "With them, they got something they can carry around and think about," he says. He still has some of the cards used during the long war with McQuade. One of them says:

VOTE FOR MC GUINNESS

MC QUADE CANNOT BE TRUSTED

QUINN (FLOPPER) HAS NO PRINCIPLES

ELIMINATE THE SOREHEADS

VOTE FOR MC GUINNESS

And another:

DON'T MIND THE DARN FOOLS

THEY DON'T KNOW WHAT IT'S

ALL ABOUT

EVEN THOUGH THEY WOULD BE

NOMINATED THEY WOULDN'T

KNOW WHAT IT IS TO

BE A LEGISLATOR

NOMINATE EXPERIENCED MEN

VOTE MC GUINNESS AND DOYLE

And still another:

GREENPOINT'S DICTIONARY

Wigwam Club; noun; a combination of political derelicts, cast on the island of Wigwam, with a sole purpose of doing nothing, only disrupting the democracy of Greenpoint.
Object of these Derelicts: Horn-blowing, wandering from one organization to another (no end) doing nothing for the welfare of the public, and trying to get a job without taking a Civil Service Examination (probably not qualified for the position they seek.)

VOTE FOR ALDERMAN

Peter J. McGuinness

McQuade's surrender was a long time coming. On two or three occasions he said he was ready to quit, then changed his mind. Late in 1927, McGuinness somehow got him to sign an actual document of surrender, which he still has on file at the Club. It read:

Between now and Jan. 1/28, I will become a member of the Regular Organization.

J. A. MC QUADE *(signed)*

O.K. JOHN H. MC COOEY THOMAS F. WOGAN *(signed, witness)*
(signed, witness)

But he did not become a member until 1932. When he did so, it was a magnificent occasion, as solemn and formal as the Japanese surrender to General MacArthur in Tokyo Bay. It came one May evening in 1932. McQuade and an even hundred of his followers met at the Jefferson Club and locked the front door for the last time. Then, with McQuade at their head, they marched slowly, as if to a dirge, down the middle of Manhattan Avenue and down Norman Avenue to the new headquarters of the McGuinness Club. McGuinness awaited them at the head of the flight of steps leading to the door. He was flanked by John McCooey, now a McGuinness enthusiast, and by James Burns, the Borough President of Brooklyn. McQuade walked up the steps, and McGuinness stepped two paces forward and took his hand. He then wheeled about and led the vanquished captain inside, where McGuinness, McCooey, and Burns watched McQuade and the hundred followers sign the McGuinness Club roster and give the treasurer their first year's dues. When this was done, McGuinness and McQuade went back to the clubhouse steps, before which a large crowd had gathered. Each made a brief address. "Peter J. McGuinness," McQuade said, "is now the undisputed leader of this district. Let no man say I am not earnest in my admiration of him. These ugly rumors must stop." McGuinness said: "From this day forward, Pete McGuinness and Jim McQuade march forward hand in hand like brothers for the benefit of the grand old Democratic Party."

In one of his speeches before the capitulation, McGuinness had said of McQuade, "He is the most despicable man in public life today. He is a man who is not even a man among men." When McQuade died in 1935, McGuinness delivered a eulogy. "You could always say of old Jim McQuade," he said, "that he was a man among men."

Most of the time that McQuade was district leader, he was on the public payroll either as sheriff or as register, and when McGuinness became leader he became eligible to succeed to those now defunct offices if he chose to do so, which he did. Some of his friends and admirers felt that he made a large mistake in deserting the Board of Aldermen for the obscurity of a county office. A writer in the Brooklyn *Eagle* compared his departure from City Hall with the "Caesars departing Rome for Constantinople or the Pope's retirement to Avignon." McGuinness in time felt the same way about it, but he thoroughly enjoys his present job as assistant commissioner of Borough Works, which he can have as long as there is a Democratic administration in Brooklyn. But he has one further ambition. He would like to be borough president. He never wanted a job that would take him out of New York or force him to relinquish his leadership in Greenpoint, but he feels that the borough presidency would be a fitting climax to what he regards as being, up to now, a thoroughly satisfying career. He has had his managers do some exploratory work now and then, and only last year a flyer was circulated around Borough Hall whose origins, according to McGuinness, were thoroughly baffling. It was somebody's trial balloon, and it read:

> Knock, knock.
> Who's there?
> Borough.
> Borough who?
> Borough President Peter J. McGuinness
> McGuinness for Borough President.

He has only once publicly avowed any interest in the job. As a rule, he has been indirect in answering reporters' questions. "I don't think I ought to be saying anything meself," he said last year, "but I will say for me sweetheart that it would make her proud as a bird of paradise." It was in 1937 that he made his one unequivocal statement. "The demands," he said to the press, reading slowly from a prepared statement, "have been so many and so general that after considerable thought and for the best interests of Greenpoint, I have decided to throw my hat in the ring and declare tonight that I am willing to accept this nomination should the County Leader see fit to honor me."

The County Leader did not see fit. McGuinness's day is past. Brooklyn's middle class may be relatively small, but it is a community of middle-class ideals. Its politicians nowadays must have a bit more finish than McGuinness has and a good many more pretensions. A man who calls himself a "boss," as McGuinness freely and happily does, just won't do. It would offend, as perhaps it should, everyone from the Bar Association to what McGuinness calls the Reverend Clergy. There is no evidence that the present Borough President, John Cashmore, is a man of greater talent or training or capacity than McGuinness, but he looks like a successful funeral director, while McGuinness looks like McGuinness, the dock-walloping son of a brass polisher. On one score, however, McGuinness could pass the purity tests of the reformers who influence the choice of candidates even when they do not control them. So far as is known, he is, by all the standard measures, honest. "They'll never show anyone," he has said time after time, "where Peter McGuinness ever stole a single vote or took a nickel for getting a pal a job." He has been investigated twice, once by Samuel Seabury for the Hofstadter Committee, and once by Paul Blanshard, the former Commissioner of Accounts. Both times his affairs were found to be in order. In 1927, his clubhouse was raided because it was found to be quartering bookmakers. McGuinness makes no bones about this matter. It was during the war with McQuade. Some bookmakers approached him and told him that many good precinct workers, McGuinness followers at heart, were being kept in bondage to McQuade merely by their love of horseflesh. The McQuade Club had facilities for betting; the McGuinness Club did not. If McGuinness would provide them with space for operations, they said, his club's membership would be increased. He provided space. Membership did increase. The police held him briefly after the raid but released him when the play-and-pay-off sheets showed that only the reasonable profit of twelve per cent was being made by the bookies and that there was no evidence that McGuinness or any other official of the club had taken any gambling money.

At the Seabury investigation, McGuinness was the most ingratiating of witnesses. Many of the district leaders called upon to testify were sulky on the stand; many refused to sign waivers of immunity. McGuinness, who came accompanied by a claque of dozens of Greenpointers, was in his usual high spirits. He strode briskly to the witness stand, where he signed the waiver with a flourish. "Gentlemen," he said to the attending members of the Hofstadter Committee, "I am glad to present me presence here today. How do you do? Shoot." Judge Seabury kept McGuinness on the stand for hours, chiefly, he later said, because he liked to hear the man talk. He questioned McGuinness about his rise in Greenpoint and his fight with McQuade, who, Seabury had just revealed, had banked several hundred thousand dollars more than he had earned. "And then you took the district away from McQuade?" Seabury asked at one point. "Judge, I didn't take nothing away," McGuinness said. "The people of Greenpoint took it away and give it to me." Seabury asked McGuinness if he had any bank deposits other than the modest ones the committee knew about or if he had any ill-gotten gains in one of the "little tin boxes" described by Sheriff Tom Farley, a large-scale grafter. McGuinness pulled out of a coat pocket a wallet, outsized and overstuffed, which he has always used as a filing case for his "contracts." "Judge," he said, "this is the only tin box I got. It's never contained anything but the heartaches of me people, me Jewish *mazuza,* and me father-in-law's front collar button. He was a great old champeen, Judge." Seabury brought up the gambling incident and asked McGuinness if he accepted full responsibility for it. "Your honor," McGuinness said, "there's only one leader of that club. Right here before you. Shoot, Judge." In time, though, McGuinness grew bored with the subject. "Judge," he said, "what do you say we bury this. I told you everything. Don't let's be talking about it any more. It's dead, and I'm tired of looking at it." Seabury agreed that the subject had been exhausted. After a few pleasantries he ended the examination. As he left the stand, McGuinness again addressed the full committee. "Gentlemen," he said, "it's been a pleasure, I assure you, having this great pleasure of coming before you. I want to thank you for being so kind and courteous to me. Good afternoon."

At times, McGuinness adopts a great air of virtue about his code of ethics. "How the hell do you think I'd feel," he says, "if I was to stand on the corner some Saturday night and see some pal coming down the street and I couldn't look him in the eye without thinking, Well, I got five hundred for getting that one the job he has today. Why, I'd just feel awful inside to think I had a nickel that should be going to feed another man's little ones." More often, however, he puts it on a more pragmatic basis. "It don't pay," he says. "There's no percentage in it. Let's say I tell a precinct cáptain to use repeaters. He gets away with it in a city election, then a state election. Then he tries it in a federal election, and bejesus it's a federal case. He says I put him up to it and I'm before a federal judge that I don't even know." He also points out that he is not exposed to the temptations that beset other politicians. He says he has never seen a horse race. His only bets have been on penny-a-point rummy. He and his wife live quietly in a four-room apartment which seems to be furnished largely with blue-tinted mirrors, golden-oak chairs and tables, and fringed lamp shades. The principal *objet d'art* is a reproduction of the "Last Supper" in butterfly wings. Mrs. McGuinness does all the cooking and housework. McGuinness takes little time off. He tries to get away from the club one evening a week and take Mrs. McGuinness to a movie. "The wife picks the shows," he says. McGuinness says he has seen very little he has really enjoyed since Marie Dressler died. Among the exceptions are Mae West movies. Mae West, he says, is a Greenpoint girl. McGuinness knew her father, a local club fighter. Mrs. McGuinness says she is not among Mae West's greatest admirers, but she goes anyway to honor local talent. "I guess she does that wiggling just to be comical," she said in one of her rare interviews with the press not long ago. "It's the way Peter says—there's worse things than that." On the same occasion, McGuinness spoke of his own ways. "Right now," he explained, "I don't drink, smoke, chew, nor gamble. And I never go to any of them Jesse James night clubs. A fellow said to me the other day, 'If you don't do none of them things, Peter McGuinness, what the hell do you do?' I said, 'All I do is take God's beautiful air and sunshine and, bejesus, I play politics.'"

⋆ En Route with Truman and Dewey

In the autumn of 1948, I spent a few weeks riding around the country on the Presidential campaign trains. I rode west from Washington on the President's train, taking a week or more to reach Los Angeles via the Pennsylvania, the Rock Island, the Denver & Rio Grande Western, the Union Pacific, the Southern Pacific, and perhaps a couple of others. (There was a good deal of backtracking and sidetracking.) In Los Angeles, I joined Governor Dewey's train and meandered up the West Coast to Seattle and east across the northern tier by Northern Pacific, Great Northern, and the Milwaukee Line. I did not realize at the time that I was covering the last tours of the country that any President or Presidential candidate would make by rail. I did foresee—and note, at the end of my letter to the New Yorker from the Dewey train—that television would alter the nature of subsequent campaigns, but it evidently did not occur to me that by 1952 the airlines would take over.

Had I realized this, I would, I imagine, have written at somewhat greater length about life aboard the trains. But I did write a bit about it, and more, I believe, than any other passenger wrote. I have reprinted the two pieces without change. I would be pleased not to have written on the assumption that Thomas E. Dewey was bound to win. But I took it for granted, and so did everyone else—including, I have always been convinced, President Truman himself at that period of the campaign. I still have notes on an interview I had with one of the President's closest friends the day after we left Washington. I find this entry: "T. says Truman knows perfectly well he can't win, is

65

doing this for the record. Besides, wants to raise hell with 80th Congress."

THE TRUMAN TRAIN

POLITICS is a branch of show business, and life aboard a Presidential campaign train—a peculiar and somewhat wearing form of existence that I have been sampling on and off during the past couple of weeks—is like life in a fast-moving road carnival. We are always either setting up the show or knocking it down. We play more towns than the World of Mirth or Brunk's Comedians (a carnival overtaken by the Truman train when I was riding on it through Colorado and Utah), and we work longer hours. The average self-respecting carnival stays for a week if a town is good-sized, and for a night in other places, but we seldom stay anywhere more than a few hours, and we frequently play ten-minute stands. Occasionally, we have been in and out of a town within five or six minutes, and have stood still for only two. On some days, we have played fourteen or fifteen places, starting at dawn and keeping at it until just before midnight. Our main concerns as we go along are narrowly professional. We worry about the tenting facilities in the town down yonder, the availability of baths, the friendliness of the law-enforcement organizations, the liquor regulations in the next state, and the size and humor of the crowds. The name of a town we have been in doesn't stand for a plot of earth and a group of buildings; it stands for a particular audience or a particular incident. To a man who has been riding the rails with President Truman, Reno isn't a famous divorce-and-gambling city but the place where our man blew a few of his lines and talked about "Republican mothbags" when he meant to say "Republican mossbacks."

Ours is, to be sure, a carnival of an unusual sort. It has just one act, and the one act is built around just one performer. For an enterprise of its size, it carries entirely too many hangers-on—twenty-odd in the President's party and fifty-odd in the press party. Still, the road-show analogy, at least on the Truman train (which, I understand, runs on a tighter schedule than the Dewey train), holds pretty true all the way down the line. We have our beaters, who travel ahead of us and make arrangements with newspapermen, police, sign painters, and soft-drink concessionaires. We have our shills, who get out in the audience and, by clapping wherever the script calls for it, help to build a good tip, as old carny hands call a large and eager crowd. Some of our beaters and shills are men of distinguished reputation. The chief advance man is Oscar Chapman, Under-Secretary of the Interior, and the boss shill appears to be Brigadier General Wallace Graham, the famous grain speculator and personal physician to the President. He is sometimes assisted by Clark Clifford, Truman's executive assistant and the chief of the ghost-writing department. Then, too, we have our Princess Bright Cloud—Miss Margaret Truman, who, wherever her father's friends have been able to stir up an audience, steps out from behind a blue velvet curtain onto the rear platform of the train to wave and smile at the crowd. This is, theatrically, the high point of the act. True, it is not followed by a spiel urging the people to lay down the tenth part of a dollar to step inside the tent and see the rest of the show. Nor is anyone advised to buy a bottle of Dr. Truman's Old Missouri Tonic. But there is a request to step inside the polling booths on November 2 and pull the right levers or "x" the circle next to the donkey. "I don't want you to vote for me," the President of the United States has been saying at county seats and railroad division points all across the country. "I want you to get out on Election Day and vote for yourselves. Vote for your own interests, your own part of the country, your own friends." It seems a rather parochial point of view to be encouraging in Americans at this stage of world history, but it is obvious that the President wants very much to stay on in the White House, and he probably feels that educating the masses toward broader perspectives can wait until he gets Governor Dewey off his neck.

It would be going too far to say that the crowds, either in the small towns or in the large cities, respond enthusiastically to his appeals for support. They don't. There is every evidence that they are kindly disposed toward him and that they sympathize with him about his difficult lot in life, but nothing that I have heard him say between Washington, D.C., and Los Angeles has drawn more than a spot of polite applause. Nobody stomps, shouts, or whistles for Truman. Everybody claps. I should say that the decibel count would be about the same as it would be for a missionary who has just delivered a mildly encouraging report on the inroads being made against heathenism in Northern Rhodesia. This does not necessarily mean that the people who come out to hear him intend to vote against him—though my personal feeling is that most of them intend to do exactly that. It may mean only that he is not the sort of man—any more than his opponent is—to provoke wild enthusiasm.

The part of the act that involves the President's daughter is invariably the most effective part, and Truman's management of it displays a good deal of canniness and trouping instinct. She comes on just before the finale at every matinee and evening performance. The show, as a rule, gets under way after "Hail to the Chief" has been rendered by the local high-school band. Next, a local beauty, a local union man, or a local Kiwanis man hands the President, depending on where we are, a bag of peaches, a mess of celery, a miner's hat, or just the key to the city. He has become quite adept at accepting these offerings graciously and then shoving them the hell inside his car. It takes, by my unofficial clocking, one and three-quarter minutes to give the mayor, the governor, and the Democratic candidate for Congress—the two last are likely to ride along with us through their state—their cracks at the audience. Whoever comes at the end of the procession has, as they say, the unparalleled honor and glorious privilege of introducing the President. During the ten-minute layovers, Truman limits his part of the act to five minutes. He begins with local scenery, local industry, local agriculture, and local intelligence; leads from this into a description of the contempt in which the Republican party holds the region he is passing through; goes on to a preview of the Good Society that he, given another term and the kind of Congress he wants, will create; and, penultimately, makes his plea for votes. Then, with a surer sense of timing than he shows in major addresses, he pauses a moment, looks quizzically at the crowd, smiles, and asks, very humbly, "And now, howja like to meet ma family?" He cocks his head slightly to catch the response; he has the appealing look of a man who wouldn't be surprised if the answer was no but would be terribly hurt. The crowd's desire to meet the Truman women, however, never fails to exceed by a good deal its desire for repeal of the Taft-Hartley Act. When he has caught the favorable response, he says, "First, Mizz Truman," and the First Lady, who, like her husband, is more relaxed before small crowds than before large ones or photographers, parts the curtain and takes her place at his right side. Sometimes, when the crowd is very small and friendly, the President identifies Mrs. Truman as "the boss" and winks knowingly at the men in the audience. After Mrs. Truman and her admirers have exchanged greetings, the President says, "And now I'd like to have you meet my daughter, Margaret." (I thought it a nice touch that, down in the border states, he said, whether artfully or not I am unable to decide, "And now I'd like *for* you to meet Miss Margaret.") It involves no disrespect for Mrs. Truman to say that her daughter gets a bigger hand then she does; this country may be run by and for mothers, but its goddesses are daughters. Margaret's entrance comes closer than anything else to bringing down the house.

As soon as the Truman womenfolk have flanked the President, a railroad official, generally a vice-president of the line, who sits at a telephone in the car ahead of the President's, calls the locomotive engineer—fifteen cars, or a quarter of a mile, down the track—and tells him to get slowly under way. As the train pulls out from the station, the family waves good-by. Mrs. Truman and Margaret then go back into the car to fix their hair for the next curtain call, leaving the President alone on the platform until the last switchman in the yards has had his look. I am certain that, no matter what the fate of the Truman administration, millions of Americans will, for the rest of their lives, have framed in their mind's eye a vivid image of the Three Traveling Trumans highballing off into the black nights of Colorado or Arizona, blending with the tall pines in the Sierras, or being slowly enveloped by the dust of the Midwestern plains. It will be a picture to cherish, and it will stand Harry Truman in good stead for the rest of his life. Traveling with him, you get the feeling that the American people who have seen him and heard him at his best would be willing to give him just about anything he wants except the Presidency.

As a rule, the Truman show does better in the small towns than in the large ones. The President is a feed-mill type of talker, and he can be excellent indeed with a small audience. Charles Ross, his press secretary and the sort of man who wouldn't stoop to inventing a literary background for his employer, tells me that Truman has worked hard at his Mark Twain, which contributes no doubt to the raciness of his conversational style and accounts for the pleasant way it falls on the ear. In Dexter, Iowa, he made a long, scolding speech to 75,000 farmers who were on hand to see the final in a national plowing contest that was being held on the farm of a woman named Lois Agg. The farmers, a happy, prosperous crew, some of whom had flown there in their own planes, were in no mood to be scolded, but they listened courteously, and applauded every now and then. A couple of hours later, after the President had inspected the plowing and some tractor exhibits, and after he had refreshed himself with some pieces of prize-winning cakes and pies, he returned to the platform, to talk informally about his early days on a farm. He carried on for quite a while about the differences between mules and machines. He was delightful, and the people were delighted. When he speaks without a script, as he always does unless he is making a major campaign address, he inflicts considerable damage on the English language, but anything he does on his own is not one-tenth as deplorable as what his ghost writers do for him. One can choose between, on the one hand, "gluttons of privilege" and "only an appetizer for an economic tapeworm," both of which are creations of his belles-lettres division, and, on the other hand, a Trumanism such as "I'm goin' down to Berkeley to get me a degree." The language of the academy seems to jinx him every time. "I'm only a synthetic alumni," he said modestly when, in Grinnell, Iowa, he was introduced by a professor as the most distinguished graduate of the local college. It can be said of Trumanisms, though, that they are genuine, that they almost always make sense, and that they occasionally, as in the line about Berkeley, have an engaging lilt.

Truman's detailed knowledge of the small towns is unexpected and remarkable. The impression one gets is that he has acquired, in his sixty-four years, a spoonful or two of information about every community west of the Mississippi and about a good many of those east of it. Of course he is briefed, by people on the other side of the blue velvet curtain, on current local problems and local interests before he hits a place in which he is going to speak, but he is always able to throw in something from his own stock-pile on its remote or recent past. If he hasn't been there before himself, the chances are that Mrs. Truman or some relative has, and that if no living Truman has connections in town, a dead Truman once had. His maternal grandfather, Solomon Young, drove wagon trains in the West a century ago, and the old gentle-man went through an extraordinary number of towns. Accord-ing to a Pennsylvania Railroad representative on the Truman train, this campaign trip is just about the most elaborate tour ever made of this country. I suspect that he is referring only to railroad trips and has conveniently overlooked, for the sake of rail propaganda, those wagon-train trips made by Grandfather Solomon Young.

In the big cities, the show loses a lot of its fun. One civic auditorium is pretty much like the next one, chicken-and-peas dinners are the same everywhere, and so are Democratic com-mitteemen and committeewomen. Even Los Angeles, from which something out of the way might be expected, put on a drab show for the President. True, there were thirty-two searchlights, but they merely showed up the bare spots in the grandstand. This is a Dewey year in the movie colony, as it probably is almost everywhere else. By the time the Truman people got around to renting a place for the President to speak in, the Dewey crowd had leased the Hollywood Bowl for the evening he was scheduled to talk, in order, as they put it, to "rehearse" the lighting effects for the Governor's appearance the following night. (When one sees the lighting effects at a Hollywood rally, to say nothing of the neon signs in Hollywood and Los Angeles, one can easily understand why federal power projects are so essential to Cali-fornia's welfare.) The Democrats had to be satisfied with a place called Gilmore Stadium. The unfortunate thing about Gilmore Stadium was not that it is smaller than the Hollywood Bowl but that it is larger. Neither Dewey nor Truman drew capacity crowds in Hollywood; as a matter of fact, they drew about the same number of people. But the vacant seats at Truman's meeting were more numerous, because the number of seats was greater.

Almost the only color in the big-city productions is provided by the automobiles in which we ride. Like a circus, we start off with a parade, and though our parades are less animated than those of most circuses, they are as musical and, thanks to the cars, have just as much glitter. Before I started on this trip, I did not realize the odd role played by the automobile in national politics. The Truman party was driven from Dexter, Iowa, to Des Moines, approximately forty miles, in a fleet of thirty-five brand-new cars, all of them convertibles with the top down. I didn't stop to wonder how so many new convertibles came to be at the disposal of the Party of the Workingmen, in Iowa, of all places. Then, riding in Car Number 30, through downtown Des Moines, I began to think it strange that the crowds that had seen the President, riding in Car Number 1, five minutes earlier, did not disperse. They were looking just as hard at the carloads of rumpled and unsmiling reporters as they must have looked at the celebrities up forward. "Sure they're beautiful," I overheard a middle-aged man say to his companion, "but I guess you have to be a Democrat to get one." "Thing about a Packard," another man said, "you can still tell one when you see it—the old pointed radiator and those red hubcaps. Hasn't changed since I've known it." "Ought to strip all that housing down," a third voter remarked. "Ever try to get a jack under one of those things?"

I didn't have time to inquire into the details of automobile procurement in Des Moines, but I did in Denver, two days later. The Truman train was met by twenty-two Kaisers and Frazers and eight new Fords. I asked our driver if he had lent his car to the President out of party loyalty. "Nah," he said. "This isn't my car. I'm just helping out a friend of mine here. He's the Kaiser-Frazer distributor in town—Northwestern Auto Company, they call it—and I guess he come out first in this agency fight. Got mostly Kaisers and Frazers here. Lucky for him. The 1949 models just come in yesterday, and he's getting a chance right off

to display them." It was the same everywhere. There was a tie-in
with the dealers in every city we visited: free transportation in
exchange for free advertising. The new cars were seen by the
President's admirers, and the President was seen by admirers of
new cars. So far, the struggle has been mainly between Ford
and Kaiser-Frazer. The Ford people seem to me to be leading
by about three to two. Denver was the only place where Kaiser-
Frazer was plainly in the political ascendancy. If the crowds
have been, for the most part, pleased with the new models, the
Secret Service men guarding the President have not. In Los
Angeles, they rebelled. They refused to let him ride through that
unpredictable city in anything without running boards for them
to stand on. A search for something with running boards was
made, and a 1934 Lincoln touring car was found. It belonged to
Cecil B. De Mille, who plans to vote for Dewey but whose
patriotic impulses are stronger than his party loyalty.

As a piece of railroading, the handling of the Truman train
is a work of art. Any Presidential campaign train demands considerable ingenuity and planning by the railroad people, but if
the man already in office is a candidate to succeed himself, the
trip is particularly difficult to organize. The problems of security
are greater, and so are those of communication. The President's
train must be a mobile White House as well as a mobile hustings.
I talked about the train with Mr. Dewey Long, a Civil Service
employee who for fifteen years has been the White House transportation and communications officer, and to Mr. Harry Karr,
who is division passenger agent for the Pennsylvania Railroad in
Washington, D.C. Both men have been on the Presidential train
from the beginning. A good part of Mr. Long's worries were over
by the time the train began to roll, but Mr. Karr, who has been
on the job of running Presidents around the country ever since
the days of Harding, has to think about each Presidential train
constantly until it pulls back into the Union Station, in Washington. Mr. Karr is a slight, tense man, physically and emotion-
ally a sort of Ernest Truex, and he says that his job has left its
mark on him. "I may not look it from the outside," he says, "but
inside I'm a nervous wreck. It's been real high-tension stuff all
along—from Harding and Coolidge on down." We were riding,

as we talked, through the Royal Gorge of Colorado, where the cut in the Rockies made by the Arkansas River is only thirty feet wide at some points. "Just look out the window," he said. "Makes you sweat blood even to think of taking a President through here. Let a few boulders roll down that thing and we'd all be shooting the rapids. Believe me, we thought long and hard before we agreed to bring this train down through here."

When the President and his political advisers have decided on a trip, they call in Mr. Long and sketch out for him the route they wish the train to travel, the places they wish to visit, and the approximate timetable they wish to keep. The White House tries to alternate between the Pennsylvania and the Baltimore & Ohio out of Washington for western trips, so whichever line is due for its turn gets it. This last time, it was the Pennsylvania, which is why Mr. Long, after getting his first instructions, called Mr. Karr in on the job. Mr. Karr put the Pennsylvania's Special Movement Bureau to work, and the Bureau, in co-operation with the Rock Island, the Denver & Rio Grande Western, the Union Pacific, and other lines over whose track the train was to go, worked out the schedule. "When we're told about a deal of this kind," Mr. Karr said, "we flash the code word 'POTUS' to every line along the way. It stands for 'President of the United States,' and it means that when the time comes, they have to be ready to do a number of things. Every grade crossing has to be manned when the train passes, and I just can't tell you how many switches have to be spiked until we've moved on." To arrange all this spiking and fit the schedule of a Presidential train into train schedules all across the country and back is, naturally, a fairly involved problem, but on this trip it was done almost without a hitch. According to Mr. Karr, only one regular train has been seriously delayed by the transcontinental movement of the President up to now. This was a Rock Island express running between Kansas City and Denver. The superintendent of one division of the line wanted to sidetrack the Truman train, which on this part of the journey was pulling up wherever two or three were gathered together, at a certain point and let the express pass it, but it was decided, after a Sunday conference of railroad

officials in Kansas City, not to let the train by. "There was just
the tiniest chance that a piece of flying steel or something like
that might have hit the President's train," Mr. Karr told me.

"Of course, nothing could have hurt the President, in his
armored car." At that, the express was only forty-five minutes late
getting into Denver.

The train that Mr. Karr had to assemble for the current trip
is a heterogeneous assortment of rolling stock. Not counting the
pilot train—usually a locomotive and a single car—which runs
five miles ahead to see that no anarchists have torn up the track,
it is seventeen cars long and includes, in addition to Pullmans,
diners, lounges, and a car in which the press can work, a communications car, operated and staffed by the Army Signal Corps,
and the Ferdinand Magellan, the President's special car, which
belongs to the government and was used by President Roosevelt
throughout the war. The communications car, which is just behind the locomotive, contains two Diesel engines to generate
power for its radio teletype and other electrical equipment. The
radio teletype makes it possible for the President to keep in constant touch with Washington and, through Washington, with the
rest of the world. News, most of it in code, is received in the
communications car and phoned back to the President's car.
The communications car can also transmit messages. Telephone
lines are kept open from the White House and the State Department to the towns the President's train goes through. He
can pull up at any whistle stop in the country and hold a long-
distance Cabinet meeting, provided he can find his Cabinet members.

The Ferdinand Magellan, which has four staterooms, a galley,
a dining room, and an observation platform, is, of course, the
last car on the train, and brings the over-all length up to the
maximum legal length for most states. In effect, it is not only a
seventeenth car but an eighteenth, for it weighs 265,000 pounds,
or about twice as much as the average Pullman. The extra weight
of the car is accounted for mainly by the armor plate, partly by
the three-inch bulletproof glass in the windows, and partly by
the extra equipment it carries, including a couple of escape
hatches and the blue velvet curtain.

THE DEWEY TRAIN

CANDIDATES notoriously promise better than they ever perform, but if Governor Dewey manages the Presidency half as well as he is managing his campaign for it, we are about to have four, eight, twelve, sixteen years of cool, sleek efficiency in government. I venture upon this prophecy after quite a spell of riding aboard the Dewey Victory Special, the train that has been hauling the Republican candidate, his wife, and his entourage of advisers, well-wishers, favor-curriers, and newspapermen up and down the country since mid-September. Before I looked in on the Dewey campaign, I had acquired some seasoning and a basis for comparison by serving a correspondent's hitch on the train that took President Truman and his similar, but far smaller, group of fellow passengers over much the same route. As far as the arts and techniques, as distinct from the political content, of the campaigns are concerned, the difference between the Democratic and Republican operation is, I calculate, thirty or forty years. It is the difference between horsehair and foam rubber, between the coal-stove griddle and the pop-up toaster. Dewey is the pop-up toaster.

Everything I've seen of the Dewey campaign is slick and snappy. This is in strong contrast to the general dowdiness and good-natured slovenliness of the Truman campaign, at least when and where I observed it. Truman's mass meetings were all old-style political rallies, brightened up, on occasion, by some droopy bunting and by Department of Sanitation brass bands. In San Francisco, the Democrats contracted a most unfortunate alliance with a musical branch of the local parent-teacher association, which called itself the Mother Singers of America. The Mother Singers were authentic mothers—and grandmothers—who wrapped themselves in yards of brown monk's cloth and sang the kind of songs you would expect them to. The Dewey group favors professional musicians, professional decorators, and professionals in everything else. All the way down the line, his effects are more dramatic and electrifying. At a Truman meeting, the President, as a rule, takes his seat on the platform and sits quietly, a slender and almost pathetic figure surrounded by

florid police commissioners and senators of heroic bulk, through
all the preliminaries. When his turn finally comes to speak, his
advance toward the microphone hardly takes the multitude by
storm. Dewey's entrances are delayed. He remains in the wings
until all the invocations and endorsements are over. Sometimes
he stays away from the meeting hall until the last moment. Then,
with a great whining of motorcycle-escort sirens to hush the
crowd and build up suspense, he arrives. The instant his name is
spoken, he comes onstage, seemingly from nowhere, arms out-
stretched to embrace the crowd and gather in the applause that
breaks the hush. It is an uncannily effective piece of business.
Dewey doesn't seem to walk; he coasts out like a man who has
been mounted on casters and given a tremendous shove from
behind. However it is done, he rouses the crowd to a peak of
excitement and enthusiasm, and he has to wait an agreeably
long while for the racket to die down.

Dewey likes drama, but he has an obvious distaste for the
horseplay side of politics. He accepts honorary memberships in
sheriffs' posses and fraternal organizations, but he is uncomforta-
ble during the installation ceremonies. On his first transcontinental tour after his nomination, he collected some fifteen cow-
puncher hats, but he refused to try on any of them in public.
The only time he got into the spirit of things was at his rally
in the Hollywood Bowl. For this gathering, his local managers,
mainly movie people, arranged a first-class variety show. In addition to assembling a lot of stars who endorsed the candidate in
short, pithy, gag-laden speeches, they hired a marimba band and
a chorus line for the preliminary entertainment. For the invocations, they recruited a minister, a priest, and a rabbi all of whom
could have played romantic leads themselves. At the end of
Dewey's speech, the marimba band struck up "God Bless America," as a recessional. Dewey was still standing at the microphone,
and Mrs. Dewey, as she always does after he finishes, came forward to join him. Perhaps the pageantry finally overcame him,
for suddenly he breathed deep and took aboard a full load of the
fine night air of Hollywood. Then he gave vent to the rich bari-
tone he spent so many years developing. ". . . land that I love,"
he sang, and, slipping an arm around Mrs. Dewey's waist, looked

encouragingly at·her. Mrs. Dewey came in on the next line, and together they went all the way through the rest of the Irving Berlin anthem.

It is one of the paradoxes of 1948 that the man in office is a much less experienced campaigner than the man who is seeking to win the office. Truman was on the public payroll when Dewey was still a college boy in Michigan, but his serious campaigning has been limited to two tries for the United States Senate and one for the Vice-Presidency. It wasn't bush-league stuff, but it wasn't big-league, either. Dewey, on the other hand, is entitled to wear service stripes for three major campaigns. In 1940, he sought the Republican nomination as vigorously as he sought the main prize in 1944 and is seeking it now. The effects are apparent in the organization and planning of every phase of his campaign travels. There is far more foresight and far better timing and scheduling than in the President's tour. Dewey's staff work is superior, too. For example, correspondents with Truman were forced, while I was aboard his train, to miss deadline after deadline because they had to wait too long for advance copies of the President's speeches. Presumably his ghost writers, some of whom were on the train and some of whom were back in Washington, were agonizing up to the zero hour, trying to make their sentences come out right. And then the sentences didn't come out right anyway. The rhetoric that Truman was given to deliver was coarse, gritty, old-fashioned political stuff, with about as much flow as oatmeal. Dewey's speeches, which reporters can put on the telegraph wires twelve to twenty-four hours before delivery time, are as smooth and glossy as chromium. It may be that, on analysis, their cliché content would turn out to be neither much lower nor much higher than that of Truman's speeches, but, as one man on the challenger's train put it, they are written and spoken in such a manner that they give one the feeling Dewey has not borrowed his clichés from the masters but has minted them all by himself.

A conscientious search for the literary antecedents of Dewey's speeches might show that the strongest influence is the *Reader's Digest*. They are full of the good cheer, the defiant optimism, the inspirational tone, and the breath-taking simplification that

have made that magazine so popular. If Dewey's speeches are
not consciously modeled on the *Digest,* there are few of them
that would not seem at home in its pages. "Your future lies ahead
of you," a catchy line that turned up in several of the speeches,
would make a splendid *Digest* title. Moreover, in sound *Digest*
fashion, Dewey is promising to start, when he gets to Washington, "the greatest pruning and weeding operation in American
history." When the thought first occurred to me that Dewey or
his advisers might have picked up a few tricks from the *Digest,*
I asked James C. Hagerty, the candidate's press secretary, if he
had any idea whether or not this was the case. "I hardly think
so," Hagerty said. "The Governor has a style all his own that he's
been working on for years." Even so, it is worth noting that one
of the important personages aboard the Dewey train is Stanley
High, a Roving Editor of the *Digest* and the author of some of
the most celebrated articles it has published in recent years. The
dope on Mr. High, as I got it from Hagerty, is that he is traveling with Dewey not as an author but as a former clergyman. His
function, I was told, is to advise Dewey on the religious implications of political issues and on the political implications of
religious issues. Still, it might be that, unknown to Hagerty, Mr.
High finds time, in between issues, to make a phrase here and
condense a line of argument there.

Dewey's effect on his audience is unquestionably greater than
Truman's. He does not, so far as I am able to judge, draw larger
crowds. The business of estimating the size of crowds is, by the
way, probably one of the most nonsensical and misleading aspects
of political reporting. Some correspondents make a hobby of it,
and conceivably their technique improves with practice, but
most of them rely on police officials for their figures. Suspecting
that a policeman can be as wrong as the next man, I made a simple test at one Dewey meeting. I asked the ranking police official
for his estimate and then asked the manager of the auditorium
for his. The policeman's count, which turned up in a number
of newspapers, was fifty per cent higher. Since the manager's
standard of living is directly related to the size of the audiences
in his auditorium, I imagine it would be safer to string along
with him. Then, there is always an element of fortuitousness in

the size of the street crowds that watch the candidates ride through the big cities. There is no way of telling how many people have come out of their way to see the distinguished visitor and how many just happen to be around. It is customary for campaign managers to take advantage of the fortuitous element. Campaign trains have an oddly predictable way of arriving for afternoon meetings just before the lunch hour and for evening meetings just before the stores and offices close. A candidate's procession never goes directly from the depot to its destination in town. The Civic Center may be only three or four blocks up State Street from the Union Station, but the motorcade is certain to follow a route that covers at least thirty blocks, and thereby catches a lot more innocent bystanders. Possibly the best way to calculate the turnout of admirers would be to estimate the number of onlookers carrying bundles and then subtract them from the total.

For judging crowds, the ear is probably a more reliable instrument than the eye. Its verdict, I would say, favored Dewey almost everywhere. No Truman crowd that I heard responded with more than elementary courtesy and occasionally mild and rather weary approval. Partly, no doubt, this was because the President has a lamentable way of swallowing the very lines he ought to bellow or snarl, and partly, I think, it was because he simply didn't have his audience with him. Dewey's ovations are never, as the phrase goes, thundering, but his applause is not mere politeness. Dewey is not an orator in the classic sense, but he is a first-class elocutionist, and when he fixes his eyes on the crowd and says that the way to avoid having Communists in the government is to avoid appointing them in the first place, as he plans to do, he gets what he wants from the customers, which means, naturally, that they are getting what they want from him.

The junior-executive briskness in the running of the Dewey campaign extends, quite mysteriously, to many phases of life aboard the train. Campaign trains become, in their few weeks of existence, compact social organizations. They develop their own mores and their own institutions. One of the most remarkable—indeed, almost weird—features of life on them is the way the spirit of the leading passenger, riding in the last car, seems to dominate and mold the spirit of the entourage. It is understandable that this should happen to the staff of the candidate, but it actually affects even the newspapermen. Candidates have nothing to do with the selection of the reporters who accompany them. In some cases, to be sure, the reporters select candidates, and it is conceivable that psychological affinity may have influenced their choices. But the effect of that affinity would be, at best, a small one, and it would govern only a few journalists. Yet I am prepared to testify under oath that the atmosphere even in the press section of the Truman train is pure Harry Truman, and the atmosphere in the press section of the Dewey train is pure Tom Dewey. One is like life in the back rooms at District Headquarters, the other like life in the Greenwich Country Club. The favorite beverage in the club cars on the Truman train, when I was on it, was the Kentucky bourbon highball, before, during, and after meals. I don't recall seeing a single cocktail served. Highballs are often seen on the Dewey train, but Martinis and Manhattans are more in vogue. The principal diversion on the Truman train was poker, generally seven-card stud. At least two games were always in progress. If any poker is played on the Dewey train, it is played behind closed compartment doors. There are, however, several spirited bridge games going on all the time.

It may be that the correspondents with Truman took to the more rugged forms of recreation because their life was more rugged. Life with Truman was not exactly primitive but, compared to life with Dewey, it was hard. If you wanted anything laundered, you did it yourself, in a Pullman basin. When you detrained anywhere for an overnight stay, it was every man for himself. You carried your duffel and scrabbled for your food. If a man was such a slave to duty that he felt obliged to hear what the President said in his back-platform addresses, he had to climb down off the train, run to the rear end, mingle with the crowd, and listen. Often, this was a hazardous undertaking, for the President was given to speaking late at night to crowds precariously assembled on sections of roadbed built up fifteen or twenty feet above the surrounding land. The natives knew the contours of the ground, but the reporters did not, and more than one of them tumbled down a cindery embankment. The Dewey organization sees that none of these inconveniences trouble the life of anyone on the Governor's train. Whenever the Dewey train stops overnight, luggage vanishes from your berth and is waiting for you in the hotel room you have been assigned. Good Republican caterers have hot coffee and thick roast-beef sandwiches waiting in the press rooms at every stop-over. Laundries are alerted a thousand miles ahead to be ready to turn out heavy loads in a few hours. There is really no need for anyone to bestir himself and risk his life to hear the whistle-stop speeches, since almost the entire train is wired for sound and the words of the Governor are carried over the public-address system.

Truman and Dewey are contrasting types, but in many fundamental ways they act on roughly the same principles and proceed toward roughly the same ends. Office-seeking is a great leveler. Most men who engage in it are sooner or later forced to abandon themselves to the ancient practices of audience-flattering, enemy-vilifying, name-remembering, moon-promising, and the like. In these matters, the 1948 candidates are just about neck and neck. Offhand, I would say that Truman is working a little harder at enemy-vilifying and name-remembering, while Dewey looks a little stronger in audience-flattering and also has a slight edge in the scope and beauty of his promises. This last is a natural consequence of the relative positions of the two men. Truman, being in office, can hardly claim the ability to deliver in a second term what he has manifestly been unable to deliver in his first. There is no one, however, to gainsay Dewey when he asserts that under his leadership "every American will walk forward side by side with every other American." Some drill-masters might quibble over the difficulty of achieving such a formation, but no one pays any attention to logic in this season of the quadrennium.

It is probably a good thing for the sanity of the republic that we do have this suspension of logic during campaigns, for the fact is that reason is outraged not only by the speeches of the candidates but by the very idea of this traveling up and down the country to make them. I have been unable to find, on the Dewey

train, the Truman train, or anywhere else, a single impartial and
responsible observer of national affairs who is willing to defend
the thesis that this tearing around will affect the electoral vote in
even one state. There are, no doubt, some people in every community who will vote for the man who says the pleasantest things
about the local crop and the local rainfall, but their number is
probably balanced by the number of intelligent citizens who will
decide, the next morning, to vote *against* the man who disturbed
their children's rest by roaring through the night, surrounded by
a hundred motorcycle cops with a hundred sirens, so that he could
deliver an address pointing out that the Republicans invented
the Depression or that the Democrats invented Communism.
Nobody knows exactly why or when people switch political al-
legiances, but it is known that an insignificant number of them
do during a campaign. Jim Farley said, in the early Roosevelt
days, that every vote in the country was frozen by October 1, and
the work done by Mr. Roper and Dr. Gallup indicates that the
results are settled long before that.

In theory, the institution of the traveling campaign is educational as well as political. It gives the voters a chance to hear
the candidates and learn their views first-hand. No doubt the
theory had great merit a century ago, but today it is possible
for any citizen to hear the candidates' voices and to learn their
views in his own home, where the acoustics are a good deal better
than in a stadium or auditorium. If an appraisal of views is the
important goal, the conscientious citizen must attend to that
matter between campaigns, not during them, for what he gets
around election time is not a candidate's idea of things but his
own, as nearly as the candidate is able to figure it out and re-
produce it. One could also argue that it is a healthy thing in a
democracy for the people to see their Presidents and Presidents-
to-be, to give them the once-over and observe what psychologists
call their "expressive movements." This notion has some measure
of plausibility, but it will be harder to find it four years from
now, when, they tell us, television will be installed in every
American home that today has radio. There will be no reason
then for not chopping the observation platform from some obso-

lete Pullman, setting it up in a television studio, and hiring a few extras to lug aboard the baskets of apples, the Stetsons, and the bouquets.

One feature of the old ritual, however, will be beyond the grasp of science for quite a while yet. That is handshaking. "Hell's bells!" a political adviser on one of the trains said to me. "Everybody knows that we don't go through all this business to win friends or influence people. We go through it to keep the friends we've already got. The only important thing that happens on this train is the handshaking and hello-there-Jacking that go on back in the caboose. We've got a party organization to keep going, and the best way to keep it going is to have the big men in the party get out and say nice things to the little men. I don't care which party it is. It means everything to the strangers you see in the club cars to go back home and tell how they rode down to the state line with the big wheel and how, when they went into his private car, he remembered them well from his last swing around the country. If you think party organizations are not a good and necessary thing in a democracy, then you can write all this off as a lot of nonsense. If you think they're important, then you can't deny the usefulness of these trips." Stated in those terms, the question is a weighty one.

* Mr. Morris Goes to Washington

On April 4, 1952, I rode from Washington to New York on the Morning Congressional with a friend, Newbold Morris, and had him tell me, in as much detail as he could recall, the story of his two months' sojourn in the capital. He had gone there at the request of the Democratic administration to try to clean up what General Eisenhower and the Republicans were, in the Presidential campaign that was shortly to follow, to call "the mess in Washington." Messes follow one another so rapidly in Washington and resemble one another so closely that the latest one tends to drive the earlier ones from our memories. Of the "mess" of which General Eisenhower spoke so often, it can be said, first of all, that it existed, and, second, that it was probably more widespread—in the sense of involving greater numbers of people— than anything in the Eisenhower administration. On the other hand, no figure of the eminence of Sherman Adams, whose troubles are briefly discussed elsewhere in this book, was implicated, and there were no scandals of the magnitude of that involving the Dixon-Yates contract. But there were on the federal payroll in 1952 a large number of people whose notions of public service were deficient and there was quite a bit of graft— "mink coats" and "deep-freezers" being the symbolic payoffs of that particular set of scandals.

At the bottom of this affair, it always seemed to me, was the fact that Harry Truman, a man whose surprising gifts and gallantry may have offset but did not overcome his limitations, decided that he would insist upon the highest standards of pub-

lic service in those parts of the government responsible for policy and strategy in foreign affairs but would not himself attempt to police those agencies that dealt with domestic affairs. This may simply have been an unconscious recognition of his inability to deal with everything at once, as well as of his politician's desire to help and protect his political friends. At any rate, a good many men who should have been elsewhere got into the Department of Justice, the outer offices of the White House, the Internal Revenue Service, and quite a few other places. In time, their misuses of office were exposed by Congressional committees, by journalistic critics, and by Republicans eager to build a case against Harry Truman.

In the early weeks of 1952, evidently, Truman told J. Howard McGrath, a former Senator from Rhode Island and chairman of the Democratic National Committee who was then presiding over the Department of Justice, that something ought to be done. Part of what followed Newbold Morris told me on the train to New York, and I wrote it as fast as I could for the New Yorker. *I republish it here practically unchanged. I have added only a few identifications and a detail or two that did not get into the first hasty report. It seems to me a revealing—and I hope amusing—bit of recent history.*

NEWBOLD MORRIS, the irregular Republican who served for two months as Special Assistant to the Attorney General of the United States and was relieved on April 3 by the then Attorney General, J. Howard McGrath, who himself resigned a few hours after firing Morris, first heard of the job on Monday, January 28. Morris was at his office, in the firm of Lovejoy, Morris, Wasson & Huppuch, at 52 Wall Street, getting ready to go home on the subway after a day he describes as having been spent, like most of his days, "punctuating wills and contracts" when he received a telephone call from Peyton Ford, who had formerly been an assistant of McGrath's. Ford was the only member, past or present, of McGrath's department with whom Morris had even a slight acquaintance. One of Morris's law partners had come to know Ford in London during the war and had later introduced him to Morris. As a friend and emissary of McGrath's, Ford had called Morris from Washington on several occasions before January 28, but never about Morris himself. Some time earlier, he had wanted Morris to join in an effort to persuade Morris's father-in-law, Judge Learned Hand, to become chairman of what was briefly known as the Nimitz Commission, which was to draw up a new internal-security code. Another time, he had wanted Morris's help in persuading another of Judge Hand's sons-in-law, Norris Darrell, a partner in the firm of Sullivan & Cromwell, to accept the position of Chief of the Tax Division in the Justice Department, a post recently vacated by T. Lamar Caudle, whose probity seemed open to serious question. Each of these requests had entailed several conversations.

On January 28, Ford said he was calling at the request of the Attorney General, who wished to know if Morris himself would be interested in a job advising the government, on a temporary and part-time basis, in the matter of "systems and procedures" for maintaining the integrity of federal employees. Morris, who is a born reformer and who, like many reformers and nonreformers throughout the country, had been reading with considerable alarm various reports that the integrity of some federal employees was not everything it might be, was very much interested. It astonished him that the Department of Justice should want his services on any basis, and at first he suspected that Ford was really after his father-in-law or his brother-in-law, but when Ford assured him that the Attorney General wished to discuss the job with Morris himself, Morris was flattered and pleased. He had considered his political career—in the course of which he served in the Corporation Counsel's office, was a member of the old Board of Aldermen, was president of the City Council during Fiorello H. La Guardia's mayoralty, and staged two unsuccessful campaigns for mayor—as over and done with. As a reformer, he took a good deal of pride in his defeats, but they seemed to him to have been so overwhelming as to preclude the possibility of his being called back into public life. "I thought I was in mothballs," he says. Since leaving the office of Council President in 1945, Morris had spent most of his time in private practice, working on wills, trusts, estates, property transfers, and corporation matters. It was agreeable and lucrative work, but

Morris, who went into politics in 1932 largely to relieve boredom, missed the stimulation of public life. His nostalgia was sometimes so great that, during the O'Dwyer administration, he would walk from Wall Street up to City Hall and wander through the building. "If Impy [Mayor Vincente Impellitteri was then president of the Council] was out somewhere," Morris recalls, "I'd go into his office—the most beautiful office I ever worked in—and check up on what kind of care he was taking of John Adams' mahogany chairs."

From reading the newspapers, Morris knew, of course, that the job Ford had mentioned to him—or at least one similar to it—had been offered to a number of other people, among them Judge Thomas Murphy, the prosecutor of Alger Hiss, and the late Robert Patterson, former Secretary of War, and had found no takers. But he felt fairly sure that if honorable terms could be agreed upon, he would accept it. He thought he would enjoy the work, and he also thought it was his duty to respond to a call of this sort whether he expected to enjoy the job or not. He communicated some of these sentiments to Ford and arranged to go to Washington on Wednesday, January 30, to meet the Attorney General and have a talk with him. Tuesday night he got on a sleeper at Pennsylvania Station, and Wednesday morning he alighted in Washington. At eleven o'clock that morning, he met McGrath for the first time. The meeting took place in McGrath's home, on the outskirts of Washington, with Ford and the Solicitor General of the United States, Philip B. Perlman, also present. McGrath did most of the talking, and Morris got along rather well with him during the two hours the conference lasted.

In a statement Morris issued on April 3, right after being fired by McGrath, he said that he was not disillusioned by what the Attorney General had done, "for I never had any illusions about Howard McGrath." What he meant by this, he says, is that he is inclined to expect very little of organization politicians in general. But on January 30, despite the poor view he takes of all the McGraths of this world, Morris had no particular fault to find with J. Howard McGrath, the Attorney General. "I explained to him that I had broken a lot of crockery in New York politics and didn't stand much better with my own party than I did with his," Morris says. "I told him that if I took the job on, I'd want my own staff and a completely free hand." McGrath said that he knew all about Morris and that Morris was exactly the kind of man the government wanted. McGrath also said that President Truman had been fully briefed on Morris's qualifications and disqualifications, and had agreed that he was the right man. By then, it had been explained to Morris that it was an investigator, and not merely an adviser on systems and procedures, that the administration was after, and this prospect, although Morris had never been an investigator of any sort before, was quite agreeable to him, provided he was guaranteed the independence he wanted. In the light of subsequent events, it is clear that there was a misunderstanding between Morris and McGrath about the meaning of "independence"; at that meeting, however, the Attorney General was, as Morris remembers it, entirely in accord with everything Morris said. He told Morris that he wanted a full investigation of the federal government, but he explained that in his view the task would not be a difficult one. "He told me that I shouldn't let the job disrupt my private and professional life too much," Morris recalls. "He said he didn't want me to work myself to death, and assured me that it ought to be possible to clean the whole thing up in a matter of months with two or three days' work each week." In enumerating for McGrath some of the things that he felt might disqualify him for the assignment, Morris did not bring up his part in the now celebrated Casey oil-tanker deal. He says it never occurred to him, though he admits that perhaps it should have. Nor did McGrath mention it, despite the fact that the Department of Justice had been looking into the deal for some time. It is difficult to see how the kind of report that McGrath said his assistants had given him on Morris could have failed to mention it.

After the Wednesday session with McGrath, Perlman, and Ford, Morris came back to New York. He had arranged to return to Washington on Friday, February 1, for another conference with the Attorney General and for a meeting with the President. Technically, he had not yet accepted the job, but he had given every indication that he would. When he got home, he immediately began making the necessary adjustments in his personal and business life. One of the first things he did was sever, formally and completely, all his connections with Lovejoy, Morris, Wasson & Huppuch for the duration of his government work. It is customary for a lawyer entering government service on a temporary assignment to make an agreement with his firm whereby he receives no part of the firm's income that derives from business connected in any way with the government. Morris drew up an agreement whereby he was to receive no part of the firm's income that derived from any source whatever as long as he was on the federal payroll. If his stay in Washington had not been so brief, this would have meant quite a loss, for his pay as McGrath's Special Assistant was $15,000 a year, which is less by far than his average income from his firm, and it cost him, as a man with a deplorable compulsion to pick up the checks of his colleagues and of newspaper reporters, just about all he was getting in Washington merely to live there. Having wound up his affairs in New York, he went back to Washington on Friday, four days after the first call from Ford. During the forenoon, Morris and the Attorney General had a fifteen-minute session with the President at the White House. Morris had met Truman only once before. That was in the fall of 1944, when Truman, who was then campaigning for the Vice-Presidency, had visited New York and had received a celebrated and, it was thought at the time, calculated rebuff from La Guardia, who chose to keep the candidate waiting in his office for half an hour while he carried on a trivial telephone conversation with one of his associates. Morris had wandered into La Guardia's office and had been shocked to find Truman standing by a window, staring out toward the intersection of Broadway and Chambers Street. He introduced himself and filled in the remaining minutes of La Guardia's phone talk by imparting to Truman some of his own esoteric information about the architecture of City Hall and the structure's close resemblance to an eighteenth-century *hôtel de ville*.

If the President recalled this encounter when he met Morris on February 1, he did not say so. Even so, Morris found the talk with the President, which was the briefest and most perfunctory of a total of three White House or Blair House conferences he had while he was on the job, altogether satisfactory. He says that he asked the President if the Attorney General had explained what an unreliable character he was generally thought to be and what a bitter-end reformer his record showed him to be. "I told him he ought to know that I was an opponent of the entire spoils system, even when it didn't result in corruption," Morris says. "I explained that I was certain to recommend that every internal-revenue collector in the country be put under Civil Service." The President replied he was aware of all this and was undisturbed by it. He went on to say that he and the Attorney General wanted nothing less than a thoroughgoing and impartial investigation of the federal government and that they would both co-operate with him in every way. Morris not only was pleased with the President's apparent enthusiasm for the undertaking but was strongly drawn by the warmth and candor he displayed even in the businesslike atmosphere of that first conference. By the end of the conference, it was officially settled that Morris would take the job and would be sworn in that same afternoon. When he and the Attorney General left the President's office, they were met by the White House correspondents and photographers. The two men posed together outside the President's office, and Morris held an impromptu press conference. In the course of the questioning, he was asked which agency of the government he planned to investigate first. At the time, he had given this problem little thought, and he didn't want to commit himself with a hasty answer. "Well, now, look here," he said after a moment's hesitation. "You fellows know that I've only just arrived in Washington, and I haven't even—" McGrath broke in and, with a flourish of his cigar, said, "I would be the first to welcome an investigation." "In that case," Morris said, "I guess we might just as well start with the Department of Justice."

McGrath, who was later to say that he regretted ever having hired his Special Assistant, has not yet said when or why he became disillusioned about Morris. Morris says his disillusionment about McGrath, as distinct from his distrust of politicians in general, began, in a small way, a short time after this conference. It is characteristic of Morris that some of the things that disturbed him about McGrath were things that would have given most other men rather a pleasant impression of the Attorney General. Morris's suspicions were aroused, for instance, by McGrath's description of him as "a distinguished lawyer" in a statement he handed out announcing the new appointment. Morris also disapproved of McGrath's insistence that he and Morris go immediately on a "Howard" and "Newbold" basis. He thought it undignified. Morris was even disturbed by McGrath's eating habits. When they left the White House, McGrath took Morris to lunch at the 1925 F Street Club, one of the most expensive and exclusive institutions in Washington. "There isn't any place like it in New York," Morris, who is in the habit of lunching on sandwiches in his office but has got around a bit in his time, says in admiration. "We had six courses and wine. It was the most wonderful lunch I ever had. But I was numb at the base of the brain when we left, and I wondered how the hell anyone with a job to do could possibly work after a meal like that." It was well along in the afternoon by the time Morris and McGrath left the 1925 Club and went to the Department of Justice. There the Attorney General himself administered the oath to Morris and then released the statement announcing Morris's appointment and describing him as being, among other things, "a distinguished lawyer." "I don't suppose I should have resented that, but I couldn't help being put off by it," Morris says. "It just wasn't so. Nobody who knows me could possibly describe me as a distinguished lawyer. I'm a pretty good lawyer, I think, but that's about the size of it, and the people who know me know it." Morris was, however, more than satisfied with most of the other things McGrath said in the announcement. It read, in part:

In asking Mr. Morris to accept this assignment, I have assured him that he will have my complete, enthusiastic, and unlimited cooperation, and that all of the facilities of the various agencies of the Government which I administer or which can be made available through the office of the President will be at his disposal. No one is more anxious than I, as Attorney General, to have the charge of misconduct in public office thoroughly and impartially sifted, for I realize that the strength of our system of government depends upon the faith that all men must have in it.

Morris started work on Monday, February 4, with a good deal of ceremony. Space had been found for him and his then nonexistent staff on the second floor of the Justice Building. His own office was a richly appointed, high-ceilinged room the size of a basketball court. "They took me into J. Edgar Hoover's office once," he recalls. "It was about as big as my closet." Morris was given elaborate instructions concerning the operation of the air-conditioning unit, a key to a private elevator for Very Important Persons, immense quantities of stationery and other office supplies, and an attractive secretary, whose usefulness was somewhat impaired by her inability to take dictation, either by shorthand or by any other method. McGrath introduced him to all the leading members of the department and asked him to deliver a talk to the division heads on the purposes and methods of his investigation. He did so. "I felt as if I were addressing the Supreme Court," he says. "Anyway they kept their enthusiasm in check."

That first day, and almost every other day until he left Justice, Morris was called upon by innumerable young men bringing him reports of one kind or another—some dealing with interesting old cases that had been tried by department members, others with the functions of the department and its various branches, still others with the relations between the department and other agencies of government. All the reports were handsomely got up, wrapped in cellophane, and neatly tied with ribbons, mostly blue, but none of those that Morris dipped into bore even remotely on the matters he understood he was to investigate. "I learned a little from the men who carried them in," he says, "but I'd never have learned a thing from what they carried."

Late Monday afternoon, Morris and McGrath had another talk. McGrath seemed to have the affair of T. Lamar Caudle very much on his mind. It was McGrath's theory, Morris says, that Caudle was an honest and conscientious public servant whose forthrightness and innocence had brought him to grief.

As an instance of Caudle's forthrightness, McGrath told Morris that before accepting a $5,000 commission on the sale of an airplane, Caudle had come to McGrath and asked if the Attorney General saw anything irregular in the transaction. The Attorney General explained to Morris, as he said he had explained to Caudle, that he personally couldn't see anything wicked in an airplane salesman getting a commission. Morris agreed with this, but added that he thought a man who wished to earn commissions on airplane sales ought to go into the airplane business. Finally, Morris says, he wearied of discussing the man McGrath referred to as "poor Lamar." "I said to him," Morris recalls, " 'Howard, how many of your assistants here do you think are practicing privately on the side?' " McGrath answered that he didn't know of any who were. "I'm sure he didn't," Morris says, "but I told him that I'd been putting the question to the nice young fellows who'd been snowing me under with reports all day and that three of the pleasantest of them had told me they had outside practices." McGrath said he certainly was surprised to hear that.

A curious episode occurred in the interval between Morris's first and second workdays in Washington. On the evening of Monday, February 4, Morris was in his room in the Carlton Hotel, where he lived throughout the two-month stay, when he received a telephone call from a man who identified himself as Rex Beach. The only Rex Beach Morris had ever heard of was the novelist, the author of *The Spoilers*, *The Silver Horde*, and other sagas of virility and adventure, most of them set in the Yukon, that were popular in Morris's childhood. Morris was under the impression that the author of these books was dead. (Morris was right. According to newspaper accounts, Beach died on December 7, 1949. He shot himself in the head with a pistol at his home in Sebring, Florida.) At any rate, when the caller gave his name, Morris said, "You mean the novelist? My God, I thought you were dead!" "Dead! No, I'm feeling fine," the caller replied. Morris said he was glad to hear this and asked what Beach wanted of him. Beach said that he had been reading about Morris's appointment and wished to discuss certain matters. He proposed that he and Morris have breakfast together in the

Carlton dining room the following morning. Morris, who knew
that it is not good practice for a reformer to meet strangers—
particularly novelists one believes to be dead—in hotel dining
rooms, dodged the invitation with the explanation that he
planned to breakfast alone in his room while he went over
some papers. He suggested that Beach call his secretary at the
Department of Justice and make an appointment for a meeting
there. He gave the affair little further thought that evening.

The following morning, Morris had breakfast in his room, as
he had planned. When he walked out of the Carlton, intending
to take a cab to his office, he was approached by a man who
introduced himself as the caller of the evening before. "He was
standing in the Carlton driveway," Morris says, "beside a Cadillac
that looked to me as if it had thirty-two cylinders and was half a
block long." Morris found the whole thing so bewildering that
he no longer remembers all the details. He remembers Beach as
a man of about his own age—fifty—and rather smartly dressed,
but he has no other impressions of him. Whatever he looked
like, Beach suggested that Morris ride down to the Department
of Justice Building with him, and before Morris knew it, he was
riding along in the big Cadillac, which had a telephone and
was lavishly supplied with fur robes. The car was driven by a
uniformed chauffeur. In the back seat were Morris, Beach, and a
third man, to whom Morris was promptly introduced but whose
name he no longer recalls, though he says it is in files he has
since turned over to the Department of Justice. It was the other
man, rather than Beach, who wished to do business with Morris.
"I don't remember his name, but I do remember what he looked
like," Morris says. "He looked like Clark Gable, but not enough
to *be* Clark Gable—I'm sure of that. He had a fortune in dia-
monds on him, all set in onyx and all in Shriners' emblems—
an onyx-and-diamond Shriners' ring, an onyx-and-diamond Shriners' tie clasp, onyx-and-diamond Shriners' cuff links. And he
was smoking a cigar so long it would have singed the chauffeur's
neck if there hadn't been a glass partition in the car. I'd only
ridden a few blocks before I recovered my senses and realized I
had no business being there, but he did a lot of talking in the
time he had." Morris must have made it apparent that he was

unaware of the Shriner's reputation, for the latter explained that such ignorance was evidence of his lack of preparation for the difficult job he was undertaking. The Shriner told Morris he was known throughout the country as one of the great private eyes of the age. "He told me there was one sure way to make a go of the investigation," Morris says. "He said that the minute I announced I was considering making him my chief investigator, I'd get co-operation from all sides. He said that he'd investigated Republicans for Democrats and Democrats for Republicans and that he'd be delighted to investigate both of them for me." Morris feigned interest for a moment and asked the man for his card, which was produced. At the next traffic light, Morris requested that the chauffeur let him out. When he got to the Department of Justice, he turned the card over to an investigator and asked for an immediate report. "His record was about what I figured," he says. "I don't have it any more and don't remember all of it, but I do remember that his last job was as lobbyist for slot-machine makers." Morris never heard from the Shriner again, but he is still curious about him and about Rex Beach.

Morris was fully conscious, during his stay in the Justice Building, that most of Washington regarded the very fact of his presence there as proof that his investigation would be a failure—probably an intentional one. He says he was not particularly bothered by this, for he wanted some time to think the problem through and he felt that his spacious office in Justice was as good a place as any to do his thinking. He might even have remained in it if he had not been strongly urged to get out by three Washington correspondents who had previously worked in New York and known him there. He had them to lunch in his room at the Carlton one day, and they told him that every hour he spent in Justice, cerebrating or doing anything else, made it less likely that he would be taken seriously when he was ready to investigate. He decided to take this problem—as well as some others that had been accumulating in his mind—up with the President, and he put in a bid for an appointment at the White House. Meanwhile, he kept busy laying his plans and trying to assemble a staff. It was his view that he could not, in nine months or ninety, look into the financial affairs of all the 2,500,000 government employees. He felt that about all he could do was study the topmost layers of the great bureaucratic onion, and that these would give him, and the country, a pretty good idea of the condition of the many layers beneath. To get the information he wanted, he needed the power of subpoena, and also financial statements from all high-ranking government employees. It was reported later that the questionnaire Morris prepared and the Justice Department refused to distribute was an afterthought and that he looked upon it as an alternative to the powers of subpoena Congress had refused him. He himself says that he decided on a questionnaire shortly after he took on the assignment and that he saw it as a necessary auxiliary to any other tools of investigation he might use. It was also reported that the questionnaire was modeled on the one circulated last year among members of the New York City police force. Morris denies this, too. When he drew it up—with considerable help, in the later stages, from members of his staff—he had, he says, nothing in mind but gathering the information needed for the job in hand, and the thought that its mere circulation might be preventive medicine for any contemplated waywardness. Although it is a formidable document sixteen pages long and calls for several hundred items of information, Morris says it is actually less detailed than the one the New York police were required to fill out. For example, where Morris asked the recipient to total his expenditures in each of the preceding five years, the police questionnaire required annual expenditures to be broken down into several categories—rent, medical expenses, liquor, entertainment, and so on.

On February 11, Morris discussed the questionnaire with the President, whose authority he would need in compelling people to answer, but in the preparatory stages he never discussed it with the Attorney General or with any other person outside his own office except his father-in-law, Judge Hand, a man who is most solicitous for the rights of the individual and who could see nothing more objectionable in it than in the many invasions of privacy to which all citizens are liable—among them, notably, the filing of income-tax returns. The only opinion Morris has ever cited in defense of the questionnaire is one expressed in the recently published *Mr. President,* in which Truman is quoted as saying, "I think that every public official who gets more than ten thousand dollars a year ought to show exactly what his outside income is, if he has any. That should include District Attorneys, Senators, and Congressmen and everyone in the Federal service. I don't see any reason why that shouldn't be done. If a fellow is honest, he doesn't care." Morris might, if he had wished, have cited a more eloquent and closely reasoned defense of the principle on which the questionnaire rested—a memorandum by Franklin D. Roosevelt on the removal of Sheriff Thomas M. Farley of the County of New York, dated February 24, 1932, in which the late President, who was at that time Governor of New York, said:

The stewardship of public officers is a serious and sacred trust. . . . Their personal possessions are invested with a public importance in the event that their stewardship is questioned. One of their deep obligations is to recognize this, not reluctantly or with resistance, but freely. It is in the true spirit of a public trust to give, when personally called upon, public proof of the nature, source, and extent of their financial affairs.

It is true that this is not always pleasant. Public service makes many exacting demands. . . . The State must expect compliance with these standards, because if popular government is to continue to exist it must in such matters hold its stewards to a stern and uncompromising rectitude. It must be a just but a jealous master.

Toward the end of Morris's first week on the job, Matthew Connelly, who arranges appointments for the President, told him that an interview had been scheduled for the following Monday, February 11, in Blair House, at eight o'clock in the evening. Morris prepared for this as if he were a schoolboy about to receive a Presidential citation for an essay on the conservation of wildlife. "I got my shoes shined, my pants pressed, and my hair cut," he says, "and I made sure I didn't get there at seven-fifty-nine or eight-one but at eight o'clock on the button." A servant met him at the front door and ushered him into the small study that the President used for much of his evening work while the White House was being renovated. The President was alone in the study. He greeted Morris warmly, and Morris started the conversation off by saying how much he had enjoyed meeting the President's daughter on a recent occasion in New York. This pleased the President, and he said that the reason Margaret was such a good girl was that her mother was a good woman; he said it was generally true in his experience that children were no better or worse than their mothers. Morris took a chair near the President's desk, which was piled high with papers. The President said he had brought them over from his White House office and expected to go through them that evening; most of them, he explained, were reports on Korea and other parts of the world beset by troubles larger than boodle and graft. Among them, however, the President went on, was a report dealing with exactly those issues, which he thought Morris ought to see, and he began riffling through the papers to find it. It proved elusive, and Morris suggested that the hunt be abandoned. He said that the time they had together would be of most benefit to him if he could talk freely for a few minutes. If, at a later date, the President found the report, Morris could read it in his own office. The President said that sounded sensible, and leaned back while Morris talked. "I talked fast," Morris says. "I told him first off that I thought I'd better stick to the top levels and not get snarled up with petty graft down below. He agreed. I told him that when I said top levels, I meant exactly that, and that I felt he shouldn't be satisfied with any investigation that didn't go right into his office. I told him I planned to look into all the affairs of Harry Vaughan and everyone else in the White House. The President said he'd be delighted if I'd give everyone there a thorough going over. I told him about the questionnaire. He said he thought it was a fine idea and that he'd always been for something of that sort. I told him that in my opinion what the federal government needed was not just a one-shot investigation but the establishment of a permanent nonpartisan commission—an agency like the Department of Investigation in New York City—to keep a running account of everything that goes on. He slapped his knee and said that was a wonderful idea. He asked me to draw him up a memorandum on it, which I later did. I told him I wanted to get out of McGrath's office. I said I'd need 20,000 square feet of floor space—somebody or other gave me that figure—and an appropriation of my own. He said that finding the space might be rough but that he'd see to it I got it. Finally, I told him that I wanted an executive order authorizing me to go ahead and directing every agency to give me top priority for the things I was after. I said I didn't want an 'administrative memorandum' but an 'executive order.' I knew they were the same thing, but the public doesn't know it, and 'executive order' would be more impressive. And I said I wanted him to use 'top priority,' or 'highest priority,' because that would show the country and the government that he and I meant business. And I said I wanted him to ask Congress to give me the power of subpoena right away. He said he'd take care of all these things, and he did."

Morris stayed at Blair House for an hour and a half, discussing, at the President's request, a good many things besides the ones he had placed on the agenda. He left in a state of exhilaration. "I'd always liked the President and thought of him as a man who'd risen above himself," Morris says. "But I'd never respected him as much as I did that night. It was the high point of the whole two months. I could see that McGrath was counting on a whitewash, and I hadn't found anyone else who was panting to help us, but I'd felt all along that it was the attitude of the President that counted, and that night I was sure he was with me." On February 14, the White House released a statement, in which the President said:

I have had a good conference with Mr. Newbold Morris about his plans for carrying out his job as Special Assistant to the Attorney General.

I am directing all departments and agencies of the government to cooperate fully with Mr. Morris . . . and to give him any information and assistance he may require and to give the highest priority to any requests made by him. Adequate funds will be provided for the activities of Mr. Morris and his staff, and they will be given separate office space outside the Department of Justice.

I intend to see to it that Mr. Morris has access to all information he needs that is in possession of the Executive branch. . . . However, in many cases where government employees have been subject to outside influence, the most essential evidence is not in

government hands. . . . Accordingly, I am going to ask the Congress
to give Mr. Morris the subpoena powers necessary to the proper performance of his duties. . . .

Mr. Morris will have my full support, and I intend to follow the progress of his work very closely. I hope that he will also have the full support of the Congress and the public.

While arrangements were being made—mainly by Carl Blais-
dell, a Defense Department expert on office logistics who was on
loan to Morris—to move Morris into the downtown building
that formerly housed the Washington *Post*, Morris necessarily
continued to put in a good deal of time at Justice. The whole
experience, in Justice and only to a slightly lesser extent later
in the *Post* building, where Morris was physically removed from
McGrath's agency but still a part of it, remains a zany memory.
No display of impatience on his part could stop the young men
from wandering in with their irrelevant reports. After he said
he was more interested in complaints than reports, he kept on
getting reports, but he got complaints, too—a mountain of them.
The first one he read came from a farmer somewhere in the
rutabaga country who was outraged because his mortgage was
about to be foreclosed; Morris was even provided with a copy of
the man's deed. In his first few weeks on the job, the only half-
way pertinent complaint he was given came from a girl who
rushed up to him in Union Station one day and said she was
employed by the Justice Department (as part of her dossier, she
carried a letter from Senator Pat McCarran asking that she be
appointed) but never was given any work to do. She couldn't
stand inactivity and thought Morris might be able to release her
from it. Morris got the impression that inactivity was widespread
in the department, though he received no other complaints about
it. Whenever McGrath, who was never less than amiable in those
days, was in Washington, he seldom missed an opportunity to
invite Morris to prolonged lunches at the 1925 Club. After accepting a few times, Morris began to plead previous engagements.
He also commenced to wonder how the department managed
to get any of its cases tried. "I found out," he says. "Every
division has a few *Harvard Law Review* types—really first-class
lawyers—working like dogs, but there are an awful lot of people

who make sure the air conditioning is right and now and then move a report from one office to another." He found no lack of legal shrewdness in the department. For example, in drawing up the formal recommendation to Congress that he be given the power of subpoena, the department went beyond the President's request and asked that Morris be given the power to confer immunity upon co-operative witnesses. Morris had not asked for this power and did not particularly want it. He realized that if he received everything the President had asked for, it would be an almost unbelievable grant of power. To ask for the right to confer immunity was, he thought, to go one step too far, and he anticipated that this request would alienate many Congressmen. In his present suspicious frame of mind, he thinks the Justice Department may have anticipated the same thing. Nevertheless, the request for immunity power was made, and Morris's fears were realized. (Hearing of the request, Senator Karl Mundt, of South Dakota, said, "It is difficult to see how Hitler himself could have cloaked his associates with more power to protect friends and to punish enemies.") If in some respects the department was eager to broaden the scope of Morris's powers, it seemed to wish them narrowed down in others. The President's order had been clear about Morris's right to have his own assistants, and the recommendation to Congress as originally drafted provided that the power of subpoena be granted to not more than three members of Morris's staff. Somewhere along the line, the wording was changed so that the power was requested for not more than three Assistant Attorneys General— in other words, three members of McGrath's staff. Morris happened to catch this change, and he protested to the President's counsel, Charles Murphy, who saw to it that the original wording was restored. Morris never got the power of subpoena or of granting immunity.

Morris was having difficulty persuading people to join his staff, and this fact was reported in, and often exaggerated by, the newspapers, a circumstance that, of course, increased the difficulty. (In one case, a man Morris had not even approached announced his refusal to join him.) Nevertheless, Morris put together the rudiments of a first-class staff. His chief assistant was a tall, loosely built man with a melancholy face named Morton Baum—a Republican who had served with Morris on the Board of Aldermen and had later joined the La Guardia administration as a special tax counsel. Morris's chief counsel, who was to function as chief investigator, was Samuel Becker; he had been general counsel to Philip La Follette, the former governor of Wisconsin, and from 1935 to 1937 had conducted the Federal Communications Commission's investigation of the telephone industry. Baum and Becker, like Morris himself, interrupted private practices in New York for the investigation. Once the three of them were together, they started building an organization. Almost immediately, they ran into that great misery of government administrators, the security check. They were told that they couldn't put anyone on the payroll until the F.B.I. had made a thorough investigation of his background, character, reputation, and reading tastes. This rigorous survey could take months. Morris and Baum called on A. Devitt Vanech, the Deputy Attorney General, and proposed that instead of actually putting people on the payroll, they hire them on a per-diem basis as "consultants." Vanech was none too sure about the propriety of this and said he would take it up with McGrath. McGrath was none too sure about it either, but finally, throwing caution to the winds, he approved the arrangement. Getting people to accept on that not so attractive basis, however, presented one more difficulty, and even that wasn't all. "One day, we thought we had a windfall," Baum said recently. "We heard that the Federal Trade Commission was going to let twelve excellent men go, because it didn't have the money to keep them. But we couldn't lay our hands on them. The F.B.I. thought they ought to be checked, even though they'd been on the F.T.C. payroll for quite a while. We suggested that to get around this they simply be kept on the F.T.C. payroll while we requisitioned their services and reimbursed the F.T.C. from our own funds. It never did work out, though I think we were right on the verge of getting them when McGrath got us."

In the dispute that ultimately arose between Morris and the Attorney General, the most widely publicized of Morris's adventures in Washington—his appearances before the Senate

Permanent Subcommittee on Investigations—played no part at all. On March 11 and 12, Morris testified before the committee, which had for some time been looking into the sale of surplus government tankers. It wanted to see what light Morris could throw on the operations of a group, headed by a former Congressman named Joseph E. Casey, that was said to have made a profit of $3,250,000 on an investment of $101,000 in surplus tankers. Morris's law firm had represented two of the tanker firms that figured in the huggermugger operations of the Casey group (the group, incidentally, had included Fleet Admiral William F. Halsey, Retired, and the late Secretary of State Edward R. Stettinius, Jr.), and Morris himself was the unpaid president of the China International Foundation, which disbursed certain tanker profits in the form of scholarships to Chinese students whose education in their homeland had been disrupted in consequence of their Nationalist sympathies. It was brought out that some of these profits had been made by the delivery, in vessels owned by the United Tanker Corporation, which was represented by Morris's firm and whose stock was owned by the Foundation, of four shipments of oil to the Chinese mainland in 1949 and 1950. As far as representing the tanker firms was concerned, Morris argued before the committee that lawyers are not responsible for any corporation they represent unless they are officers of the corporation; Lovejoy, Morris, Wasson & Huppuch, he said, had not counseled any illegal actions on the part of the corporations. He was aware, he said, that some of United's ships had delivered oil to Communist China (the four trips to the Chinese mainland were part of a total of more than two hundred trips United's tankers had made throughout the world during the two years in question), but he was also aware that the oil deliveries, all of which took place before the Korean war, had been sanctioned by the State Department and had been discontinued promptly when the Economic Cooperation Administration urged that this be done. Morris said that he himself had not received a dollar from the operations of any of the tankers, but he did admit that his share of the legal fees for representing the owners was probably in the neighborhood of $30,000.

A fair number of people in Washington felt that Morris's role in all this would prove a continuing source of embarrassment to his investigation. A larger number, while not necessarily holding this opinion, felt that Morris's petulant response to some of the questioning was censurable, despite the fact that the provocation had been great. Senator McCarthy talked about Morris's reaping profits "soaked in American blood." Morris accused McCarthy of subjecting him to an ordeal similar to the one Joseph Cardinal Mindszenty endured at the hands of Hungarian Communists. In the opinion of almost everyone in Washington, both McCarthy and Morris overstated their cases. None of this, however, bore on the conflict between Morris and McGrath, for McGrath, the President, and just about everyone else in the administration shared Morris's view that the affair of the tankers in no way disqualified him for the task at hand. Many members of the administration were inclined to think better of Morris because of his defiance of Senator McCarthy. In any event, he felt encouraged to stay on in Washington.

The tanker question, the difficulties of getting a staff together, the problem of operating without the power of subpoena, and most of Morris's other troubles seemed—outwardly, anyway—to have been reasonably well surmounted by the week of March 31, the week that began with McGrath's statement that he was sorry he'd ever hired Morris and ended with Morris's firing and McGrath's resignation. From around the middle of March on, things had appeared to be going smoothly, on the whole. A staff of about fifty had been put together and preparations were being made to double it, complaints were being received in fair volume, and the staff investigators were getting their work well organized. Morris had had another highly satisfactory interview with the President. It had taken place shortly after Morris appeared on a television program called "Meet the Press," in the course of which he said some characteristically severe things about General Vaughan and Ambassador William O'Dwyer. The President wanted Morris to know that he bore Morris no resentment for these judgments and was still behind him. About General Vaughan he made what seemed to Morris an odd but touching point. The President directed Morris's attention to a small piece of sculpture on the mantelpiece. "Do you know who gave me that?" the President said, quickly answering his own question. "Harry Vaughan's daughter did. She made it, and she's just graduating from art school. I have a daughter, too, you know, and Harry Vaughan is my friend. You say what you want about him; that's what you're here for, but Harry Vaughan is still my friend." When Morris left, he received still another assurance that the President, as President, was behind him.

A grand jury was to be set up on Monday, April 7, and although Morris did not expect to be in a position to seek any indictments by then, he was hopeful that the jury could be kept sitting until something good broke. He planned to use it the way Miles McDonald, the District Attorney in Brooklyn, used the grand jury whose sessions resulted in the exposure of Harry Gross's bookmaking ring—that is, not chivvying witnesses and trying to get them to admit specific crimes but leading them along more or less at random in the expectation that they would sooner or later talk themselves into trouble. Meanwhile, the questionnaire had been printed and Morris was planning to distribute it. There was a rather nightmarish touch in connection with his efforts to do so. It turned out that nowhere in the government is there any file or index that tells who occupies what job. The Budget Bureau has a complete list, by grade and title, of all the jobs in all the agencies, but neither it nor any other body has a list of the people who fill the positions. It might seem reasonable to suppose that there are officials in every division of the government (when the Hoover Commission counted up a few years ago, it found a total of 1,816 "component parts") who know who their own employees are, but no one knows or can easily find out who anyone else's employees are. Thus, when Morris, with the aid of Baum, studied government charts and job descriptions to determine which employees should get the questionnaires, he found he had no way of taking the next step—mailing them out to the jobholders. He and Baum decided they would have to deliver the questionnaires to the heads of the various agencies and ask them to fit the names to the jobs before passing them along. In Justice, to which Morris, aided by a platoon of porters, delivered the first bundles by hand, it was maintained for a while that not even in the department itself was there any way of finding out the names of the 596 employees who were to receive the documents. But Morris and Becker protested, and finally a list was found. The copies of the questionnaire, though, remained in McGrath's office until, presumably, the garbage men got them.

Morris is now inclined to the view that the investigation never had any chance of succeeding. He feels that the smooth sailing of the penultimate weeks was a mere illusion. This illusion, he thinks, rested on the illusion on the part of McGrath and others that Morris would not do a really serious job of investigation. "They let us alone for a while because they thought we were going to let them alone," he says. He believes it probable that if he had started with some other department, he would have encountered the same kind of resistance. The only administration leader besides McGrath with whom Morris discussed the questionnaire at any length was John Snyder, the Secretary of the Treasury. Snyder said he felt that its distribution would demoralize his department. Morris pointed out that the public had the impression that the Treasury Department, which was next in line after Justice, was already in an advanced state of demoralization. Snyder said he thought the public had the wrong impression. It was clear that he was against the plan and would be a reluctant collaborator. Although it was in the course of testifying about the questionnaire before the Chelf Subcommittee of the House Judiciary Committee that McGrath indignantly said he was out of sympathy with Morris's program—an eruption that led directly to the departure of both men—what actually brought matters to a head, in the opinion of Morris and his associates, was a far less controversial question. In the absence of any statement by McGrath, there can, of course, be nothing but speculation as to the real basis of his conduct during the week of March 31, but Morris and most of those who were associated with him argue that it was McGrath's resistance to disclosing *any* information about the conduct of his own office that caused the blowup. Just as Morris was on the point of getting to work on McGrath's office—that is, of accepting the invitation issued by McGrath in the White House on February 1

—McGrath's attitude began to change. An order came through stating that there were to be no more additions to Morris's staff without the Attorney General's approval. When Morris tried to get this order set aside, he was unable to find McGrath anywhere. McGrath was in Rhode Island—McGrath was out to lunch—McGrath hadn't arrived in the office yet—McGrath had left early—McGrath was in conference—McGrath was indisposed. "I finally did see him on March 25th," Morris says, "and he agreed to junk this order and to do most of the other things I asked, but I had a kind of sense that we were heading into the biggest crisis yet, even while outwardly the investigation appeared to be building up steam in a hurry. I felt there was real trouble ahead, though I can't say I had any premonition of the way it was all going to work out. The truth is I never doubted that we would succeed. I thought the President wanted us to succeed and that his support was all we needed."

On March 26, Morris and Becker decided that the time had come to force McGrath to put up or shut up. An appointment was made for Becker to call on McGrath that afternoon and make arrangements for beginning the investigation of the Attorney General's office. The appointment was set for half past three. Becker arrived then and was alone with McGrath for forty-five minutes. In a memorandum on the interview that Becker prepared for Morris, he wrote that he started out by "telling [McGrath] that we had no reason to doubt that the affairs of the Department were properly handled." This was not quite as disingenuous a remark as it may appear to be, Morris and Becker say, for it was understood that they were talking not of efficient and intelligent management but of the financial honesty of McGrath and his immediate subordinates, which, they say, they still have no reason to question. "I said," Becker continued in his report, "that my guess was that if any improprieties or irregularities turned up, they would probably be on the same administrative level as in the Treasury. Under such circumstances, it was to the interest of the Department to make the facts known promptly, so that any rumors or charges could be set to rest." McGrath seemed to be in agreement with all this—and, indeed, with most of the things Becker said. The copies of the questionnaire still had not been distributed, and when Becker brought this up, McGrath assured him they would go out before the end of the day. Becker made certain proposals for speeding up the process of getting the people Morris wanted to hire cleared by the F.B.I. and put on the federal payroll. McGrath said he thought these proposals reasonable, and asked that he be supplied with a list of those Morris wanted most urgently to employ, so that he could attend to the speed-up himself. On all matters of organization, McGrath was, on the evidence of Becker's memorandum, more co-operative on March 26 than he had been at any time since early February.

At last, Becker arrived at the question that he expected trouble about. "I suggested," he wrote in his memorandum, "that we would want promptly to commence our regular, routine examination of the files in accordance with the procedure that is customary and usual in investigations of this nature, similar to public investigations in which I had been engaged and very much like the investigations that the Anti-Trust Division [in the Department of Justice] now makes." Becker went on to explain that the simplest procedure, in his view, was to start at the very top of the heap and work down. McGrath asked Becker exactly what records he wished to have, and Becker said he wanted all the records. He mentioned specifically "correspondence, diaries, appointment books, records of telephone calls." It has lately been reported in the press that when Becker asked for these, McGrath grew angry and shouted his refusal. Becker, whose laconic memorandum does not deal with McGrath's attitude, says that this was not at all the case. He says that McGrath was calm and extremely courteous throughout the interview, that he recognized Becker's role as Morris's emissary—Morris had sent Becker to McGrath instead of going himself because he felt that Becker was a more adroit and self-controlled interviewer— and that he did not raise his voice once in the forty-five minutes they were together. But when Becker explained in detail what he was after, McGrath, according to the memorandum, "informed me that he would not consent to such examinations and would not give access to the files except on a most restricted basis; that is to say, if any evidence were furnished suggesting any misconduct or impropriety and specific files were called for, he would make them available." Becker pointed out that this would help very little, since it was in the records themselves that he expected to find the evidence McGrath was demanding as a prerequisite for turning over the records. McGrath said that that was too bad, but he had made his mind up on this point. Furthermore, Becker went on in his memorandum, McGrath "said that he would in no case permit examination of his own records. . . . I told him that I thought the Presidential directive was in the nature of a subpoena to all government departments to make available and to give access to all the records of the departments or persons in the departments relating to their general work." McGrath said that he didn't think it covered the things Becker was asking for. Becker reminded him that the President had authorized Morris to have "all information he needs that is in possession of the Executive branch" and that he couldn't see how this excluded anything. "I suggested," Becker wrote, "that the limitations he imposed were contrary to the executive order and it seemed to me that matters of that nature were not open to discussion between us or between him and you." McGrath said that this might be true but that he intended to discuss it himself with the President. McGrath also said that he felt there was a certain unfairness about Morris's having singled out the Department of Justice for attack. "I told him," Becker wrote, "that this was the purest coincidence; it originated [in] his invitation to you at the time of your appointment and the press conference which followed." McGrath said he considered it unfair nonetheless. With that, the interview ended, and Becker returned to his office to write his memorandum, which concluded with the statement that "unless this question [of the conflict with McGrath] is answered satisfactorily before the end of next week, I see nothing further for us to do."

That was March 26. Neither Morris nor anyone in his office saw McGrath or any of McGrath's assistants after that. On Monday, March 31, McGrath testified before the Chelf Subcommittee. He said he was undecided whether to distribute the questionnaire and whether to fill out his own copy. Asked if he would hire Morris if he had it to do over again, he said he would not. On Wednesday, April 2, McGrath saw the President in the White House for fifteen minutes. It is not yet known what was said at that meeting. McGrath saw the President again in the afternoon, at the National Airport, and a few snatches of conversation were overheard by reporters, but no one is sure exactly what was under discussion. The following morning, Mc-Grath fired Morris. At a few minutes after four that afternoon, the President, in his press conference, announced that McGrath had resigned and had been succeeded by Federal Judge James P. McGranery. At the conference, the President was asked a number of questions about Morris's dismissal, but he contributed very little information in his replies. These are some of the exchanges that bore on the mystery:

QUESTION: Did Mr. McGrath fire Morris with your knowledge and approval?

ANSWER:* The President said he saw it in the paper.

Q.: I take it, Mr. President, that you didn't know about it before McGrath—

A.: The President said it was under discussion but that he was not consulted when it was done.

Q.: Were you consulted before it was done?

A.: The President said he was talked to about it but that he made no suggestion about it.

Q.: Why was Mr. Morris fired? Do you think his dismissal was justified?

A.: The President said he couldn't answer the question.

Q.: Do you intend to reinstate Mr. Morris?

A.: The President said he couldn't answer the question. He said that he had a new Attorney General.

Q.: I wonder what is your opinion of the celebrated questionnaire of Mr. Morris?

A.: The President said he had never seen one so he couldn't answer a question like that.

Q.: Mr. President, could I ask whether you have any reason to feel dissatisfied with Mr. Morris's work?

A.: The President said he couldn't answer the question.

* President Truman did not authorize direct quotation.

Q. (by Mrs. Elisabeth May Craig, a correspondent for a number of papers in Maine): Mr. President, I'm, I'm . . .

A.: The President observed that Mrs. Craig was kind of tangled up, wasn't she?

Q.: Well, sir, I am, because we understood that Mr. Morris was your man to conduct [the investigation] and now he is fired and you don't tell us whether it is in your opinion a justified dismissal. It leaves Mr. Morris under a cloud.

A.: The President said Morris was hired by the Attorney General, brought down by the Attorney General, and the Attorney General fired him.

Q.: And we were wrong in thinking he was your man?

A.: The President said he wasn't his man. He said he never was.

The next morning, Morris went down to the Washington *Post* building, gathered up a few belongings, and taxied to Union Station with a friend—a New York journalist who now and then looks in on Washington. They boarded the Morning Congressional and, over drinks in a compartment, rehashed the whole affair.

When Morris reached Pennsylvania Station, it looked fine to him.

* The Kept Witnesses

1 9 5 5

ON FEBRUARY 3, 1955, a press conference was called at the Hotel Biltmore in New York City for the purpose of providing a young man named Harvey Matusow with an opportunity to make a public confession of fraud and perjury. Along with the confession—and necessary as a foundation for it—went some items of biography.

In 1947, Matusow, who was then twenty, joined the Communist party. He claims to have taken this step as a dedicated revolutionist. Within a year or two, he said, he became disillusioned and penitent. The way of transgressors is hard. Matusow did not leave the party he no longer believed in. Instead, he stayed on as a voluntary agent of the Federal Bureau of Investigation. In 1951, he abandoned this masquerade and in 1952 appeared as a witness for the prosecution in the trial, in federal court, of thirteen leaders of the Communist party charged with conspiracy under the Smith Act.

Matusow's performance under oath—some seven hundred pages in the trial record—pleased the government attorneys, who won their case, and gained him an honored position as a kept, or professional, witness. That is to say, he made his living—and a very good one, he now maintains, for a man of his age and station—by being sworn and saying what those who paid him wished to have him say. Between 1951 and 1954, his services were sought, and easily obtained, by the United States Department of Justice, the Subversive Activities Control Board, the Permanent Investigations Subcommittee of the Senate Judiciary

Committee, the House Committee on Un-American Activities, the Ohio Committee on Un-American Activities, and the New York City Board of Education. He claims to have testified in twenty-five trials, deportation proceedings, and the like, and to have made 180 identifications of Communists, or of persons he chose to call Communists, for the various agencies that employed him. He found a good deal of additional employment. He hired out as a speaker in Congressional campaigns, in which, for a fee, he would damage this candidate or that one with intimations of subversion. He composed memoirs and revelations for the Hearst newspapers, lectured on the American Legion circuit, and now and then exploited himself and his past as a night-club entertainer and radio disc jockey.

In his New York press conference and in subsequent testimony before a federal grand jury and two committees of Congress, Matusow repudiated his career as a professional witness. He explained that he had walked down a city street one day and had been deeply moved by an eloquent call to piety and virtue which he found inscribed on a sign outside a synagogue. He had not been living the good life. The testimony he had given was riddled with lies. In case after case, he told the assembled reporters, he had fabricated evidence, sometimes on his own initiative, sometimes at the instigation of government lawyers.

He was now filing affidavits in support of requests for new trials for many of those he had helped convict. Such was his remorse that he was willing, he said, to risk the penalties of perjury to undo the damage he had done.

This, at any rate, is Matusow's story. And it appears to have something in common with the stories of at least two other people. Mrs. Marie Natvig and Lowell Watson, government witnesses in a recent proceeding before the Federal Communications Commission, have given the lie to their testimony. Both swore before the F.C.C. that they had known as a Communist one Edward Lamb, an Erie, Pennsylvania, newspaper publisher whose right as a television licensee had been called into question. Mrs. Natvig, a gaudy triple divorcee from Miami Beach, now says she lied not only about Lamb's Communist record but about her own. She had invented a Communist past for herself in order to identify others as Communists. Watson, a Kansas farmer who, like Matusow, had worked often for the Justice Department, disowned only his avouchments in the Lamb case.

The recantations necessarily leave many matters in doubt. It is the misfortune of skillful dissemblers that their fellows can never give full faith or credit to anything they say. The regeneration of Matusow, Mrs. Natvig, and Watson may be causing unbounded joy in heaven, but here it must be received with the cool skepticism that should have greeted their sworn testimony. "A liar is always lavish of oaths," Pierre Corneille wrote three hundred years ago in *Le Menteur*, one of the great definitive works on the subject. The courts, the committees, the commissions, and the security panels before which Matusow and Mrs. Natvig were lavish of oaths will be a long time working over the tangled skein of evidence put in the record by this bedeviled youth and this odd woman.

And certainly in Matusow's case those who preside will, if they are possessed of the thoughtfulness the task requires, be haunted by the possibility that he has not really recovered his amateur standing—that he is, in point of fact, as much a professional as ever. Now he has written a book about his experiences. His press conference was called by the publishers of the book, the firm of Cameron & Kahn. There was a distinctly promotional air about the whole enterprise, and there was a distinctly Stalinist air about it, too. Cameron & Kahn is a house that up to now has specialized in Communist literature. In any case, Matusow, whether genuinely purified or merely reverting to form, is once again capitalizing on the confidences of former associates; now he is putting the finger not on Communists but on anti-Communists—on Senator Joseph McCarthy, on Roy M. Cohn, on all his collaborators of the last four or five years. Is he once again on somebody's payroll? It is an uncharitable thought but an inescapable one.

"This is a good racket, being a professional witness," Matusow told the reporters when Cameron & Kahn broke out the Scotch at the Biltmore. Immediately the conference was over, he hurried to the Columbia Broadcasting Company studios for a telecast.

The Department of Justice announced, soon after Matusow's

confession, that it would be among the agencies reviewing and re-evaluating the recanted testimony. The anonymous spokesmen for the Attorney General were a bit grudging and condescending about it. They pointed out that Matusow had given only "corroborative" testimony, as though this were some unimportant species of testimony, hardly worth the bother of looking into. (Actually, there is no special category of evidence known as "corroborative." It merely means, in this instance, that Matusow testified to facts also testified to by one or more other witnesses. Not only can two witnesses be wrong, but there are circumstances in which the withdrawal of one witness's testimony destroys the legal value of another's.) But after Matusow appeared before the grand jury, and after Mrs. Natvig and Watson revealed their fabrications, the Department of Justice promised a full investigation. Bearing the honorable name it does, it could hardly do less. Men are in prison today in part because of evidence drawn from a confessed perjurer by department lawyers.

Neither the Department of Justice nor any other agency of government, however, has given any indication that the Matusow incident has led it to reconsider the moral, juridical, and political effects of the whole practice of retaining professional witnesses. On the contrary, it would appear that the government's principal concern at this stage is to prevent Matusow's latest set of confessions from discrediting the testimony of its other professionals. A federal judge has jailed him on the ground that his recantation is false and contemptuous and the department has indicted Mrs. Natvig, not for the perjury she admits, but for having lied to its lawyers.

In a sense, of course, the government is profoundly right in wishing to protect its employees. One embezzler does not make thieves of all bankers. One spy in the State Department does not prove all diplomats disloyal. One perjurious witness for the government does not make liars of all the rest. Yet there is a difference. Matusow was asserting not the unverifiable but the self-evident when he said that it had been "a good racket, being a professional witness." As rackets must be judged, it was a good one for him, certainly; and, since Matusow's talents are unusual but not unexampled, it may, at this moment, be equally good for others. And if it is a good racket for anyone, it is a racket for which the government of the United States must bear the heaviest responsibility. For it is the government of the United States—"that august conception," as Samuel Taylor Coleridge once called it—that originated this racket and that continues to encourage and pay for it. Matusow was in partnership with the government.

The government's use of professional witnesses has at least this much in common with a racket—that information about it is exceedingly difficult to come by. The whole affair is veiled in secrecy. The government will not talk. It does not, because plainly it cannot, plead that the safety of the nation would be imperiled if it revealed the number and the identity of those whom it hires to testify according to the wishes of its lawyers. It does not plead the right to withhold the names on the ground that these people are confidential informers; obviously it cannot do that in the case of men and women who appear in open court. The government gives no reasons for its unwillingness to discuss or even to defend this phase of its operations, but it evidently holds to the view that it would not be in the public interest to make any sort of public accounting in this matter.*

* On December 20, 1954, I wrote the Attorney General to request facts on the use of professional witnesses and the department's "response, if it has made one, to critics of the practice." I pointed out that there had been, even then, a good deal of public discussion of the question, and I noted that it suffered from the lack "of the kind of solid information I imagine the Department of Justice could provide." I got no reply until February 10 of this year, which was a few days after the Matusow recantation. I then received a letter from William F. Tompkins, Assistant Attorney General in charge of the new Internal Security Division. Mr. Tompkins merely acknowledged receipt of my letter and enclosed copies of two speeches, one by Assistant Attorney General Warren Olney, III, delivered before the Michigan Association of Prosecuting Attorneys on July 23, 1954, and one by himself, delivered before the Camden County, New Jersey, Bar Association on September 28, 1954. Both speeches are addressed to the problem, but neither really deals with it. Both assume that the sanction the courts have given to paid informers can be extended to professional witnesses. Both contain some rather handsome specimens of question-begging. For example, Mr. Tompkins: "The testimony of these witnesses has been weighed by numerous American juries and found to be credible. Of the eighty-four defendants who have been tried thus far for conspiring to violate the Smith Act, eighty-one have been convicted and only one has been acquitted by a jury. A more convincing yardstick of the credibility of those witnesses I

In mid-1954, though, some enterprising Washington journalists came into possession of a Department of Justice list which contained the names and earnings of thirty persons "regularly used as witnesses" and of fifty-three "occasionally used" in the period, spanning two administrations, between July 1, 1952 and May 31, 1954. This list has been made public, and the department has not to date challenged its authenticity.

Whether the list was complete is not known. It was specified that the eighty-three named were all under contract to the Immigration and Naturalization Service of the department. There are others in other bureaus of the department and in other executive agencies, and there are known to be several working for the legislative branch and the state governments. American public life on almost every level today is characterized by what can only be described as an obsession with problems of loyalty and internal security; it is a rare public agency that does not have at least one division devoting itself to these problems, and it is a downright underprivileged one that does not have some judicial or semijudicial apparatus for making the kind of distinctions the ruling obsession demands. These apparatuses require witnesses.

At all odds, the Department of Justice had at least eighty-three kept witnesses in 1954. It seems wholly reasonable to assume that, despite the defection of Harvey Matusow, the number is not smaller today. More likely than not, it is larger, for the new Internal Security Division of the department, which came into being on July 9 of last year, has announced that it plans greatly to accelerate its work in this field and aspires to produce an ever-mounting volume of prosecutions under the Smith Act, the Communist Control Act of 1954, and all other available statutes.

Of the eighty-three persons retained by the department in 1954, all were, by their own admission, former members of the Communist party. Some, like Benjamin Gitlow, one of the first

---

cannot imagine." Neither speech provides any solid information. More recently, in testimony before a Senate committee, Tompkins has said: "It has become increasingly clear that the current attack against government witnesses . . . has its roots in a Communist effort."

American Bolsheviks and once Communist candidate for Vice-President, had been true believers; others, like Matthew Cvetic, whose exploits as an undercover agent were celebrated in a radio serial called "I Was a Communist for the FBI," had been quite the opposite but had infiltrated the party at the direction of Mr. Hoover's famous agency. A few, like Harvey Matusow, had made the transition from revolutionist to counterrevolutionist inside the party. Those who are public servants now receive $25 a day plus $9 "in lieu of expenses." These, at least, are the sums that have been brought out on cross-examination in several trials and hearings. Some witnesses may receive more, others less; $34 a day appears to be the prevailing fee.

By government standards, this is fairly high pay. And it is high in comparison with what some of the kept witnesses made before entering government service. Harvey Matusow was earning $35 a week in 1951. The job formerly held by Paul Crouch—who earned $9,675 from the department in two years of witnessing —was as an airline employee at eighty-five cents an hour. Leonard Patterson was a New York taxi driver. Many of the others were paid functionaries of the Communist party, which means that their pay was low and infrequent. To satisfy the statute under which the payments are authorized—the General Services and Administrative Act of 1949—the people who receive them are carried on the books not as kept witnesses but as "expert consultants." But kept witnesses is what in fact they are; such usefulness as they may be said to have derives from their ability and readiness to identify people as Communists, to describe Communist activities for the enlightenment of judges, juries, and security panels, and to interpret Communist doctrine in such a way as to bring it within the area proscribed by the Smith Act.

Some critics—notably Joseph and Stewart Alsop, who first brought the problem of kept witnesses to public attention—have urged that a distinction be made between those who have been paid large sums and those who have been paid small sums. It is proper, they point out, to describe a witness such as Manning Johnson, who is credited with earnings of $9,096 in a two-year period, as a professional. However, some on the department list are credited with amounts that can only be considered as pin money: $200 or $300 in twenty-six months. Obviously, some sort of distinction ought to be made between those who earn enough to live on and those who do not. But because of the department's refusal to provide information, it is impossible to do this. In an act of high magnanimity, the Alsops accepted the bootlegged list from the department and concluded that there were only twelve witnesses "who have earned enough so that one may reasonably presume the sums were meaningful to them." Harvey Matusow was not one of the twelve, for the Department of Justice had him down as a witness "occasionally used" and listed his earnings as only $75. It has since developed that the one list so far circulated tells only part of the story. Matusow got $75 from the Immigration and Naturalization Service and $1,407 from a separate account with the Attorney General's office.

There are certain ironies connected with the purely procedural aspects of the department's relations with its paid witnesses. The General Services Act, which provides the legal authority for their retention, was passed by the Eighty-first Congress very largely because it had the formidable endorsement of the Commission on the Organization of the Executive Branch of Government, headed by Herbert Hoover. The Hoover Commission had been distressed to learn that certain agencies of the federal government very often had to forgo the advice of eminent American specialists in such fields as science and education because they lacked any means for retaining them on a part-time basis. The commission prepared a plan to enable certain agencies to draw up and offer contracts retaining specialists on a per-diem basis. It was accepted with enthusiasm by the Congress.

An additional advantage of the scheme, it was thought, was that it made it possible to obtain the services of qualified advisers without the delays and embarrassments caused by the protracted rituals of loyalty and security checks. So far, the most conspicuous use to which the law has been put is the hiring as "expert consultants" of the former Communists and police agents who make up the department's corps of professional witnesses. And one of the most conspicuous uses to which the professional witnesses are put is in establishing by sworn testimony that certain other employees of the government are loyalty and security risks.

Thus, the key figures in the field of loyalty and security clearance are men and women who are themselves—almost alone in the whole teeming structure of federal bureaucracy—exempt from the need for clearance. More than that, they compose a group whose individual members would have almost no chance of getting clearance if it were required of them. It reflects not at all on their present condition of rectitude and probity to say that their pasts reek of subversion and sedition and that a number of them are convicted felons. One of the most prominent, for example, is Morris Malkin, formerly a union hoodlum and twice convicted for felonious assault. Another is Paul Crouch, generally regarded as the professional witness with the most experience and highest earnings, who was once court-martialed for offenses against the Military Code of Justice, sentenced to forty years of hard labor on Alcatraz Island, and dishonorably discharged from the Army. Fortunately relieved of any accountability for these aspects of their past, they play a crucial role in determining who is and who is not of sufficient uprightness to work for the United States government.

And as witnesses in other proceedings, the professionals play a crucial role in determining many things. There is, indeed, no end to the number of places where they may turn up in the course of their service to the Department of Justice and apparently in fulfillment of their agreement with it. While under contract to the department, Matusow was a witness in departmental trials of a number of New York public-school teachers. Paul Crouch, the dishonorably discharged buck private, filed with Senator McCarthy's Committee on Government Operations a bizarre memorandum describing a plot to subvert our entire military establishment which he claims to have hatched with the late Mikhail Tukhachevsky, Marshal of the Red Army, thirty years ago. This bit of delayed intelligence provided, according to Roy M. Cohn, the impetus for the investigation of the Army Signal Corps' radar laboratories at Fort Monmouth, New Jersey —a piece of work that uncovered not a single Communist but did incalculable harm not only to government research but to the government's relationship with the whole scientific community. Called by Congressmen hostile to the admission to statehood of the Territory of Hawaii, Crouch took the oath before the House Committee on Interior and Insular Affairs and deposed at length on Communism on the islands. William Garfield Cummings, one of the most ubiquitous of the breed, testified, along with Mrs. Natvig and Lowell Watson, before the F.C.C. in the Lamb case. In Louisville, Kentucky, an obscure journalist was indicted for promoting civil disorder; to the good fortune of the state attorney trying the case, there chanced to be on the Department of Justice's list a Mrs. Alberta Ahearn, who was prepared to say that she knew the defendant as a Communist. Manning Johnson and Leonard Patterson, seasoned performers on the Smith Act wheel, appeared as witnesses against Dr. Ralph Bunche, of the United Nations Secretariat.

Because the government takes the view that its dealings with its professional witnesses are privileged, it is impossible to take the true measure of their influence. But it is clear beyond all dispute that one agency, the Department of Justice, is subsidizing testimony not only in many of the cases it is legitimately prosecuting as the legal arm of the federal government but in a number of other cases, some of them flagrantly political. Even the subsidy it provides for witnesses in its own prosecutions is a problem serious enough to warrant investigation and examination.

It is a novel arrangement, this hiring of people to take a solemn oath and testify favorably to the government. American history offers no precedent for it. The use of paid informers by police departments and federal agencies such as Internal Revenue is neither precedent nor true parallel. The paid informer's job is to aid the authorities in the uncovering of crimes and the apprehension of criminals. He may sometimes be called as a witness, just as the paid witness may sometimes be used as an informer, but generally speaking the functions are separate, and the witness enters upon the scene only when the work of the informer is done. It has long been recognized that the maintenance of order in a society such as ours requires the use of paid informers, but the professional witness up to now has made an appearance only as the creature of disreputable law firms and private detective agencies and of certain businesses, reputable except in this particular, which are frequently engaged in litigation.

Up to now, he has not been associated with the United States government. Circumstances may justify the association today, but it nevertheless violates the spirit of our law and jurisprudence. We do not ask witnesses to meet rigorous tests of disinterestedness, as the Romans did, but we have always insisted that the giving of testimony is a bounden duty of citizenship, like the payment of taxes. It is expected that it will be done freely and in good faith. When expectations fail, the law steps in. The subpoena power exists to compel testimony. Our courts are empowered to require witnesses to furnish bonds under certain conditions, and witnesses may be jailed to assure their appearance and prevent their being tampered with. Failure to meet certain prescribed rules and standards may lead to citations for contempt of court. It is recognized that the discharge of this responsibility of citizenship is in many ways onerous and that it generally entails some financial sacrifice; the courts, therefore, pay modest witness fees. But these, like payments to jurors, are deliberately kept so low that they cannot in any sense be regarded as rewards or even as just compensation. Four dollars a day is the regular Department of Justice fee.

In certain cases, it is true, the courts tolerate payment by one side or the other to witnesses who can provide highly specialized knowledge. The general rule of law is that this may be done in the case of men upon whose observation and counsel, outside the courtroom, society itself sets a price. Doctors, alienists, and property appraisers are perhaps the most frequently encountered types. These may be paid by principals in the case, provided the fact of their payment is made known to the court and provided there is no contingency basis for the agreement; the payment of witnesses can under no circumstances be made to depend upon the outcome of the case.

But even with these conditions the practice has always been regarded as a dubious one, and jurors are allowed to give whatever weight they choose to the fact that a witness testifying before them is being paid for his version of the truth. "The experience of the ages," Justice Chadwick of the Supreme Court of the State of Washington once wrote, "sustains the legal conclusion that where the truth is made to depend upon the pecuniary interest of the witness . . . his utterances wear a cloak of suspicion, and they should not be accepted unless the taint is removed by the testimony of credible witnesses or by circumstances that cannot be denied."

The cloak of suspicion is a garment that must be wrapped several times around the witnesses for whose services the Department of Justice has contracted. For one thing, their pecuniary interest—assuming, for the moment, that $34 a day constitutes one—has the unusual character of a continuum. Ordinarily, where the possibility exists that the cupidity of a witness, or even his simple exigency, will color his testimony and thereby thwart justice, it exists only for a specific case at a specific time. The experience of most men and women just is not rich or varied enough to give them direct knowledge of more than a few matters that may be subject to litigation during their lives. But an accident of history puts the ex-Communist, whether his faith was feigned or authentic, in possession of an extraordinarily negotiable thing—his past.

As Whittaker Chambers, who has given testimony but has never become a professional and who has confronted the problem of negotiable pasts with candor and deep insight, has written, "He [the ex-Communist anti-Communist witness] risks little. He sits in security and uses his special knowledge to destroy others. He has that special information to give because he knows those others' faces, voices, and lives, because he once lived within their confidence. . . ."

Such an ex-Communist has acquired an expertise for which the demand is, apparently, inexhaustible. His patron, the Department of Justice, seems to measure its usefulness by the number of people it has jailed, by the number of deportations it can claim, by the number of loyalty and security risks it can process out of the government. It appears to be the department's hope to prosecute the 30,000 or so American Communists one by one; it recently got a start in this direction by convicting one Claude Lightfoot in Chicago for violation of the Smith Act

—not as a leader of the Communist conspiracy, not as a teacher of the doctrine of violent overthrow of the government, but as a mere member of the conspiracy, a mere adherent of the doctrine. With this conviction, which may well be justified by both the law and the public interest, whole new horizons open up for the department and its witnesses.

What is wanted now, what is likely to be wanted more and more in the immediate future, is identifications—identifications in great numbers. Plainly enough, there could be rewards for an elastic memory. The possibility exists, almost without end, of the truth being made to depend on the pecuniary interest of witnesses. Putting aside what may be the singular case of Matusow, there have been, to date, no clear instances of fraudulent identifications. But certain matters of record suggest the nature of the lurking dangers.

Louis Budenz, a former editor of the *Daily Worker*, who has testified that his income from all sources as an anti-Communist witness and publicist has exceeded $10,000 a year, spent what he maintains was 3,000 hours giving the names of Communists to the F.B.I.

In none of those sessions, Budenz has conceded, did he offer the name of John Carter Vincent or Owen Lattimore. But when Senator McCarthy named both these men in various connections, all of them unfavorable, it came to Budenz, quite certainly, that they were Communists. He so testified before several Congressional committees and grand juries. Likewise, Paul Crouch talked to the F.B.I. on many occasions, testified in numerous trials, and submitted to Congressional committees the names of all Communists he had known aside from rank-and-file members. Not once did he list a certain Jacob Burck, a Chicago newspaper cartoonist. When, however, Burck was the subject of a deportation hearing, Crouch testified that he had encountered him often at meetings of the Central Committee of the Communist party.

The memory is notoriously the most vagrant of human faculties, but there are few cases on record of a bent for mnemonic topicality as powerful as that revealed by Paul Crouch. In some instances, it is possible to rule out avarice altogether as an explanation for the weather changes his recall has undergone. In a large number of documents that he prepared and read in evidence before the Subversive Activities Control Board and a number of Congressional committees, he recounted at length his experiences in the Soviet Union during the period in which he was preparing the campaign to subvert the American military establishment. In these, he mentioned associations with Russian leaders so numerous and so mighty in power as to expose himself to reproaches for name-dropping. Up to 1953, there was one name that did not turn up on any of the lists—that of Georgi Malenkov. In March of 1953, Malenkov succeeded to the premiership of the Soviet state, and in March of 1953, Crouch, filing the statement that led to the Fort Monmouth investigation with the Committee on Government Operations, revealed for the first time that the new Premier was among those with whom he had conferred in 1927.

Crouch has acknowledged a weakness that may in his case help explain such quirks. Before an Army court-martial in 1925, he testified: "I am in the habit of writing letters to my friends and imaginary persons, sometimes to kings and other foreign persons, in which I place myself in an imaginary position. I do that to develop my imaginary powers." In the *Leviathan*, Hobbes wrote that "Imagination and memory are but one thing, which for divers considerations hath divers names." No free man's rights are put in jeopardy, no principle of law is dishonored when Crouch either imagines or abruptly recalls Georgi Malenkov as an old comrade-in-arms. But he has had frequent lapses and recoveries involving persons who do qualify for our law's protection. At the trial of Harry Bridges in 1949, Crouch denied acquaintance with a Communist agitator named David Davis. "I have never heard of David Davis," he told the court. "I had no knowledge of David Davis." By 1951, however, he had not only heard of David Davis, he had encountered him as early as 1928. He was examined by a federal judge about a Communist meeting allegedly held in 1928:

Q. Was Mr. Davis present?
A. Yes, your honor.

On May 6, 1949, Crouch testified before the House Committee on Un-American Activities and was asked if he knew a man named Armand Scala, an officer of Miami Local 500 of the Transport Workers Union:

A. Very well, with Local 500.
Q. Is he a member of the Communist party?
A. I do not know. . . . I do not know of my own knowledge what his party affiliations are.

But on May 11, five days later, Crouch put into the record of the committee a statement and several affidavits amplifying his earlier testimony. In one, he said: "Another member and officer of Local 500 I knew to be active in Communist work in Miami is Armand Scala. Scala had been the chief Communist courier to Latin American countries." In an article published in the Hearst newspapers a few days after that, he made an even more explicit identification of Scala as "the chief courier of the party in Latin America . . . traveling to Buenos Aires and Rio de Janeiro frequently on party business." In a subsequent libel suit, he swore to the truth of these assertions. Since the newspaper stories had not been privileged, Scala was awarded $5,000.

It may well be that Crouch was, as he presently insists, testifying to the best of his recollection on each specific occasion. No more can be asked of anyone. But the fact cannot be blinked that the use of subsidized testimony increases the danger of subsidized perjury. The rule of law against contingent fees is not directly violated by the contractual agreements the Department of Justice has with Crouch and other witnesses. These agreements are signed, sealed, and delivered in advance of testimony—sometimes very far in advance. A witness named Daisy Van Dorn has testified that she received $125 a month for two years simply to hold herself ready to take the witness stand. However, the clear moral principle upon which the rule of contingency rests is abused by the practice.

The department's list of the names and earnings of the "persons regularly used as witnesses" shows wide variation in income among the professionals. An element of contingency accounts for the variations. A witness gets his fee whether the case is settled favorably or unfavorably for the government, but common sense—and even the solicitousness for the taxpayer of which the government boasts—must suggest that the witness who can assist in the production of the greatest number of convictions is the witness who should get the most work. In the Department of Justice—as, for that matter, in most lesser prosecuting agencies throughout the country—success is quantitatively measured. It has been customary in this country to take what steps we can to prevent the quantitative measurement of truth. The use of professional witnesses, though it may be warranted by many present needs, should at least be recognized as a step in the other direction.

Justice Chadwick's cloak of suspicion is becoming to the professional witness for reasons other than those of pecuniary interest. If a heavy risk is run of his memory being stimulated by the prospect of increased emoluments, there is an equally heavy risk that he will visit, not the truth as he knows it, but the fury of disenchantment as he feels it on those against whom he testifies. There is no way of being certain of how many of the professional witnesses are genuine apostates and how many are merely former police agents.

(It is F.B.I. policy never to confirm or deny an individual's statement regarding instructions he claims to have had from the Bureau, and this has led to a certain amount of confusion. Matthew Cvetic told the House Un-American Activities Committee that George Dietz and Joseph Mazzei were members of the Communist party in Pittsburgh. Dietz and Mazzei, fired from their jobs, indignantly declared that they, too, were F.B.I. agents and had in fact been reporting to the Bureau on Cvetic's numerous subversive connections. Similarly, doubts were cast on the *bona fides* of William Garfield Cummings as an F.B.I. agent when it was revealed that his membership in the Communist party antedated his recruitment by the Bureau and that he encouraged continued service to the party by friends and relatives after he left it.)

In any event, a considerable number of the professional witnesses are disaffected Communists and clearly carry the stigmata and disabilities, along with the special insights, of their kind.

Many of them display what may be regarded as a touching eagerness to serve the society they once sought to destroy; in some of their cases, this laudable sentiment is fused with what may more reasonably be described as a thirst for revenge. Men's defects are often only the flaws in their virtue; the flaw may render the virtue nugatory. Manning Johnson, once an ardent Communist and more recently an ardent patriot, testified before the Subversive Activities Control Board that it is an article of his present faith that some things are more important than truth:

> Q. In other words, you will tell a lie under oath in a court of law rather than run counter to your instructions from the FBI. Is that right?
> A. If the interests of my government are at stake. In the face of enemies, at home and abroad, if maintaining secrecy of the techniques of methods of operation of the FBI who have responsibility for the protection of our people, I say I will do it a thousand times.

Again Manning Johnson, this time in a sedition trial in Pennsylvania and undergoing examination on his testimony in a deportation proceeding that had taken place earlier:

> Q. That testimony was not correct, was it, Mr. Johnson?
> A. No, it wasn't, precisely, because I could not at that time reveal that I had supplied information to the FBI. . . . I think the security of the government has priority over . . . any other consideration.

The fear of systems of priorities such as Mr. Johnson's has given rise to the legal doctrine of *testis unus, testis nullus*— one witness is no witness. But a difficulty raised by the Justice Department's use of professionals, and by its policy of withholding information about it, is that two or more witnesses may share this view, or a similar one. We do not know how many people have been convicted, deported, and discharged from government service on evidence supplied wholly by kept witnesses.

Throughout the history of societies living, or trying to live, under the rule of law, the role of the witness has been a vexatious problem for judges, lawyers, and all others who have concerned themselves with it. Broadly speaking, the tendency in most Western nations has been a steady easing of restrictions. When systems of law are young, jurists cling to the hope that truth will be received only from undefiled sources. This is sooner or later found to be an impossible aspiration, and in some respects a false one, though it is unquestionably noble in spirit. The judicial process, to be sure, must always be, or should always be, a relentless search for the truth. But we know from long experience that the truth is often found in the unlikeliest places. The fact that a Manning Johnson hates and fears Communists, feels betrayed by them, and regards every living one of them as a menace to the whole of humanity does not mean that he is incapable of ever telling the truth about them. What it does mean is that he may possibly tell something other than the truth—and that those who use him as a source of information must be vigilant against the possibility of receiving misinformation.

It is doubtless necessary to use the Manning Johnsons of this world. Society has little choice in the matter. As police and prosecuting officials like to point out—when they are rebuked for their use of low, untrustworthy characters as informers and witnesses—it is very seldom possible to find bishops and cardinals who are widely acquainted among felons and well-informed on the workings of vice syndicates, counterfeiting gangs, dope peddlers, smuggling rings, and the like. Society, through its law-enforcement agencies, must deal with these aspects of itself, and it cannot afford to scorn information about them that comes from persons it regards with distaste and does not entirely trust —even from persons deeply implicated in the crimes under review. Though it would be agreeable to adhere to the view of Lord Langdale, who ruled in a famous nineteenth-century judgment, that "a witness has no business to concern himself with the merits of the case in which he is called," we must realize that in many cases no such witness exists.

Because truth often turns up where it is the least expected, and because we have a steady need of truth from whatever source, we have progressively reduced the number of factors disqualifying witnesses and progressively increased our reliance on the power of the witness's oath, the perjury laws, and cross-examination. Up to now, though, we have not accommodated ourselves to the idea of witnesses who make a business of being witnesses. It may be that the time has come when we must do so. It may be that internal security is our overriding need and that we must accept this device for coping with it. But if this is the case, it would seem as if the problem ought to be squarely faced. The Department of Justice should, in that event, abandon its present furtiveness and give a full public accounting of the terms and conditions upon which it purchases testimony. It should recognize, as Justice Holmes did in his weighing of the merits of wire tapping, that the government is caught in a conflict of competing "objects of desire"—the desire to catch criminals and the desire to maintain governmental integrity. ("We have to choose," Holmes said, "and for my part I think it less evil that some criminals should escape than that the government should play an ignoble part.") There may be an equitable and decent way of resolving the conflict, but no conflict can be resolved without first acknowledging that it exists.

In any serious weighing of the issues, it would be necessary, also, to recognize that more is at stake than justice to individuals. That is, of course, the largest question of all in any free and open society. But it is not the only one. When the federal government subsidizes a group such as its present corps of professional witnesses, it finds itself, willy-nilly, subsidizing a special political interest. Many of the larger categories of cases tried under federal law involve political principles, political ideas, political organizations. The Communist cases manifestly do, and not the least of the effects of the government's policy has been to give those professional witnesses who are also professional politicians and ideologues an opportunity to exert a considerable influence on public opinion and public policy in matters on which they have a special, if not an eccentric, outlook.

It should not strain credulity to suggest that if there has been prevalent in recent years a somewhat distorted view of the dimensions of the problem of domestic Communism the fault can in large part be charged to the account of the Department of Justice and its professional witnesses.

No man, for example, has had any greater influence on the public view of the Communist problem than Louis F. Budenz. On the basis of his reputation as the government's leading witness in Smith Act cases and before Congressional committees, he has established an almost universal acceptance of himself as a high authority and of his books, articles, lectures, and television discourses as bearing some imagined seal of official approval. Elizabeth Bentley, J. B. Matthews, Benjamin Gitlow, Howard Rushmore, and Joseph Kornfeder run not very far behind. (Whittaker Chambers has also been enormously influential, but of him it must be said that his writings lend more authority to his testimony than his testimony lends to his writings. He is not, therefore, of this company.)

Lesser witnesses have established lesser reputations on the strength of their endorsement by the government. Moreover, they have had and are having a direct influence on policy and law—not through appeals to public opinion but through direct appeals to the governing powers. Paul Crouch tells the Senate what to do about Hawaii and how the Army should be run. Matthew Cvetic is called by the Senate Rules Committee to advise on the thorny question of rules for Congressional investigations. Maurice Malkin, the ex-convict, himself eligible for deportation and denaturalization, is called before the Senate Subcommittee on Naturalization and Immigration to make recommendations. (He thought there were too many avenues of appeal. He said that once it is proved that anyone is a member "of a certain organization, he should be deported without further hearings of any sort.") Almost the entire membership of the department corps was summoned before the Internal Security Subcommittee to help produce the enormous and enormously influential report "Interlocking Subversion in Government Departments"—a document that more perhaps than any other has formed the prevailing image of Communist infiltration in the nineteen-thirties and forties. The kept witnesses have been given an opportunity to foul American due process and quite a bit else besides.

* At a Baize-Covered Table on the Isle of Rhodes

1 9 5 8

ONE OF THESE DAYS, perhaps, some gifted historian will undertake to explain how and why it was that the early autumn of this year turned out to be a period of upheaval and unrest in most of the countries that have asserted national sovereignty since the end of the last war. In Asia, three of them gave up—temporarily, at least—the struggle to maintain free institutions and passed into military dictatorship. The President of Pakistan, a soldier named Iskander Mirza, said he had come to the conclusion that democracy couldn't work in a country where eighty-four per cent of the people were illiterate; he therefore abolished democracy. He suspended the constitution, dissolved the Parliament and the Provincial Assemblies (in one of them, the Deputy Speaker was recently killed by flying microphones, desk tops, inkpots, and other artifacts of parliamentary government, in the midst of a brawl on the floor), outlawed all parties, arrested many politicians, and turned the state power over to General Mohammed Ayub Khan, the head of the Army. In Burma, the Premier, U Nu, a gentle Buddhist philosopher and the Burmese translator of Dale Carnegie's *How to Win Friends and Influence People,* said that the chaos and corruption in the country were more than he could cope with; he put the Army in charge and made arrangements to turn his own job over to General Ne Win, the commander in chief of the Burmese defense forces. In Thailand, where the military had several times seized power in the last few years but where the constitution had remained in force, Field Marshal Sarit Thanarat, who had just returned home after spending almost a year in London and New York undergoing treatment for cirrhosis of the liver, took over the government and junked the constitution—justifying his action by citing the need to "build a stronger bulwark against Communism and to drive Communist elements from the country." While the lights were going out through much of Asia, a small one was turned back on in Ceylon, whose Prime Minister, S.W.R.D. Bandaranaike, voluntarily relinquished certain powers of censorship, arrest, and seizure that had been granted him some time back to deal with racial disturbances. But the Prime Minister himself was not sanguine about the future of democracy in Ceylon or elsewhere in the Orient. "I have always had doubts whether the system is quite suitable to some of our countries," he said. In Iraq, where a bloody palace revolution took place last July, there was an attempt at another one, and the government of Lebanon, which had received protection from the United States Marines after the Iraqi revolution, came very close to collapse. In Indonesia, Ghana, and Tunisia, where the rulers are eloquent in their professions of democratic and liberal sentiments, severe repressive measures were taken against critics and opponents of the regimes. The Jakarta authorities decreed that henceforth no one could start a newspaper without the approval of the Jakarta military command. Kwame Nkrumah, the Prime Minister of Ghana and a man often described as an African Thomas Jefferson, banned public meetings of the opposition party, on the ground that such meetings "might provoke ill-disposed persons to indulge in breaches of the peace." In Tunisia, President Habib Bourguiba, another leader widely admired as an evangel of a free society, had the leading opposition paper put out of business. (The paper had accused Bourguiba of holding a political trial of a former Premier, who had been charged with "treason" because he helped the old Bey of Tunis flee the country with all his jewels.) "Freedom is dangerous," Bourguiba said. "The state and its existence are essential before everything else. All this preoccupation with liberty is not serious. . . . I am creating a nation."

While some of these melancholy developments were being announced and others were in the making, I had the luck to find myself on the Isle of Rhodes, in the eastern Mediterranean, attending a series of discussions by informed and eminent persons —the majority of them public officials or leaders of opinion— from the countries that were the scene of so much turbulence. These discussions, which were officially and ponderously called "An International Seminar: Representative Government and Public Liberties in the New States," were planned and managed by the Congress for Cultural Freedom, a worthy organization, anti-Communist and generally libertarian in outlook and associated with no government, that has its headquarters in Paris. Some forty people, mostly from the so-called new states but including a few from democracies that have been in more or less successful operation for a longer time, talked together, or made speeches at one another, for a week and a day in the Hôtel des Roses, a seaside resort built by the Italians during their occupation of Rhodes before World War II and now mainly patronized by prosperous German vacationers. The costs of the gathering were met by the Ford Foundation, itself a new and awesome sovereignty in the world.

The seminar was organized back in the spring, when it could hardly have been guessed that the talk would be punctuated by bulletins that would seem to make a good deal of what was being said academic. (The announcement that the Army had taken over in Pakistan came only a few hours after a Pakistani told the gathering how fortunate his country was in having an Army whose officers hadn't the slightest interest in politics.) But the organizers knew well enough that the new states were having their troubles as well as their triumphs, and that these troubles were being shared, willy-nilly, with the old states. (The term "new states," incidentally, satisfied no one, and the Persians, Siamese, and Egyptians who were cast as representatives of "new" sovereignties could hardly have been more uneasy than the "old" Americans, cast as avuncular, ripe-with-experience types.) And they knew, too, that if present trends continue through the next ten or fifteen years, there will be an even greater proliferation of sovereignties than occurred in the last ten or fifteen. By 1970 or thereabouts, Africa could easily have more representatives in the United Nations than the entire Western Hemisphere, and Asian irredentism could just about double the number of nations on that continent. The Cultural Freedom people thought, in good Western fashion, that it might be helpful if some of the formidable intellects from the present new states were seated, along with a few from the older states, at a baize-covered table, provided with a moderator and an agenda, and given eight days in which to talk.

Rhodes, which lies only fourteen miles off the coast of Turkey and affords a magnificent view of the coastal ranges of the Anatolian Mountains, was chosen as the site for the seminar partly because it is more or less conveniently situated for the new states and partly because it is an agreeable place to be in mid-October. The fact that it was allied, a few millenniums back, to the Athenian democracy was no doubt an extra inducement, even though the government that now has Athens as its capital and Rhodes as its easternmost province is not a particularly shining example of either representative government or public rights. Midway in the seminar, the Athens radio and newspapers brought the participants the news that two Greek editors had been clapped into jail for the novel offense of "misinterpreting" a newspaper article by Joseph Alsop. However, this did not prevent innumerable allusions to the glory that was Greece, the grandeur that was Rhodes, and the great charm that the Platonic ideal of philosopher-kings held for a group of political intellectuals.

The Congress for Cultural Freedom is more interested in philosophers than in kings, and in the Western nations it is easy to tell one class from the other; indeed, it is almost impossible to confuse the two. In Western Europe, intellectuals may find their way into government a trifle more often than they do in this country, but, by and large, the rule in the West is that intellectuals and politicians stay out of each other's way. Of the fifteen or so Europeans and Americans at Rhodes, only four had any official connections. These were the Right Honourable John Strachey, M.P., a son of Bloomsbury who has a Labour constituency in Dundee and was Secretary of State for War under Clement Attlee; Frode Jacobsen, a member of the Danish Par-

liament and a sometime Cabinet Minister; Judge Charles Wy-
zanski, Jr., of the Federal District Court in Massachusetts; and
Gunnar Myrdal, the famous Swedish economist and sociologist
(and the author of what is often said to be the most comprehensive study ever made of race relations in the United States), who
has now and then worked for his own government and for the
United Nations, and whose wife is at present the Swedish Ambassador to India. There were four other Americans, three French-
men, and one Italian (the novelist Ignazio Silone), none of
whom held either appointive or elective office, and none of
whom, as far as was known, had political aspirations.

In most of Asia, the Middle East, and Africa, though, things
are very different; scratch an intellectual in those parts of the
world and the chances are better than even that you will find a
politician—possibly a President or Prime Minister, almost certainly a member of, or candidate for, Parliament. There are at
least two good reasons for this. One is that the independence
movements have been mostly led by intellectuals, who thus find
themselves on the ground floor when nationhood is achieved—
as men like Jefferson, Hamilton, Madison, and the Adamses did
in the early days here. The other is that illiteracy is so widespread
in most of the areas that have become or are about to become
self-governing that any man of any education has to be pressed
into service *pro bono publico*. In fact, the scarcity of competence
is so great that a good many new states have had to hire foreigners to get things going for them. For instance, one participant
in the Rhodes seminar, a seminarist from Tunisia, was Cecil
Hourani, a man of Lebanese-Arab ancestry who was born in
Manchester, was formerly an Oxford don, and at present plays
a Harry Hopkins–Sherman Adams role for President Bourguiba.
The Israeli intellectual was the journalist Moshe Sharett, a
former Foreign Minister and Prime Minister, and at present
a member of the Knesset, Israel's Parliament, while the man
from the United Arab Republic was Ibharim Abdel Rahman,
an astrophysicist who serves President Nasser as secretary-general
of the National Planning Commission in Cairo. (After the opening session, neither of these showed up when the other was
present.)

The people invited to the seminar were chosen not for their political attainments but for their presumed ability to participate in a free and rational discussion of the state of democracy and liberty in the countries they came from. But in the new states the men who have the intellectual equipment for such a discussion almost invariably turn out to be either running the show or hoping to run it soon. It was largely on this account, I think, that the seminar failed to provide anything very striking in the way of polemics. One thing it did provide was evidence that the doubling in brass of the intellectuals itself constitutes one of the major problems for the new states. The Westerners, lacking political responsibilities and political hopes, could speak with detachment of the societies they represented; only a few of the non-Westerners could do so. This first came to light when an Indian politician with an iconoclastic turn of mind—Minocher R. Marsani, a former mayor of Bombay and a member of the Indian Parliament who is among the sharpest of Mr. Nehru's critics—said that in the course of a visit to Brazil a few years ago he learned that the Brazilians had established literacy requirements for the exercise of suffrage; the thought had then crossed his mind, he said, that his own country might have given some thought to this possibility when its constitution was drawn up in 1949. Mr. Marsani did not say that he opposed universal suffrage; he said merely that he had been struck by the fact that the idea of limiting the franchise to people who could read and write had never even been examined by the founding fathers of Indian democracy. The effect of these observations on his compatriots and on certain other Asian and African politicians was roughly comparable to the one that might be produced in the Congress of the United States if someone took the floor to recommend that all members of the American Legion, the A.F.L.-C.I.O., Rotary International, the League of Women Voters, the National Grange, and the Methodist, Baptist, and Presbyterian Churches should be stripped of the rights of citizenship. Illiterates constitute about eighty-five per cent of the population of India, and are thus an enfranchised bloc a good deal larger than the combined membership of these respectable American organizations. One after another, the highly literate Indian participants, reinforced by allies from other countries where illiteracy is widespread, rose to denounce Mr. Marsani's heresy and explain what splendid citizens, what wise electors, what shrewd judges of character, what incorruptible spirits the illiterate peasantry were. The speakers were not content to point out that there could be educated boobs and men of unlettered wisdom; they were trying to suggest that it was unfair and undemocratic to make any correlation between judgment and knowledge, and they carried this so far that an impressionable observer might have drawn the conclusion that a convocation of some of the world's most highly trained intellects was advancing the argument that illiteracy was a blessed state indeed, and that the world would be better off if only it were more widespread. Some unimpressionable onlookers drew the conclusion that few democratic politicians, Eastern or Western, highbrow or lowbrow, from new states or old, will ever allow themselves to be put in the position of questioning the virtues of any sizable bloc of voters—certainly not a bloc that is eighty-five per cent of the whole and about 325 million in number.

At Rhodes, moments of candor and self-criticism were rare, and most of them were provided by Westerners. Robert M. Hutchins, the former president of the University of Chicago and now the president of the Fund for the Republic, drew a portrait of American society not "with warts and everything," as Cromwell wished to be drawn, but with warts and almost nothing else, and in a brief talk on political parties Ignazio Silone seemed to be saying that in the West—and, by implication, everywhere that Western practices are followed—all mass parties must come to approximately the same bad end as the monolithic, doctrinaire, intellectually corrupt Communists. It was not that the men from the new states were complacent about the way things were going back home; it was, instead, that they preferred to dwell on the obstacles placed in their way by such large, unmanageable forces as history, tradition, and the uneven distribution of natural bounties rather than to discuss difficult but conceivably assailable problems like the scarcity of educated men and women, and the need that democratic societies had for the kind of critical and analytical minds that were so obviously in short supply even at this select gathering. Edward A. Shils, an American sociologist who acted as chairman of the seminar for most of its meetings, wrote a brilliant paper on this very subject, which was circulated to the participants—a paper arguing that democracy and public liberties can hardly exist unless there are, outside the state apparatus, a number of people dedicated to the job of examining and appraising the workings of the apparatus. The argument aroused little interest or sympathy; in fact, a session devoted to discussing it was sidetracked by an impromptu and interminable exposition of Islamic polity by a learned Lebanese who lectures on such matters at Oxford—the brother, as it happens, of the Lebanese who is the strong right arm of the President of Tunisia. (Oxford was a great presence at the seminar; it had sons on hand from many countries, and they made as distinct a fraternity, socially and intellectually, as the Americans, the French, or the Indians.)

A few non-Westerners attempted hard analysis and criticism, but they met with little success in inducing others to undertake this exercise. The most notable attempt was made by a Siamese named Kukrit Pramoj, a Bangkok publisher and a prince of the ruling house, who had barely managed to make the seminar, having been acquitted only a few days before of charges of sedition and libel over some unflattering observations about the American Ambassador. Prince Pramoj, an old Oxonian himself, was a worldling beside whom most of the other participants seemed like so many Dr. Panglosses. He delivered himself of some home thoughts from abroad, whose tenor was that democracy (an ideal he respected as much as anyone else at the meeting) had in his country just about succeeded in wiping out public liberties —such as free speech and a free press—that had been fairly secure under an absolute monarch; in fact, it had merely led to the replacement of one absolute monarch by two hundred of them. Representative government, he said, could have little meaning in a country whose people had not accepted or had not grasped the idea of a conflict of economic interests or of a conflict between private and public interests. There are, he said, about thirty parties in Thailand, practically all of them co-operatives or benevolent associations for politicians. He pointed out that Thailand's situation is a bit different from that of the former colonies. Illiteracy is not above thirty-five per cent, which means that there are a good many people qualified by schooling, if not by devotion to the general welfare, for political jobs. And just about everyone wants a political job, he declared; the arrival of democratic politics in Thailand was like the arrival of television or air-conditioning in an industrialized country—it opened up an entirely new field for employment and money-making. Since the politics were mostly concerned with nothing political (there simply can't be thirty different approaches to the problems of Thailand), they turned out to be mostly about money-making. Representative government, he said, had developed into organized corruption, and when public liberties got in the way of this important enterprise—as when someone risked giving offense to the American Ambassador—the tendency of the state was to deny them.

At the conclusion of his talk, Prince Pramoj, who had manifested a great impatience with the oratory and pedantry that characterized much of the seminar, threw out a challenge to the other participants from the new states to put aside hopes and distant prospects for the moment and describe, as factually as they could, the present condition of democracy and freedom in their countries. He said that this would redeem for him the long trip to Rhodes and the long days of sitting in a hotel ballroom listening to talk. He was roundly applauded, but no one rose to accept his challenge, and the discussion quickly soared back to the high level of theory and historical perspective from which he had dragged it down. (Later in the seminar, a newly arrived Burmese lawyer and journalist, Dr. Maung Maung, spoke in the same spirit as Prince Pramoj, but not in response to his challenge.) At the instance of Mr. Strachey, the left end of the Oxford team, a good deal of time and huge stores of heavy irony were spent in pursuit of the question of whether there existed in the new states the "class struggle" that Mr. Strachey (though no longer as pure a Marxist as he was twenty years ago) still regards as the first fact of life in the old states. Now and then, there were promising starts at discussing how far essentially European institutions, such as common law, could or should be adapted to non-European cultures. There was always someone ready to remind the Europeans and Americans that their ideas of right and wrong and good and bad were not the only ones in the world of men, but there was very seldom anyone who could be specific in making distinctions. At one point, a noted specialist in African affairs said flatly that much of Negro Africa found the system of law introduced by the British repugnant to the local perceptions of reality. M. Raymond Aron, the distinguished columnist of *Le Figaro*, of Paris, and a man who made a large contribution to the seminar by repeatedly asking "How?" and "Why?" and "Where?" and "When?," said that this piqued his curiosity; he wished to be set straight on exactly what perceptions the man was talking about. The specialist said that it wasn't easy to think of an example just then, but that one would surely come to him. In a moment, one did: An African villager who discovers that the tracks of a missing domestic animal lead directly to the pen of a neighbor, he said, cannot follow the principle of Anglo-Saxon jurisprudence that holds a man innocent until he is proved guilty; he will assume the neighbor's guilt, leaving it up to the suspect to prove his innocence. One had the feeling that if the difference between cultures went only this far —that if African villagers held roughly the same view of things as Wyoming ranchers—then one man's meat would be another man's meat, Anglo-Saxon democracy would be a universal value, and life would be quite simple; on the other hand, however, one had the stronger feeling that life was not this simple, that the example did not exemplify but showed, perhaps, only the difficulty of putting profound differences into words at an international conference paid for by the Ford Foundation, and that possibly the very notion of trying to get at the truth by seating a lot of people around a table in a first-class hotel was culture-bound and foolish.

Yet the worldling Prince Pramoj did not succumb to such doubts. Twice more he challenged the seminar to deal with concrete problems. Once, after a lush bit of rhetoric by a French West African named Thomas Diop on European and American inhumanity to the darker-skinned peoples of the earth, he said that his "boredom would be relieved" if he could receive an encouraging report on the steps being taken to eliminate class and caste and color distinctions in the parts of the world not dominated by Europeans and Americans. And on another occa· sion he raised the question of whether certain groups of people that had achieved, or were soon to achieve, nationhood were not too small and too poor for so difficult and costly an undertaking. Africa, he said, seems well on its way toward being cut up into a host of nations (many of them no larger in population—and, in some cases, in size—than Connecticut or New Jersey), with each, unless fashions change greatly or history stops repeating itself, striving to maintain an army, a navy, an air force, foreign em· bassies, and, in time, no doubt, an atomic-energy establishment. Does it all make sense, he asked. No one answered him directly, but an answer emerged: Sense or no sense, this is what the people seem to want. A Nigerian spokesman, after hearing Moshe Sharett proudly describe the way the Israelis had used their army as an educational institution, said that this was exactly what his countrymen planned to do after 1960, when they would achieve independence. The armed forces, he said, would not be a bunch of idlers; when the troops were not defending the father· land, they would be learning to read and write and operate lathes and drive tractors and repair sewing machines, and so forth. At this point, someone propounded an extraordinary question: Would it be necessary for Nigeria to *have* armed forces? The spokesman—Mr. Ayo Ogunsheye, director of the department of extramural studies at University College, Ibadan, and one of the most interesting speakers at the seminar—said that of course the country would need armed forces. What for? To protect the frontiers. But Nigeria will be completely surrounded by French colonies and a United Nations trust territory; is France likely to attempt to subdue an independent Nigeria in the world of 1960? Probably not, Mr. Ogunsheye said, but, after all, an army is an attribute of nationhood; every nation has one. Not Costa Rica, it was pointed out. Mr. Ogunsheye was unmoved. The Tunisian Mr. Hourani came to his aid. He remarked that an army needn't be such a great expense, because it isn't really necessary to arm every soldier. The Tunisians, he explained, have a fine army with only one rifle for every four riflemen. Professor John Kenneth Galbraith, of Harvard, rose to suggest that in time the new

African states would prove themselves capable of cultivating the tensions and hostilities that Europe had so brilliantly achieved and that made the maintenance of armies seem so worth while. Mr. Louis Fischer, an American journalist who has made something of a specialty of the new states, said that he found Mr. Ogunsheye's attitude entirely understandable. "A gentleman needs a necktie," Mr. Fischer said.

The seminar touched only lightly on the questions that seemed —from what may be the narrow and parochial point of view that came naturally to at least one American—to be the most important ones for the new states. The new states are mostly in what we used to called "backward regions" and now call "underdeveloped areas"—though for several, particularly in the Middle East, "overdeveloped" might be a more accurate term. They are poor, and at the present time their prospects for riches are not great. The United States, in contrast, had a virgin continent to develop, and there are parts of it that remain virgin to this day, thousands of years after much of North Africa and Asia was— agriculturally, at any rate—worked almost to death. The United States is only now feeling the first faint tremors of the population explosion that is rocking many of the new and burgeoning sovereignties; while we have the technology to cope with it for a century or two, at least, there are grounds for suspecting that it is already beyond control in certain parts of the world. We achieved national unity (though not without a hideous war that, if it had been fought with modern weapons, might have destroyed us altogether) because we had plenty of time in which to assimilate aliens and teach them our language, and because the aliens were persuaded to come to us by their admiration for what we were doing. This nation grew organically; the majority of the new states achieved mere growth long ago, far in advance of nationhood, and in most cases they now seek to achieve unity within boundaries that were never intended to be national ones but were merely drawn to mark off the outer limits of some European empire's power or interest. Many of the new states—even the minuscule ones—lack so much as a common tongue. If the characteristics of a nation are common loyalties and a common language, then India, which, of the lot, appears to have the most representative government and the widest public liberties, should be not one nation but a dozen—and, in the opinion of some authorities, it may be, one sad day. In the continental United States, there have never been very many people who, if asked what temporal authority their loyalties were pledged to, would answer anything but "the United States." In India, on the myriad islands of Indonesia, in nomad Iraq, and even in little Ghana, there are vast numbers of people who have little awareness—if they have any at all—of the fact that they are nationals of the recognized governments of those territories. The United States had a hundred years in which it ignored and was largely ignored by the rest of the world; the new states are under enormous pressures, both Communist and anti-Communist, to take part in the world struggle for power.

It could only be hoped that one American's view of the prospects of the new states was as myopic as some of the people at the seminar must have thought it, and that American experience was not as relevant as it seemed.

PART THREE

A FEW ENTHUSIASMS AND HOSTILITIES

* Holmes, J., Sage

1 9 5 8

"IN COMPRESSION OF STATEMENT," Stimson Bullitt has written of Mr. Justice Holmes, "he was a rival of Tacitus and an equal of Bacon." He was in any case a splendid writer—as accomplished a stylist, at least in the narrow sense, as this country has produced. There is a liveliness and tension and rub about the briefest of Holmes' letters and the least controversial of his opinions from the bench. He never spoke or wrote except crisply. He never committed a soggy sentence.

Holmes may not endure the centuries as Tacitus has, or Bacon. One certain fact, though, is that he lived in that state of grace we call maturity as long as any man in history. Holmes, who knew John Quincy Adams and Alger Hiss, was intellectually adult in adolescence, and he reached his middle nineties without being overtaken by senility. Aged nineteen, in the summer before Lincoln's election, he wrote a Harvard theme on Albrecht Dürer that only recently was cited by Wolfgang Stechow, an eminent German critic, as making Ruskin's essay on Dürer sound hazy, hasty, and trivial by comparison. Three-quarters of a century later, Holmes was cracking jokes with Harold Laski and advising him that Franklin Roosevelt was "a good fellow with rather a soft edge"; urging the soft-edged one to "form your battalions and fight"; shooting off prickly commentaries on current cases to his friend Sir Frederick Pollock; gossiping with Walter Lippmann; eying Washington flappers through his Georgetown window; reading Ernest Hemingway; and talking on the radio. George Bernard Shaw started as early as Holmes and ended as late and was flashier all the way, but in most things Shaw lacked

Holmes' finish and judgment. ("He seems to me," Holmes said, "to dogmatize in an ill-bred way on his personal likes and dislikes. Of course I delight in his wit.") "Maturity" was never the word for Shaw, but it was for Holmes, who had no flibbertigibbet stages, though he was sometimes undone by flipness, a quite different thing. It took him forty years to appreciate Lincoln. "Few men in baggy trousers and bad hats are recognized as great by those who see them," he had explained, lamely, to a lady in 1909. He early decided that most liberals and radicals "drooled," so he not only withheld his sympathy but missed most of what they had to say. But though he may have often been wrong, he was never stupid and never foolish. And never, above all, banal. No platitude was ever known to cross his lips.

Holmes was a sage—probably the truest one this country has produced. The term seems to have occurred to everyone who has written of him. "A sage with the bearing of a cavalier," Walter Lippmann said. "He wears wisdom like a gorgeous plume." A sage is a man, generally old, who wears wisdom, but the wisdom need not be particularly original, though it should always seem to be fresh. Holmes was more original in expression than in thought. He was not a philosopher in any creative sense. He was more—to use a distinction of his own, but not one that he applied to himself—"a retail dealer in notions" than "the originator of large ideas." He belongs, I think, with Montaigne, Dr. Johnson, and all the great apostles of common sense. Someone has said that his was the profoundest intellect that ever dispensed Anglo-Saxon justice, and this may well be so, but his gift was for criticism and elucidation, not for invention and construction. It is not clear that he ever acknowledged this, and certainly he wished it to be otherwise. He hungered shamelessly for immortality in the sense of remembrance beyond the grave. He had high hopes that the "little fragments of my fleece that I have left upon the hedges of life" would not be blown away. He spoke of anticipating "the subtle rapture of a postponed power"—and he said that "no man has earned the right to intellectual ambition until he has learned to lay his course by a star which he has never seen—to dig by the divining rod for springs which he may never reach." But he did not ever really do this; he was no dowser; the revolutionary urges were wholly alien to him. It may be that he was too skeptical and mordant to wish to break through to new territory. He did not much like new territory, anyway, or innovation. He had a way of fixing his gaze on the funny part of every landscape. "I think pragmatism an amusing humbug," he wrote Pollock, "like most of William James's speculations, as distinguished from his admirable and well-written Irish perceptions of life. They all of them seem to me of the type of his answer to prayer in the subliminal consciousness—the spiritualist's promise of a miracle if you will turn down the gas." Metaphysics he regarded as mainly "churning the void to make cheese." He read more history and science than philosophy. Most moralities, theologies, and antitheologies were "human criticism of or rebellion at the Cosmos, which to my mind is simply damning the weather." Holmes' *The Common Law* is still judged a considerable work by authorities in the field, and it is a joy to read now simply for style and logic, but it is essentially, as it was intended to be, a piece of nineteenth-century exposition—a history and commentary lighted by the best of what was then, and largely still is, modern thought. What Holmes could do superbly was state a case or extract an essence in a few clear and compelling words. Other men in his time labored and produced fat books to make some point that he could clinch in a single declarative sentence. Toward the end of his life, there was, for example, a school called "legal realism." The core of its doctrine had been expressed by Holmes, in 1897, in a now famous asseveration: "It is revolting to have no better reason for a rule of law than that so it was laid down in the time of Henry IV." That is the totality of the case against *stare decisis,* or abiding by the judicial precedents. Much of the rest of the case for "legal realism" was summed up by Holmes in these few words: "The Common Law is not a brooding omnipresence in the sky but the articulate voice of some sovereign or quasi-sovereign that can be identified. . . . [The law is] what the courts do in fact."

The great thing about Holmes was that he faced the dilemma of the modern mind—he snorted at phrases like that—unflinchingly, merrily, and responsibly, while such contemporaries as Henry Adams and John Jay Chapman turned into cranks and helpless neurotics, some of them going clean off their rockers and others, like Henry James, averting their gaze and dwelling (to the world's vast profit, in this instance) on other things. Holmes came to believe, at his father's knee, that "we're in the belly of the universe, not that it is in us." He thought this anguishing, and he never stopped thinking about it, but he discovered a way of living with it. He was a moral and—though it did not come easily to him—a compassionate man, and he knew that he was so partly by choice, partly by breeding. All his values were, in any case, elected ones; a few he had deliberately chosen, the rest he deliberately accepted from his forebears and the community, but none of them without reluctance and a certain amount of grumbling. Perhaps one of the reasons he was not truly a philosopher was that he found it convenient to go through life believing no more than he had to believe and investigating only the irresistible problems. "All I mean by truth is what I can't help thinking." He hated the bleakness of the world he saw and the even bleaker horizons that came into view when he squinted. He could not avoid thinking that "the sacredness of human life is a purely municipal ideal of no validity outside the jurisdiction." But he forced himself to accept the municipal ideal because his moral instincts told him to and because he was social—that is, because he enjoyed being part of the municipality. Politically, his bent was conservative. He simply decided, early in life, to accept the community values and moralities he found defensible on terms other than those of truth. "Morality is simply another means of living," he wrote, "but the saints make it an end in itself." Nevertheless, he liked it as a way of living. His morality was conservative and conventional, too. Theodore Roosevelt once said he could carve from a banana a judge with more spine than Holmes. This was unfair. Holmes had no faith in democracy or social welfare or the common people or the uncommon people, or even, ultimately, in justice, another municipal ideal. But he could not help thinking that some things ought to be sacred—"I do accept a rough equation between isness and oughtness"—and he settled on some of these. And he worked up the closest thing he could to fervor. Of free speech, he said that "in the abstract, I have no very enthusiastic belief, though I hope I would die for it."

Holmes was hugely aided, in getting through life in a serviceable way, by this ardently felt need for knight-errantry. He quickly elected to value the idea of dying for sacred principles even if he could not find any. This at times misled him, at least from a mid-twentieth-century point of view. Holmes went into the Union army thinking little of the Union. He regarded Lincoln as rather a fathead. As for abolitionism, he waxed sometimes hot, sometimes cold, but mostly tepid. He gave twenty-five cents to the Anti-Slavery Society, which was, even by the standards of the day, pikerish of him. Now and then, he worked up a degree of conviction, but it never lasted. Yet he fought like a tiger and toward the end of the war began to take the view that philosophies should be judged by their power to compel sacrifice. He held it into the next century. "The faith is true and adorable," he wrote Harold Laski, "which leads a soldier to throw away his life in obedience to a blindly accepted duty, in a cause which he little understands, in a plan of campaign of which he has no notion, under tactics of which he does not see the use." True and adorable, indeed! Had he lived a few years beyond 1935, he would not have said this. Some of his views —his admiration for the martial virtues, his fatalism, his belief in the futility of most efforts to improve life—made him at times hard and imperious and possibly even cruel. But there was a warmth to him that pessimism could not reduce by very much, and there was an immense *joie de vivre*. "I was repining," he once wrote Pollock, "at the thought of my slow progress—how few new ideas I had or picked up—when it occurred to me to think of the total of life and how the greater part was wholly absorbed in living and continuing life—victuals—procreation —rest and eternal terror. And I bid myself accept the common lot: an adequate vitality would say daily: 'God—what a good sleep I've had.' 'My eye—that was a dinner.' 'Now for a rattling walk—' in short, realize life as an end in itself. Functioning is all there is—only our keenest pleasure is in what we might call the higher sort. I wonder if cosmically an idea is any more important

than the bowels." Not more important cosmically, perhaps, but
—other things being equal—more important in lesser ways and,
as a rule, more interesting. "My aim below," he wrote Pollock
at another time, "has been solely to make a few competents like
you say that I had hit the *ut de poitrine* in my line." The chival-
rous assumptions, the pleasure he took in the stuff of life, and
the reaching for high C combined to give us a sage, a noble
jurist, and a very fine writer.

* White Mountaineer

I. SHERMAN ADAMS AND BERNARD GOLDFINE

1 9 5 8

THE DIE WAS CAST, the dew was off the meadow the moment it became known that it was seldom a Dutch treat when Sherman Adams, the Assistant to the President, and Bernard Goldfine, the woollens man, were together. From then on, it mattered very little whether the House Committee on Legislative Oversight turned up any new evidence in the case. "I need him," said the President, knowing the worst, but the correspondents gathered in the Indian Treaty Room knew what all the king's horses and all the king's men couldn't do. The political mischief had been done. When chastity gets lost, it is for keeps. Eisenhower could have spared himself some awkward times in press conferences by a stout repudiation of a double standard of political morality, but consistency is a mean virtue, and in any case the damage to his system for subcontracting political authority was beyond repair. For one thing, Sherman Adams could never again be protected from the Congress. His vicuña coat might shield him from the elements,* but it and the Oriental rug and the hotel bills worked like a radiologist's dose of barium in making him accessible to close scrutiny. As the President's agent extraordinary, he had been like the Secret Service and the Central Intelligence Agency in that he could not function effectively while others looked on; if he was to be a watched pot, he would never boil.

* Cozily or otherwise, depending on the quality. After all, the reason Goldfine got in trouble in the first place was that the Federal Trade Commission took the position that there was not as much wool of a certain grade in Goldfine's yard goods as Goldfine's labels said there was. Had this question not arisen, there would have been no need for Adams to call the F.T.C. in Goldfine's behalf.

Until last month, he successfully avoided examination. Senator McCarthy wanted to put him on the stand in the Army-McCarthy hearings. Senator Kefauver sought his expert testimony during the fuss over the Dixon-Yates contract. Both times Adams spoke the magic words about separation of powers and the privileged character of executive communication, and that was that. But now, thanks to Goldfine's handsome benefactions, this will no longer do. Having once admitted a certain confusion of private affairs with public ones, he has forfeited the right to claim that he never acts except on behalf of the President. The claim won't wash. What is more, Mr. Adams has probably made it impossible for any successor to enjoy the immunity he has enjoyed. If he quits and a successor is found, the new man will be under surveillance.

From the start, Adams and his White House associates, including the President, have relied on defensive strategies that are just about as damaging as an outright admission of malfeasance. One is the *tu quoque,* or you're another, argument, which consists in pointing out that most members of Congress and many members of the press have received favors from private citizens and done favors in return. The noted entertainer and public-relations authority Tex McCrary has been installed in the Mayflower to gather bushels of documents to support this argument, which, putting aside all questions of relevance and logic, has the disadvantage of making enemies in exactly those places where friends are most needed. The other line of defense has even graver flaws. To assert his integrity, Adams has had to concede a lack of good sense. With an innocence that would have done him credit if innocence were of much value in his calling, he told the Harris Subcommittee that he had made errors "of judgment but not of intent," and the President seconded this by saying that, as he saw it, his Assistant had not been wicked but only "imprudent." Some defense of Adams' virtue was certainly called for, but to explain that what may have had the appearance of moral delinquency was only bad judgment is hardly, in this case, more helpful than it would be to say of a banker, for example, that the man did not lack a knowledge of finance but was merely, on occasion, larcenous. To put it rather coarsely,

Adams was put on the payroll not to exercise his honesty but to apply good judgment. As between a defect of virtue and a defect of prudence, the latter may be, from the point of view of the general welfare, the more serious. The commonwealth as a whole would not have suffered greatly if in fact Adams had put in the fix at the Federal Trade Commission so that his friend could label his merchandise as he chose. But a few lapses from good sense by a man wielding such powers as Adams is reputed to have had could be costly and painful to everyone.

He will not again wield great powers, even in the unlikely event that he stays on through the end of his patron's term. There is, of course, a certain amount of doubt as to whether the powers he wielded deserve to be described in the terms the press has generally used. Adams was never a high-policy man. John Foster Dulles has had complete charge of diplomacy, George Humphrey has called the tune on ways and means, and the President himself has laid down the administration line on welfare issues. Adams has had a hand in patronage and politics and office management. He has checked the mail; handled visitors who cannot be turned away at the front door yet do not rate an audience with Himself; and settled arguments that arise among administration officials. His work has not required unique gifts, but this, probably, does not alter the fact that his presence has been important. When Eisenhower came to office, necessity mothered the invention of a deputy President. The new President lacked, on the one hand, political experience, and, on the other, a zest for acquiring it. Most of the tasks that have taken up most of the time of Presidents interested him hardly at all, and most of the people a President normally sees were not to his taste. There simply had to be a Sherman Adams, and it is interesting now to recall that Eisenhower knew this from before the start; he came back from Europe to enter the New Hampshire primaries and right away hired the Governor of New Hampshire, one of the first politicians he met. Adams has been essential to him. The kind of work he does makes him expendable, provided he is replaceable. A willing successor might easily enough be found, but the very fact that he was Adams' successor would make him vulnerable. For a time, at least, no one will be allowed to work in the shadows. It appears very much as if Eisenhower will have to do for himself whatever it is that Adams has always done for him.

The question that everyone in Washington has been trying to answer is: How on earth did Sherman Adams get into this mess in the first place? What weakness of perception allowed him to accept, of all things, a *coat* from a man he knew to be at odds with the authorities? The hotel bills one can perhaps understand, despite the fact that a member of the Truman administration owed his downfall to a few days on the cuff at the Saxony in Miami Beach; still and all, hotel bills can be regarded as entertainment. And a rug for one's living-room floor, particularly if there was some talk of returning it one day, could just possibly be regarded as what the President described as "a tangible expression of friendship." But for a man charged, as Adams was, with most of the work in cleaning up "the mess in Washington" to accept the symbolic garment of corruption, a coat, from a businessman petitioning the government for relief—this has flabbergasted all of Washington. What was Sherman Adams thinking of? How could any man in his right mind have been so foolish? Adams' admirers have never been great in number in the capital (no one in his position could hope for too many admirers), but it has never been suggested that the man is a fool. Thus far, his association with Goldfine is his only really striking error of judgment. Nor is it credible that he is simply one more venal politician. If he were, he would have covered his tracks more artfully, and the chances are that he would have had far less to do with such compulsive name-droppers as Bernard Goldfine and Goldfine's odd associate of former times, John Fox. Also, if personal gain had been his central motive, he would have left the administration some while back and exploited his connections from the outside, where the exploiting is really good. Whatever else may be said of the Assistant to the President, the length of his service testifies either to his loyalty to his President and his party or to his fondness for power and conceivably to a combination of these. Moreover, he has served, as far as anyone now knows, selflessly; it is impossible to detect in any of the transactions in which he has been known to have had a part any self-serving decisions or resolutions. Members of the Harris Subcommittee have said that they have not yet unfolded the whole story of Sherman Adams, but it is a fairly safe bet that if the files currently held anything juicier than what has been spread on the record over the past month, some indication of the character of this intelligence would by now have been given.

If Adams is neither stupid nor venal, the flaw must lie somewhere in his political education and perhaps, too, in the political atmosphere that envelops him. He must simply never have understood that his relationship with Goldfine would be interpreted by most people as being quite as improper as anything that came to light in the Truman administration—and at the same time downright hilarious to those who have always regarded him as the sternest of the deacons in the Eisenhower administration. When he ordered the late Harold Talbott to resign as Secretary of the Air Force because Talbott had attended to some personal affairs on office time and written some private letters on office stationery, he must have thought of his action not as a defense of morality but simply as the enforcement of a house rule. This confusion of values, if that is what it was, might be explained by the fact that his whole training has been that of a provincial politician. When he met Eisenhower, he was a lumber merchant who had served briefly in the New Hampshire legislature, a single term in the House of Representatives, and two terms as governor of New Hampshire. Before he became an Eisenhower enthusiast (he had, he once explained, been on Senator Robert A. Taft's side on most matters of policy, but he became convinced early in 1952 that the then General was "the fastest horse in the stable"), he had had no experience in national politics aside from his two years in the House, which is an extraterritorial jungle inhabited by tribesmen whose chief concern while there is with what is going on around the council fires at home. As a New Hampshire politician, Adams had gone to a school in which the prevailing moral philosophies are as greatly at variance with those professed in Washington as if they came from two wholly different societies in wholly different stages of development. In most state governments, and notably in that of New Hampshire, the idea of conflict of interest simply does not exist. On the contrary, a mutuality of interest between government and business is taken for granted, and men often go into the legislative branches to represent their businesses. Adams used to have no hesitation in telling his early biographers that he had entered the New Hampshire legislature—which is, incidentally, one of the world's largest parliaments, with 424 members, or one for every one thousand citizens of the state—at the instance of his superiors in the Parker-Young Lumber Company and primarily for the purpose of representing the firm. In state politics, especially in those states that have not yet got what they regard as their full share of capital investment, a man who speaks for a prominent industry is very much *pro bono publico.*

A good many politicians take the statehouse view of life to Washington, but as a rule the view undergoes certain modifications. They come to regard themselves, particularly if they are Republicans, as spokesmen not for a particular business but for an entire industry or for business in general. And the quicker ones learn in good time that the gratuities that may be accepted in state politics (all forty-eight governors gratefully accepted bolts of vicuña from Bernard Goldfine) can get a man in serious trouble in Washington. In Adams' case, quite evidently, no such change occurred. This could be because he is an excessively provincial man and an excessively insensitive one. He has been one of the largest figures in the administration right from the start, but the conditions of his work and the austerity of his life may have made it impossible for him to appreciate that Washington is different from Concord in fundamental ways. He has been unaccountable not only to Congress but to the press and to other members of the administration. He has worked behind closed doors in the White House and, as the President's accredited deputy, has had everyone except Eisenhower himself come to him when he called. So far as is known, his off-duty life has not been a broadening one; he has always been thought of as a Yankee villager who kept Epworth League hours, except on choir-rehearsal nights, and few things have been more surprising to his colleagues about the recent revelations than that he had so gay and worldly a friend as Bernard Goldfine and that he frequented such places as the Carlton, the Sheraton-Plaza and the Waldorf-Astoria. The general belief even now is that these were novel associations for him and that their very novelty and glamour blinded him to the consequences of enjoying them. The cruel word "hick" has been a good deal used in discussions of the mystery of his behavior. It was surely a countryman speaking when his first response to the charge that he had received an $800 coat was that this was untrue because he had looked into the matter and found that its real value was $69.

Yet the mystery is not dissolved by any amount of digging into Adams' past or by speculations about his life in Washington. He had, after all, assimilated enough of the spirit and rhetoric of political uplift to make acceptable speeches and to register hot indignation when other men embarrassed the White House by their associations. He has been quick to learn all the other rules of political self-preservation. If it was mere self-righteousness, a belief that it was all right for him to do what he had fired other men for doing, his New Hampshire canniness should have warned him at least to be more careful and artful than he was. And if, on the other hand, some Yankee-trader instinct was working deep within him, the concern with appearances that all politicians—provincial or otherwise—have, should have told him that this would at least *look* bad and that by far the better deal, in the long run, would be to pass up the opportunities his friendship with Goldfine afforded. His needless, pointless fall from grace is easily the most baffling problem in political behavior to come along in years.

II. SHERMAN ADAMS AND DWIGHT D. EISENHOWER

1 9 6 1

MOST OF Sherman Adams' *First-Hand Report* is not first-hand at all, but second- or third-hand. Adams recounts at length crucial

events in which he had little or no part—the Suez crisis, Dienbienphu, the Bermuda Conference of 1953, the Geneva Conference of 1955, and the recurrent alarms over Quemoy and Matsu
—and his reports appear to benefit very little from his intimacy
with the President. It seems, on first thought anyway, odd that
this man, whose talent was narrowly executive and whose competence, so far as is known, was limited to insular affairs, should
now be so preoccupied with matters of high policy abroad. But
perhaps it is not so odd: these were the memorable affairs, and
it may well be that if he had stuck to matters he knew intimately,
he would have been writing almost exclusively about trivialities.
Even in those days when everyone in Washington spoke of him
as the power behind the throne and the closest thing to a deputy
President in American history, it was difficult to learn or even
to imagine exactly what he *did* with his time. Here and there,
the suspicion grew that his work might not be as demanding and
as important as it was said to be. The Goldfine affair and the
other difficulties that led to his departure, in 1958, strengthened
this suspicion. A power behind the throne who had time to stop
by the Carlton in midafternoon; who was frequently on the
telephone discussing the affairs of nonscheduled airlines, textile
manufacturers, and television operators in provincial cities; and
who ran up sizable bills at the Sheraton-Plaza, in Boston, obviously was not burning himself out as a Richelieu. Adams' book
is not of much help in explaining his role. In a chapter called
"At Work in the White House," he remarks that he could not
sit in on many of the discussions of policy "that Eisenhower
wanted me to attend" because "I had too many telephone calls,
too much paperwork, and too many appointments at my own
office, as well as a White House staff to supervise." He goes on
to say, "Somebody who made a count of such things once estimated that my outgoing and incoming telephone calls were usually 250 a day and that figure was probably not far from right."
It sounds quite far from right. At two minutes a call, with no
rest at all for voice and ears, he would have been on the phone
for more than eight hours and would never have made the
Carlton or got much paperwork done. Still, the record does show

that he was on the telephone quite a bit. But the importance of it all is another matter. Adams could not have thought it altogether vital to the welfare of the administration, for he says that after a year at the White House he was offered a job that paid better money and was eager to take it. "I talked to the President about it, reminding him that he had often urged us to speak up if any opportunity came along that we felt, for our own economic security, ought not to be turned down." Eisenhower remembered, and was ready to let Adams go if Henry Cabot Lodge could be persuaded to stop arguing with Andrei Vishinsky and become the new power behind the throne. Adams knew then what Eisenhower was to learn—that Lodge was having a great time in New York and could not be talked into helping the President run the country from Washington. "I was sure," Adams writes, "that Lodge, if he could help it, would have nothing to do with scrubbing the administrative and political backstairs as I was doing at the White House."

Adams' memoir is rough going most of the way. Its length is excessive, its tone is flat, its detail is boring and mostly insignificant, its revelations are depressing. Still, it does contain revelations—most of them, one suspects, unintentional. Adams says of Eisenhower that "temperamentally, he was the ideal President." But Adams plainly understands that temperament is not everything. Even what Adams considers an ideal one was no defense against naïveté and lack of firmness. Adams knew that the President was kidding himself in thinking for a moment that Lodge would go backstairs in the White House, and he knew that the President was naïve about many other things. So did others in the administration. When it was pointed out that restrictions sought by business in our trade arrangements with the Japanese might drive the Japanese into deals with Peking, Eisenhower (according to Adams) asked George Humphrey if American businessmen might "make some sacrifices in such a situation in the interests of world peace." "No," Humphrey replied. "The American businessman believes in getting as much as he can while the getting is good." The President accepted this judgment but said—"seriously," according to Adams—

"Maybe that's the trouble with businessmen, George." Adams' Eisenhower is an almost hopeless idealist surrounded by men with a superior knowledge of the world. Senators Taft, Knowland, and Styles Bridges, the Secretary of Defense, the Secretary of State, and half the rest of the Cabinet were always setting him straight about the realities of life and about the impossibility of fulfilling his pleasant hopes. Adams speaks of Everett Dirksen, the last of Eisenhower's three leaders in the Senate, who had "with considerable political gallantry come around to accept more and more of Eisenhower's views and solutions to major foreign problems." When such considerable gallantry was lacking, as it was most of the time, Eisenhower did nothing. "Before I worked for him," Adams writes, "I assumed Eisenhower would be a hard taskmaster. . . . But he seldom called anybody down when he was displeased with his work and I never knew him to punish anybody. . . . Though contrary to his nature, a tougher . . . line would have brought better results." Adams mentions only two cases in which Eisenhower took a real stand with Congress. One was in backing up his Secretary of Agriculture. "If I can't stick with [Ezra Taft] Benson," Adams reports the President said, "I'll have to find some way of turning in my own suit, or I'll just be known as a damned coward." The other was his announcement of his intention to prevent any Democratic attempt to enlarge the Tennessee Valley Authority. "It's time to stop being bulldozed!" he said. The President felt no call to valor in the matter of Senator McCarthy's bulldozing, and Adams says that, as a matter of principle, Eisenhower "did not make a decision, or take a public stand on an issue, when it was not necessary." It was on this account that he did not make firm statements on several aspects of racial integration. The President was intermittently aware of the pain he gave his party comrades by the positions he chose to defend and by those he chose to leave undefended, and he could be hurt by the lack of respect accorded his judgment. Adams recalls Eisenhower's reactions after a Republican strategy meeting in Denver in 1952: "When Humphreys [Robert Humphreys, a National Committee public-relations man] finished with the presentation, Eisenhower said nothing. I could see that beneath his usual outward composure something had annoyed and upset him. I asked him later what had bothered him. 'All they talked about was how they would win on my popularity,' he said. 'Nobody said I had a brain in my head.' "

The most interesting sections are those on the President and his first Secretary of State. "In the quiet of Eisenhower's home," Adams writes, without saying how he knew what went on there, "Dulles had talked about [their] relationship before they had begun their official association. 'With my understanding of the intricate relationships between the peoples of the world and your sensitiveness to the political considerations involved, we will make the most successful team in history.' " It is hard to believe that Dulles actually dared to put it this way (it was close to saying "with my brains and your popularity"), but it is easy to believe that he thought of it this way. By Adams' account, Eisenhower feared the consequences of Dulles but hesitated to restrain "the best Secretary of State he ever knew.' " "Eisenhower, of course, was well aware that his own approach to foreign problems was far more conciliatory than Dulles's. . . . Dulles was readier to fight for Quemoy and Matsu than Eisenhower was." Eisenhower tried to assert his own views through other people. He had C. D. Jackson, Harold Stassen, and Nelson Rockefeller working on psychological warfare and disarmament. Dulles couldn't abide any of them and eventually got the President to drop them. At Geneva in 1955, while Eisenhower was talking up Rockefeller's "open skies" scheme, Dulles "passed the word to his staff that he wanted disarmament talks 'closed out quietly.' " Dulles, of course, wished that Eisenhower himself would stay out of diplomacy. Adams writes, "When Eisenhower's Paris summit conference with Khrushchev collapsed in 1960, I could hear Dulles saying, 'Now do you see what I mean?' " Not long after the Paris disaster, Adams came down from Franconia Notch for a reunion with Eisenhower at Newport, Rhode Island. "Foster Dulles's opposition to what he regarded as foredoomed summit conferences now takes on more aspects of wisdom," he observed to Eisenhower. "Foster Dulles was a great man," the President said. "Foster had one great quality—somebody could disagree with him violently but he never bore any ill feeling after the argument was over."* It is doubtful if this really was Dulles's most striking or most admirable quality, but it was one that the most amiable of Presidents rated highly indeed.

* In the summer of 1961, Drew Pearson had an interview with Nikita Khrushchev, who, according to Pearson, said, "I came to have admiration for Dulles before he died. He could disagree with you, but you knew exactly where he stood."

* The Importance of George Orwell

THE LATE George Orwell was a novelist, a journalist, an essayist, a literary critic, a political polemicist, an occasional poet, and a man whose mark on his contemporaries was and is large and clear and good. He was central to his time, which is our time from the late twenties to the fifties and into the plausible terrors of *Nineteen Eighty-Four*.

He was born in India in 1903 and died in England in 1950, of a lung ailment contracted in childhood. George Orwell was a pen name he took in 1934; he had been christened Eric Blair. At the time of his death, he had been a writer for less than twenty years, and for almost half of that period he had been quite obscure. Nevertheless, it is difficult to call to mind any figure of the twentieth century, apart from the seminal thinkers like Freud and Dewey and the literary innovators like Joyce and Eliot, whose influence has been as sharp and visible and cleansing as Orwell's. In the closing years of his life, when *Animal Farm* and *Nineteen Eighty-Four* were being read everywhere, the world had a sense of him as a prophet. *Animal Farm* was published here in 1946 (many publishers rejected it on the ground that it would have a disturbing influence on Soviet-American relations), and I do not think it would be going too far to say that it did as much to clear the air as Winston Churchill's "Iron Curtain" speech of the same year—an oratorical salvo often cited by historians as the starting point of Western resistance to Soviet imperialism. By 1949, when *Nineteen Eighty-Four* appeared, Orwell was by no means a lonely prophet; by then, the wilderness was full of voices. But Orwell's had a stunning clarity and edge.

167

Anyone could see the flower of totalitarianism in Stalin's Russia or Stalin's Poland or Stalin's Czechoslovakia. It took Orwell to uncover the living roots of totalitarianism in contemporary thought and speech, in the puritanism of civic virtue, in our slackening of ties with the usable past, in cravenness before the gods of security, in mass entertainment's deadening of impulses. He put Newspeak and Doublethink into the language, and our habits of speech and thought are the better for this. If we and our offspring never have to endure *Nineteen Eighty-Four*, we and they will have Orwell partly to thank.

Nineteen Eighty-Four was a dazzling illumination, and I suppose that for most people it will always be the first thing to spring to mind whenever Orwell's name is mentioned—just as most of us, in free association, would respond to "Swift" with *"Gulliver's Travels."* Yet it was not Orwell's first illumination but his last. Years earlier, even before *Animal Farm* had won him his first really wide circle of readers, he had exerted a liberating and strengthening influence on a whole generation of writers and intellectuals. That generation, of which I am a member, knew him first as a journalist. In my own case, I did not even know that he had written any fiction until some time after I read his political and literary criticism. (A few of his early novels were published here in the early thirties, but they attracted little attention and quickly went out of print. They were not reissued until 1950 or after.) I think my own awareness of him must date from late 1939 or more probably early 1940; in any case, I knew enough about him by 1941 to go to some lengths to get hold of a copy of *The Lion and the Unicorn,* a wartime study of English life and ideals that has never been published here. Orwell was a socialist when he wrote it, as he was to the day of his death, and the book may justly be regarded as a piece of socialist literature, though it spends less time telling how socialism might improve England than how England might improve socialism.

I followed *The Lion and the Unicorn* with *Homage to Catalonia* and all the fugitive pieces, in English periodicals and in *Partisan Review,* that I could lay hands on. It was Orwell's view of any particular question that made his work as a journalist so exciting and his example as a writer so bracing to his colleagues. Nor was it merely the verve and acuity of his writing, though this was indeed part of it: quite apart from any special tendencies of his thinking, he was a magnificent performer. But the important and stirring thing was the way he coupled contempt for all the "smelly little orthodoxies" of his time with a continuing interest in ideas and a decent respect for the opinions of mankind. He was free, on the one hand, of pieties of any sort and, on the other, of flippancy. He was at once responsible and absolutely independent, and this in a day when responsibility and independence were customarily disjoined. He fused a moral commitment with a fiercely critical mind and spirit, and if today there are more writers who approach this ideal than there were twenty years ago, it is largely because they have profited by his precepts and have been moved by the magnificent gesture of his career.

Orwell was a writer of great force and distinction. He would be remembered today if he had been only a journalist and critic. But he was far more; he was—among other things, though certainly first among them—an artist, and a many-sided one. The thrust of his moral imagination has been felt by all those who read *Nineteen Eighty-Four,* but that was by no means the end of it, nor was it the beginning. Though *Nineteen Eighty-Four* was no doubt his most important book, that work of apocalyptic fury did not provide the most impressive display of his gifts. The reader of *Burmese Days* and *Coming Up for Air,* which seem to me the two most successful of his early novels, will discover that his imagination was more than moral. He could deal superbly with the individual consciousness and with the intercourse of character. He could be wonderfully evocative of moods and times and scenes and conditions of life. No one who has seen anything of England or encountered any members of the British lower middle class can miss the verisimilitude of *Coming Up for Air.* We have it on excellent authority that *Burmese Days* is as sensitive a rendering of Indian and Anglo-Saxon life; in any case, it could scarcely be more memorable. I would rank *Down and Out in Paris and London* with these two novels if I did not think it too directly autobiographical and reportorial a work to be described as a novel at all; whatever its category, it is a match-lessly vivid description of the life of poverty and unemployment and squalor. It is impossible to read the *plongeur* passages without having the sensation of gray soapy water sloshing about the arms up to the elbow. Though Orwell's bent was for such description and for a manner that is ironical, astringent, and detached, he could on occasion be lyrical and quite astonishingly tender, as one may learn from the sections on Tubby Bowling's boyhood in *Coming Up for Air* or from the haunting and pathetic scenes between Julia and Winston in *Nineteen Eighty-Four*.

In all of his novels, including those that might, on balance, be described as failures, one feels oneself always in the presence of a writer who is fully alive and has eyes and an intellect and a vibrant character of his own. The conventions of criticism demand, I suppose, that he be placed as a "minor" novelist. He was not in any crucial sense an innovator, and he did not penetrate the mysteries to the depths reached by Dostoevski or Conrad. He did not people a world as Balzac did—though one has the feeling that something like this would have been within his powers if he had devoted himself entirely to fiction or if he had lived and written longer. He was of the second rank, but he was never second-rate, and to my mind and taste the distinction is anything but invidious. All of us, I think, get major satisfactions from certain minor novelists, and minor satisfactions from certain major novelists. Stendhal, for example, means less to me than Samuel Butler, and Orwell more than Joyce. I believe that Orwell is, as Irving Howe has said, "one of the few contemporary writers who really matter."

John Atkins, the author of a useful critical study of Orwell, has said that "his uniqueness lay in his having the mind of an intellectual and the feelings of a common man." I cannot quite accept this, for I recognize no sentient state that can be described as "the feelings of a common man." As for "the mind of an intellectual," that is what every intellectual has. Still, I think Atkins is reaching for a central truth about Orwell and one that is not easy to grasp. Perhaps one could say that his uniqueness lay to some degree in his almost studied avoidance of the unique.

The experience he chose to deal with was the kind of experience known to large numbers of people, to whole social classes, to entire nations. He did not often concern himself with the single instance. As a novelist, he was rather old-fashioned in the sense that he did not explore the extremes of behavior. The merely anomalous, the merely phenomenal, the exotic, the bizarre—none of these attracted his interest very much. In fact, the most obvious and persistent of his faults was an intolerance of eccentricity and neurosis. As a critic, he was rather old-fashioned in the sense that he paid the most attention to books that have been read by millions and left to other critics those works of genius that are admired chiefly in genius circles. It was Dickens and Kipling, staples in a national culture, rather than, say, Henry James or Gerard Manley Hopkins, who drew forth his greatest critical efforts. He pioneered in the serious analysis of popular culture, writing brilliantly of "good bad" books, boys' magazines, patriotic verse and marching songs, penny dreadfuls, and even the bawdy postcards on sale at seaside resorts. In a striking essay on Henry Miller, which was, I think, one of his few appreciations of what some people would call a "coterie" writer, he found it necessary to convince himself that the lives of the odd fish of whom Miller wrote "overlap fairly widely with those of more normal people." Had he been unable to say this, he would have been unable to admire Miller.

He set great store by normality. This is not to say that he despised the extraordinary or placed no value on the uncommon or superior. He was an extraordinary person himself, he detested conformity, and he never celebrated mediocrity. "The average sensual man is out of fashion," he wrote, and he proposed to restore him, giving him "the power of speech, like Balaam's ass" and uncovering his genius. Because we know that he believed there was a great deal in a name, we can assume that in *Nineteen Eighty-Four* he did not settle lightly on one for the central character, Winston Smith, who linked the memory of a most uncommon Englishman with the commonest of English patronymics. What Orwell cared about most deeply was the general quality of human experience in his time. The virtues he honored were the universally accessible ones—candor, courage, love, common sense, integrity, decency, charity. The tyrannies he anatomized were those that could hurt us all.

Orwell, who was fascinated by the English class structure and enjoyed drawing fine distinctions of status, spoke of his own family as members of the "upper lower middle class." His father was in the Opium Department of the Indian Civil Service and was at Motihari when Orwell was born. Orwell was one of three children; his home life, he said, was drab, and he felt "isolated and under-valued." It is safe to assume that he changed his name because he disliked the memory of the years in which he had borne it. He told friends that he found the name itself unpleasant; he said he did not care for the Scottishness of Blair or the Norseness of Eric and felt more content wih a surname taken from an English river he had loved and a resoundingly British Christian name. If his home life was dreary, it was also brief. "I barely saw my father before I was eight," he wrote. And at eight he was sent to a boarding school on the South Coast, the inferior place he calls Crossgates in "Such, Such Were the Joys . . . ," an essay full of that anguishing vividness he scarcely ever failed to achieve. It is possible that the reality of Crossgates was not quite as bad as the memory of it. Cyril Connolly was there at the same time, and in *Enemies of Promise* makes the school, which he calls St. Wulfric's, sound a somewhat happier place and Orwell a somewhat happier boy than we find in Orwell's account. But with childhood, it is always the memory that counts. At Crossgates, Orwell did what was expected of him and won a scholarship to Eton. He finished Eton and acknowledged in later life that he had rather liked the place, but he did not go on to a university. He thought it better to see something of "real life." He went back to India and served five years in Burma as a member of the Indian Imperial Police. He was to some extent at least the Flory of *Burmese Days,* a guilt-ridden servant and beneficiary of the Raj.

In the essay "Why I Write," Orwell says that he had known his vocation from the age of five or six but that from the age of seventeen to twenty-four, a period that included all the Burma years, he had sought to escape it, "with the consciousness that

I was outraging my true nature." So far as I know, he never explained why he sought to flee what he regarded as his destiny or whether he had in mind some other fulfillment. As a matter of fact, it is difficult to find one's way about in the years between Eric Blair's adolescence and the emergence of George Orwell in 1934, when he was thirty-one. His own writings are vague as to dates and sequences in this period. I think it is quite clear, though, that he was a young man who suffered a good many torments of mind and spirit. His attempt to avoid writing could have resulted from an admixture of insecurity, or fear of failure, and self-denial. There are traces of Calvinist asceticism all through his work. At any rate, not long after his return from Burma, he entered upon the mortification of the flesh that provided him with the materials for *Down and Out in Paris and London.* He sought out poverty, whether to write about it or merely to suffer it we cannot tell. "What I profoundly wanted at that time," he wrote several years later, in *The Road to Wigan Pier,* "was to find some way of getting out of the respectable world altogether." But why did he seek out misery? Why did he embrace poverty instead of Bohemia? John Atkins has said that the moment Orwell thought of anything beyond endurance, he put himself to the test of enduring it. I think there is something to this. It was compulsive behavior, almost masochistic in character, and it makes Orwell's retention of independence and cool judgment all the more interesting and all the more impressive. The most powerful critic of fanaticism in our time was a man who had a good many fanatical impulses.

He has said that he spent about two years in all in the lower depths of Paris and London. It is hard to tell whether or not this was one continuous experience. At some point between 1928 and 1934, he taught school for a while, and at another time he worked as a clerk in a bookshop. After 1933, there are few uncertainties. In that year, his first journalism began to appear—articles and reviews under the name of Eric Blair in *Adelphi* and other magazines. *Down and Out* was published in 1933 and *Burmese Days* in 1934, when he became Orwell. His surrender to destiny was now complete. He did a book a year for several years, in addition to the newspaper and magazine work that kept him alive. After *Burmese Days,* there were three more books dealing with poverty. *A Clergyman's Daughter,* published in 1935, and *Keep the Aspidistra Flying,* published in 1936, are novels of English life. They have their particular distinctions—the Trafalgar Square scene from *A Clergyman's Daughter* may well be the finest thing in all of Orwell's fiction—but they are not his best work. In them, however, one can trace his growing concern with politics and his drift toward socialism. He was a socialist by the time he did the fourth of his books on poverty, *The Road to Wigan Pier,* which was published in England in 1937 and has not yet been published in this country,* doubtless because, being largely a factual report on the mining communities of South Wales in the worst part of the depression, it has been thought to have too antiquarian a flavor. But then the bubonic plague of which Defoe and Pepys wrote had lost a good deal of its topicality, and Orwell on life in Swansea and Wigan and Newcastle in 1936 seems to me fully the peer of Defoe and Pepys on London in 1664.

The Road to Wigan Pier is a masterpiece. It is also a basic document in the intellectual history of this century. The book had been commissioned by Victor Gollancz, the publisher, on behalf of the Left Book Club, an organization whose tendency is evident in its title, as a study of human misery in an exploitative social order. The first half is exactly that. Orwell was never more brilliant as a journalist. The second part is an examination of socialism as a remedy. It was perhaps the most rigorous examination that any doctrine has ever received at the hands of an adherent. It was so tough, so disrespectful, so rich in heresies that Gollancz, who, as proprietor of the Left Book Club was the shepherd of a flock that scandalized as easily as any Wesleyan congregation, published the book only after writing an introduction that could not have been more strained and apologetic if he had actually been a Wesleyan minister who for some improbable reason found himself the sponsor of a lecture by George Bernard Shaw on the Articles of Religion. Gollancz's plight was in some respects even more difficult than that hypothetical one,

---

* Since this piece was written, *Wigan Pier* has been published in the United States—by Harcourt, Brace & World in 1958.

since it was necessary for him to concede that the early chapters
"really *are* the kind of thing that makes converts."

In discomfiting his fellow socialists as he did, Orwell performed, for the first time, what was to become his characteristic
service to his generation. In 1956, I find it rather awkward—
indeed, I find it downright embarrassing—to have the responsibility of explaining exactly what this service was. For it was
really nothing more or less than clearing minds of cant, and the
service should never have been necessary in the first place. It
has to be understood that the typical intellectual of the thirties
was a man so shocked by social injustice and the ghastly spectacle
of fascism that his brain was easily addled by anyone who proposed a quick and drastic remedy. The humanistic mind in those
days was poorly equipped to deal with social and political ideas,
and grappled with them almost as awkwardly as in recent years
it has grappled with the problems of nuclear physics. We tend
now to recall Communism as the only brain-addler of the period,
but there were others. Non-Communist liberalism had a way
of stiffening into illiberal orthodoxies, as did pacifism. Fascism
itself won over a few essentially humanistic intelligences, and
so did extreme conservatism. Almost at the onset of social and
political consciousness, intellectuals surrendered their critical
faculties. Many of them thought they had excellent reasons for
doing so. It was perfectly obvious, they would argue, that the
conditions that cried out for change would not be changed by
individuals. Still less would they be changed by acts of cerebra-
tion. They would be changed only by the action of large numbers
of people—by parties, by armies, by collectivities of one sort or
another. Parties and armies require discipline. Discipline necessarily calls for a ceding of rights and privileges. *Ergo,* for the
benefit of mankind, for the prisoners of starvation, for the
greatest good of the greatest number, for the Cause, it is necessary
to give up the right to be critics, iconoclasts, Bohemians, indi-
vidualists.

It can be objected, I know, that I am only describing a species
of conformity and that conformity continues to be quite a problem. Certainly it does, and that is one of the reasons why Orwell
is needed today. But today's conformity is one of assent, and

I am talking about a conformity of dissent, which is in many ways a more terrible thing. Twenty years ago, it was the critics of society who allowed their critical powers to atrophy; it was the independent-minded who threw away their independence. W. H. Auden, the poet of the decade, wrote the apologia in a quatrain that stands as the dedication to Erika Mann in *On This Island,* published in 1937, the *Wigan Pier* year:

> Since the external disorder, and extravagant lies
> The baroque frontiers, the surrealist police;
> What can truth treasure, heart bless,
> But a narrow strictness?

To some of us, it seemed a compelling and quite lovely bit of poet's logic. To Orwell, it was a *non sequitur*—illogical and unlovely.

Orwell arrived on the scene in the middle thirties and proceeded to fire the camps of the orthodox wherever he found them. How he came to this role is, I think, quite a mystery. His acquaintance with social and political ideas and practices was, if anything, even slighter than that of most of his contemporaries, and there were, as I have suggested, aspects of his temperament that seemed to make him rather a promising candidate for fanaticism. Nevertheless, he stood almost alone in his generation as a man of consistent good judgment and as one who never for a moment doubted that it was possible to be at once humanistic and tough-minded, to make commitments and avoid the perils of commitment. He was no less shocked by social injustice and fascism than the next man. He had known poverty and had written four books on it, at least two of which, *Down and Out* and *Wigan Pier,* are classics. He saw the point about parties and armies and took more than his share of responsibilities. For all his heresies as a socialist, he was no stranger to the grubbiest of political chores, and in 1936 he went to Spain and bore arms against fascism—an experience that led to another classic, *Homage to Catalonia.* He was not, of course, alone in seeing the perils of Commitment, but most of the others who saw the perils either withdrew their commitments or made silly counter-commitments. Orwell did neither. He felt that withdrawal was out of the ques-

tion "unless you are armored by old age or stupidity or hypoc-
risy." But of the committed writer he said, "His writings, in so
far as they are to have any value, will always be the product
of the saner self that stands aside, records the things that are
done and admits their necessity, but refuses to be deceived as
to their true nature." He was seldom deceived as to the true
nature of anything.

"He was the conscience of his generation," V. S. Pritchett said,
meaning, of course, his generation of writers. Up to 1945, he
was very little known in this country, and his British audience
was pretty well limited to the readers of the weeklies and
monthlies of opinion. He was becoming established as a critic
and journalist when he went to Spain. He was wounded in the
neck and hospitalized in Lérida; he had joined the P.O.U.M.,
which opposed the Communists and was critical of the Popular
Front government from a more or less Trotskyist point of view,
and he left Spain with some difficulty and with a price on his
head. He published *Homage to Catalonia* in 1938: though it was
a passionately Loyalist book, it gave as great offense to the passionate Loyalists as *Wigan Pier* had given to socialists and Communists, and by the time of his death had sold only nine hundred
copies. From 1938 to the middle years of World War II, he had
a difficult time of it; he was held in great admiration by people
whose admiration was worth having, but partly because of his
political views and partly because of the general dislocations of
the period he had little work and little sense of function. He
wanted to join the army, but the army would not have him. In
1939, he published *Coming Up for Air,* and in 1941 *The Lion
and the Unicorn,* but these did little to help keep him alive or
relieve his sense of frustration. He served in the Home Guard,
did occasional scripts for the British Broadcasting Corporation,
and wrote brilliantly from London for the *Partisan Review* in
New York. It was not until fairly well along in the war that he
attracted a sizable British audience for his periodical writing,
most of which appeared in the Laborite *Tribune.* His tubercu-
losis, which he never seems to have done much about, had
progressed during the war; it was in an advanced and incurable
state by 1945, so that for the short period in which he had

a large number of readers, from the publication of *Animal Farm* until his death in a sanatorium a few months after the publication of *Nineteen Eighty-Four,* life held many agonies and few rewards. He once said that *Nineteen Eighty-Four* would have been a less bleak and bitter book if he had not been a dying man when he wrote it.

In the past decade, critics in large numbers have been drawn to Orwell's work and have found him for the most part a thorny problem. The truth is that his work does not much lend itself to theirs. His novels were direct and fairly simple narratives in an old tradition. Their meanings are mostly on the surface. Orwell posed no riddles, elaborated no myths, and manipulated no symbols. Even *Nineteen Eighty-Four* offers limited possibilities for exegesis. One need only be alive in the twentieth century to grasp its significance. There is not much to do with Orwell's novels except read them. Nor is there much to be said about his style. It was colloquial in diction and sinewy in construction; it aimed at clarity and unobtrusiveness and achieved both. Cyril Connolly once performed an experiment by scrambling some sentences of Orwell's with some of Ernest Hemingway's and some of Christopher Isherwood's. He defied the reader to tell the writers one from another and argued that, since identification was impossible, all writers who strive for the colloquial throw away a good part of their heritage as writers. He felt that those who worked in a Mandarin Dialect—those, that is, who strove for elegance of phrase and exquisiteness of texture—were at least using all the resources of their language, while those who worked in what he called the New Vernacular needlessly confined themselves to a narrow range of rhythms and tones. I think Connolly was wrong in saying that his three novelists could not be told apart and wrong in his dispraise of colloquialism. But beyond saying that Orwell's was simply the style most commonly used in modern English and American writing and that Orwell employed it with great vigor, there is really not a great deal for a critic to say. A writer of Orwell's sort does not give the modern critic much of a chance to draw upon his imposing collection of critical utensils and contrivances.

In consequence, there has been a search for the sources of
Orwell's strength in Orwell's character. No doubt that is where
the sources are to be found; *le style est l'homme même,* and so
forth. But it cannot be said that the search has been very productive. What nearly everyone seems to find in Orwell is rectitude and more rectitude. Lionel Trilling has said that the
profoundest statement he ever heard about Orwell came from a
college student who said: "He was a virtuous man." John Atkins
has said, "The common element in all George Orwell's writing
was a sense of decency." Atkins also calls him a "social saint."
The idea of saintliness turns up everywhere; there is a touch
of hagiography even in the arguments directed against it. Irving
Howe, poking fun at the "old maids of criticism, hunting for
stray bits of morality as if they were pieces of tatting left in the
parlor" and pointing out that Orwell himself had said that
"sainthood is a thing human beings must avoid," has ventured
the opinion that Orwell was a "revolutionary personality." But
what is that except another term, one with secular and socialist
overtones, for a saint? A "revolutionary personality" is what the
Ethical Culturist calls Jesus Christ.

Orwell was an uncommonly decent person, and his moral and
physical courage survived many hard tests. He was not a saint,
or even saintly. I do not think he was any *more* virtuous or decent than his contemporaries. What is probably behind the use
of these terms is a confusion of the prophet and the saint—that
and an appreciation of the fact that Orwell saw through all the
pretenses of his time and never made a fool of himself. None of
this really has much to do with personal "goodness." On the contrary, there is often a rather direct and visible relationship
between folly and purity of spirit. We all know about the paving
stones on the road to hell. "The surrendering and humbling of
the self breed pride and arrogance," Eric Hoffer has written, and
of course pride and arrogance breed folly. The obverse of this is
the old set-a-thief-to-catch-a-thief principle. It takes a certain
amount of wickedness to understand the mechanics of wickedness
as Orwell did and to perceive that "the essence of being human is
that one does not seek perfection, that one *is* sometimes willing
to commit sins for the sake of loyalty, that one does not push

asceticism to the point where it makes friendly intercourse impossible, and that one is prepared in the end to be defeated and broken up by life, which is the inevitable price of fastening one's love upon other individuals." I think it clear that Orwell's asceticism furnished him with a knowledge of the point to which asceticism should not be pushed and that his impulse toward fanaticism furnished him with a comprehension of it and a determination to resist it. Naturally, there was more than that to it, else he would have succumbed to impulse.

In any event, Orwell had his share of wickedness. He could say cruel things and his fairness of judgment did not always extend to individuals. He called Kipling a "gutter patriot" and W. H. Auden a "gutless Kipling." (He could be remorseful, too; he publicly apologized for this characterization of Auden.) His judgments were not always as charitable as they were sound; there was a bit more to be said for the radical intellectuals of the thirties than he could find it in his heart to say. I do not see how, on logical grounds alone, he could be as indulgent as he was toward P. G. Wodehouse and at the same time as bitter about the liberals and radicals, to whom he had a way of referring as "the pansy left." Standing alone, his plea for Wodehouse would have seemed an act of generosity and understanding. But it seems only fair that if one is going to excuse Wodehouse for allowing himself to be exploited by the Nazis, one should be approximately as forgiving to those who allowed themselves to be exploited by the Communists. Orwell was quite frequently unfair in this way, but his unfairness flowed not, I think, from self-righteousness but from ill-temper, from his passion for the truth, and, part of the time, from his use of overstatement as a device of rhetoric. His choler and intemperance had something in common with that of Dr. Johnson and with that of the author of *Gulliver's Travels,* of whom he once wrote: "Politically, Swift was one of those people who are driven into a sort of perverse Toryism by the follies of the progressive party of the moment." It was Orwell's distinction that the follies of his friends never drove him to abandon them, but now and then he did manage to sound like the spokesmen for a perverse Toryism.

Orwell, thank God, was no saint. He was burdened by no

excess of purity. I do not think it within the province of the critic to determine what properties of the pneuma account for what we find in a man's work. It should be enough that we find something to which we can respond and that we seek to understand what it is that moves us. In Orwell, we find a mind that did not have to be cleared of cant because it evidently had none to begin with. He had sense and sensibility, a love of language, a nose for fraud, a hunger for truth, a resolute heart, a robust and inquiring intellect, and whatever it is that makes a man an artist.

* Arthur Hays Vandenberg: New Man in the Pantheon

1 9 6 2

DEAN ACHESON has lately reminded us of the eminence of Arthur H. Vandenberg, a Republican Senator from Michigan from 1928 until his death in 1951. "Without Vandenberg in the Senate," Acheson writes in *Sketches from Life of Men I Have Known*, "the history of the postwar period might have been very different." Quite probably this is so. Acheson goes on: "Vandenberg stands for the emergence of the United States into world power and leadership, as Clay typified the growth of the country; Webster and Calhoun the great debate of the ante-bellum days; and Robert M. LaFollette the turbulence of the Progressive Era." This puts him in fast company, but perhaps he belongs there. He performed, according to Acheson, "a service for which this country should forever be grateful."

Vandenberg's career was certainly an interesting and important one. But, as now and then happens in this world, the things that made it important were not the things that made it interesting. Vandenberg was, even by the standards his contemporaries set, a mediocrity. He was a nice, immensely likable mediocrity, to be sure, and often an entertaining one, but his only gifts of consequence were for political survival, friendship, and the production of prose that seemed to have been influenced chiefly by Mr. Micawber and Sam Goldwyn. Yet there is no doubt that in his later years he performed the services of a statesman. His story teaches a rather stirring lesson in the political uses of rectified error. It was Vandenberg's conversion, in the last days of the last war, from isolationism to internationalism that made him a large figure in the postwar world. Without Vandenberg's help, it is at least conceivable that Roosevelt and Truman might have suffered the fate of Woodrow Wilson. Vandenberg, a powerful Republican leader in 1945, supported the Democratic administrations in most of our postwar policies—among them, membership in the United Nations, the Marshall Plan, the North Atlantic Treaty, the peacetime dispatch of American troops to Europe, and the resistance in Korea. Before and even during the war, he had been isolationist. "This war is about nothing but twenty-five people and propaganda," he said not too long before Pearl Harbor. He supported the war once we were in it, but on strictly nationalist grounds. He opposed the nomination of either Dewey or Willkie in 1944. His man was General MacArthur. But then, on January 10, 1945, he took the Senate floor and said, in one of his typically overblown speeches, "No nation hereafter can immunize itself by its own exclusive action." This broke the back of Republican isolationism in the Senate. It made Vandenberg a central figure in the diplomacy and politics of the years that remained to him. He gave the country a bipartisan foreign policy—which Vandenberg, a compulsive tinkerer with words, said he preferred to describe as an *"un*partisan policy." (In earlier days, he had said, "I am more insulationist than isolationist. But if forced to elect between the designations isolationist and internationalist, I am proudly the former.") He could not have done this except as a recent convert. Dean Acheson would not have accredited him to the pantheon if he had been an internationalist all along.

The conversion itself was rather a commonplace affair. If one wished to sail easily before the wind in 1945, one talked about international co-operation, the community of nations, collective security, the smallness and oneness of the globe, and all that sort of thing. For politicians, especially Republican politicians, internationalism was the great success school of the period. The isolationists, like Representative Hamilton Fish, were being voted or gerrymandered out of Congress. The prewar leader of the movement, Senator Burton Wheeler, of Montana, was in disgrace for having made some unsavory associations—something Vandenberg, incidentally, never did. Wendell Willkie, Thomas E. Dewey, and Harold Stassen were internationalists in one degree or another and doing very well at it, while in November 1944, Senator Robert A. Taft, unregenerate as always, barely squeaked through in Ohio. Eisenhower Republicanism was in the making. Vandenberg was unquestionably in earnest about seeing things in a new light in January 1945, but he was lucky in having come upon one of those delicious moments in life when self-interest and conviction unite in urging the same course of action. He would be up for re-election the following year, and both the internationalist Republicans and the Democrats would have given him a hard time if he had had to conduct a defensive, grousing campaign as an isolationist. His change of heart made him, immediately, a national and international figure. He was able to win re-election without making a single speech or even visiting Michigan. He learned of his victory in 1946 while enjoying the amenities (he was a great one for amenities) of the Hotel Meurice on the Rue de Rivoli and lending powerful support to the Secretary of State, James A. Byrnes, in his tangles with the Russkis. Conversion led to a fascinating career and, it would seem, immortality. If he had not had his blinding illumination, he would be recalled today—if he were recalled at all—only as a gassy and pompous Michigan politician whose saving graces were an indefatigable friendliness and a talent for self-mimicry. He was a windbag ("What is right? Where is justice? There let America take her stand") who stood a certain distance apart from others of the breed by virtue of his joviality and sweetness of nature. He was one of the few men I have ever known whom one could describe as inoffensively pompous. For one thing, he was the sort of whom pomposity was expected—he was big, fleshy, jowly, well-looked-after. For another, he was the soul of charity. In his diaries, which were published by his son in 1952 as *The Private Papers of Senator Vandenberg,* he describes his response to an extraordinary display of bad manners by President Roosevelt and some members of his family. The Senator was at a White House reception for the King and Queen of England. He had lately been making Presidential noises. When it came his turn to be presented to the King, Roosevelt did not introduce him by name, as he had everyone else, but merely said, "Here's a chap who thinks he's going to succeed me. But he isn't." Two of the Roosevelt boys, standing behind their father, doubled up with mirth. Vandenberg's only comment was: "I was surprised because the President is usually very charitable to me in his greetings. Perhaps he was trying to be funny." He gave everyone the benefit of the doubt—especially if it was possible to say they were trying to be funny.

If he is to stand in history alongside the great figures of the second rank, he will make an odd and amusing addition to their company. He came to Washington in 1928 after two decades as a small-city newspaperman and free-lance writer. The paper was the Grand Rapids *Herald,* whose owner, and Vandenberg's patron, was William Alden Smith, himself a Senator. As a writer, he had turned out innumerable short stories in the Oliver Optic–Horatio Alger vein for Eastern magazines and three dreadful books about Alexander Hamilton, the best known of which is *Hamilton: The Greatest American.* He combined with his Merry Andrew nature a powerful hero-worshiping bent, and early in life, he said, he had settled on Hamilton. "He stood at my shoulder like a big brother in my youth," he once wrote. This seems, at first glance, a somewhat astonishing assertion. Hamilton has not appealed to many boys. Why should the charitable, easygoing Vandenberg have revered a believer in the knavery of men? Actually, Vandenberg never grasped and never tried to grasp Hamilton's view of life or his place in the history of political theory. Of this side of Hamilton, he merely wrote: "To epitomize his omniscient services the contributions of a Titan would be impossible"—and let it go at that. What he found in Hamilton was an absorbing rags-to-riches saga, an exciting Tattered Tom or Ragged Dick story of the sort he was selling to *Pearson's.* He wrote that there is nothing in American history "more wonderful than the contrast between Hamilton, a friendless immigrant upon the docks of Boston at the tender age of fifteen and Hamilton, by sheer force of human intelligence, whiplashing a snarling New York convention majority into unwilling acceptance of the Constitution at the age of thirty-one." When Vandenberg was appointed to the Senate in 1928, he had one aim he set above all others—the erection on the banks of the Potomac of a monument to Hamilton of a tonnage equal to, or greater than, those that honor Washington and Lincoln.

In his early days, and to some extent later on too, he was a combination hick and roué. He was a sort of Grand Rapids *boulevardier*. He seemed hardly more serious about politics than the Honorable Jimmy Walker, the song writer and soft-shoe virtuoso who, during Vandenberg's first years in the Senate, was mayor of New York. As a matter of fact, Vandenberg was also a songwriter. He was the author of a popular ballad in praise of the movie queen Bebe Daniels entitled "Bebe, Bebe, Bebe—Be Mine." This was the *boulevardier*. The small-town boy, a harness maker's son, turned out editorial after editorial denouncing Sinclair Lewis for *Elmer Gantry* and wrote a lengthy commentary on the sordid Snyder-Gray murder case called "Sin and Justice—Both Naked." In the great days, toward the end, he was mostly *boulevardier*. Having been a prohibitionist before Volstead and bone dry as long as Prohibition lasted, he became a conspicuous friend of the highball and a busy and quite charming ladies' man. When history found an important role for him, he took to the black Homburg as Douglas MacArthur took to gold braid and handled his cigar with a new elegance. He was very impressive and very Senatorial in all the pictures of him talking things over with Anthony Eden, Guy Mollet, Trygve Lie, the King of Greece, and all the others.

As a writer, he could be faulted for many things, but he had one endearing asset. He loved words—in fact, he loved them almost to death. He was very proud of having been called to duty in the Republican campaign of 1920 and of being responsible for the slogan "With Harding at the helm, we can sleep nights." He was once asked if "Back to Normalcy" was his. "Normalcy," he said. "That sounds like one of my words." It surely did. A man responsible for "sheer magicry" might be responsible for anything. His love of words was of the purest, most elevated sort; he loved them not just for their meanings but for themselves alone. Who else could have come up with such phrases as "our mirific inheritances," "pursuant to the pattern of the rapes of yesterday," "dream ourselves and others into delusions," "extinguish the jeopardy," "marcescent monarchy," and "knock-out admonition"? He was a lover not only of words but of punctuation. He worked into everything an ungodly number of useless quotation marks, exclamation points, parentheses, capitalizations, and italics.

I have said that he would have been forgotten but for his conversion in 1945. It can be argued, though, that his conversion was entirely predictable. He was being converted all the time. He could have found his way along the sawdust trail blindfolded. (His "favorite Biblical character," according to his son, "was St. Paul, the dynamic convert to Christianity.") He came to the Senate a conservative. But when he ran for re-election in 1934, it was as a New Deal collaborationist. He had steered through the Federal Bank Deposit Insurance Act and took all the credit he could get for it. He described the Wagner Act, which he voted against, as "labor's hard-won bill of rights." He coined a phrase: "Social-mindedness, not Socialism." He wrote an article called "The New Deal Must Be Salvaged." ("The New Deal must be melted over, recast in a new engine, going slowly and rather on the bias in several directions.") It is worth noting that in 1934 he was one of two Republican Senators to make it. He picked up in one election as much seniority as he might normally have gained by winning two or three elections.

It is inaccurate, or at least incomplete, to describe him as having been, in the post-1945 period, an isolationist-turned-internationalist; it is more nearly accurate, though still not completely so, to describe him as an internationalist-turned-isolationist-turned-internationalist. As editor of the Grand Rapids *Herald* in 1916, he favored intervention in Europe while Wilson and Hughes were dead set against it. His prose had not attained its full lusciousness by then, but he was going pretty good, and he wrote, close to thirty years before he had his blinding vision in the Senate:

One right yielded up invites the loss of a second—then a third. The endless chain. Soon infringements pyramid, and assailants, encouraged by ease of unchallenged conquests, commence to plot against the nation itself. Somewhere a stand has to be made.

Once the stand was made, the war appeared to Vandenberg as "the greatest revival the world has ever known since Christ came upon the earth." The revival spirit cooled (as it always must—if it didn't, one revival would be enough), and by the time the League of Nations fight came along, Vandenberg had turned isolationist. This development may have had some connection with the fact that the owner of the paper, Senator William Alden Smith, took a stand against the League. Smith, a great contemporary of Cut-Rate Carpenter and Rise-Up William Allen, had not been conspicuous on any side of any issue up to 1919. His most famous contribution was his raising of the question, during the investigation of the *Titanic* disaster, of why the passengers did not climb into the watertight compartments. But the League of Nations somehow offended him, and he gave powerful support to Henry Cabot Lodge's fight against it. The League offended Vandenberg, too, and in the days when he was pleased with this phase of his record he talked a lot about an interview he had with William Howard Taft. As an interviewer, as in all his other roles, Vandenberg did most of the talking, and the notable thing, according to him, about this encounter was that he talked Taft right out of opposition to the Lodge amendments to the League treaty and into support of them. Taft's switch, he always maintained, was what *really* defeated Wilson. Vandenberg also used to enjoy recalling that he made a contribution by supplying Lodge with the sentence: "Unshared idealism is a menace." Lodge used it, and it had, Vandenberg thought, great impact.

He was isolationist pretty much throughout the thirties. He cast one of the two votes against recognizing the Soviet Union. He was a leading participant in Senator Gerald Nye's investigation of the munitions makers. He said that testimony before this committee persuaded him he had been in error in 1916. He supported the Neutrality Act of 1937 and voted against the repeal of its Arms Embargo in 1939. He went through a brief but hot interventionist phase in the winter of 1939-40. He wanted to put an immediate stop to the Russian invasion of Finland, and he regarded the Japanese as a distinct menace. He was a sponsor of the Senate resolution which abrogated the Japanese trade treaty of 1911—a measure described by Walter Lippmann as "the longest step on the road to war that the United States has taken since President Wilson announced . . . that the United States would hold the German government strictly accountable for its acts." It was shortly after this, however, that he entered the isolationist phase from which he did not emerge until 1945. From the fall of France to Pearl Harbor, he was against everything the administration proposed. He supported the war but continued to be isolationist. He opposed the Ball-Burton-Hatch-Hill Resolution, which sought, in 1943, to commit the country to a postwar United Nations. Then, just before the Dumbarton Oaks conferences that were preliminary to the San Francisco meeting at which the U.N. Charter was adopted, he made the great speech. In his diaries, he says that he rewrote it "at least a dozen times." It may be that each time he rewrote it, he found room for one more use of the gorgeous tautology "honest candor," which appears a good dozen times, now and then reinforced—as in "honest candor devoid of prejudice or ire" and "honest candor on the high plane of ideals." In the speech, he announced that he had come to believe isolation impossible and he put forth a program of sorts for the disarmament of Germany by the victorious powers. What he had to say could have been said in a few simple words. But those twelve revisions led to the creation of a great mountain of platitudes, topped by glittering redundancies:

We must have maximum Allied cooperation and minimum Allied frictions. . . . We cannot drift to victory. . . . There are critical moments in the life of every nation. . . . We confront such a moment now. . . . A global conflict which uproots the earth cannot submit itself to the dominion of any finite mind. . . . Each of us can only speak according to his little lights—and pray for a composite wisdom that shall lead us to high safe ground.

This is the indispensable point. Our basic pledges [the Atlantic Charter] cannot be dismissed as a mere nautical nimbus. They march with our armies. They sail with our fleets. They fly with our eagles. They sleep with our martyred dead. The first requisite of honest candor, I suggest, Mr. President, is to relight this torch.

Our oceans have ceased to be moats which automatically protect our ramparts. Flesh and blood now compete unequally with winged steel. War has become an all-consuming juggernaut. If World War III ever unhappily arrives, it will open new laboratories of death too horrible to contemplate. I propose to do everything within my power to keep those laboratories closed for keeps. We stand by our guns with epic heroism. I know of no reason why we should not stand by our ideals. . . . I do not wish to meddle. I want only to help. I want to do my duty. It is in this spirit that I ask for honest candor in respect to our ideals.

In Vandenberg's own modest words, "The electric effect of the speech was instantaneous." "It cannot be said of many speakers," Walter Lippmann wrote, "that they affect the course of events. But this can be said of Senator Vandenberg's speech if the President . . . will recognize promptly and firmly its importance." Roosevelt was no slouch in this matter. He took fifty reprints along to Yalta and handed them out as promissory notes from the Republican party. The speech sent Vandenberg to the peaks immediately; it became practically impossible—certainly unofficial—to hold an international conference without him. His defection had made a repetition of 1919 impossible. If one can imagine the devastation that would be wrought among right-wingers today if Barry Goldwater defected and tagged along behind Dean Rusk everywhere Rusk went, one has some picture of the devastation Vandenberg wrought by his famous switch.

Dean Acheson compares his role to that of Clay and Calhoun in ante-bellum days. The analogy conceals the irony of the situation. Clay and Calhoun were great controversialists and they played unique historical roles. Vandenberg contributed only his large and amiable presence. He never really *did* anything. When he went to San Francisco, Moscow, London, Rome, Geneva, or Rio, his function was to weaken Republican resistance in Washington and to prove to allies and adversaries that we had something approaching national unity in this country. He was a kind of property eagle. He could fulfill his function without opening his mouth—though he generally opened it quite a bit. Still, many things might have been different, and worse, if we had not had him.

The moral of the Vandenberg story can be formulated in some such fashion as this: it is very often better to be wrong first and right afterward than to have been right all along. As Scripture tells us, it makes a man more precious in the sight of the Lord. Virtue is its own reward, but there is nothing that quite matches the combination of virtue's reward and the wages of sin. There are times when uprightness has practically no meaning unless it rests firmly on the foundation of waywardness. Whittaker Chambers might have ended in the near-anonymity of the *Time* masthead if he had not been a spy; now there are those who think of him as a modern St. Augustine. Vandenberg, in his day, was far from being the only Republican internationalist in the Senate. To name another, there was Warren Austin, of Vermont. But Austin's record was grievously flawed: it contained no recent isolationist phases. Truman made him ambassador to the U.N. and he served with distinction, but there is no one to propose that Clay, Calhoun, Webster, and La Follette move over and make room for him.

But one cannot begrudge Vandenberg his place. He would appreciate it greatly if he knew about it and would think of himself as being much closer to Big Brother Alex Hamilton. And his service was not small: what he did, by switching from isolationism to internationalism, was to make it possible, by a process resembling vicarious atonement, for lots of other isolationists who knew, if not that they were wrong, at least that they were licked to make an honorable peace with the administration and thereby to enable the country to have something like a workable foreign policy.

✳ Willkie, Another Happy Warrior

1 9 5 3

JOSEPH BARNES' *Willkie* is an instrument of justice, restoring to its subject some of the vitality, audacity, and firmness of character that are not among the features our wayward memories have fixed upon. Over the years, Willkie has shrunk to a symbol of gullibility—a windy, well-meaning, heavy-drinking promoter who got religion and became a sap about it, allowing himself to be hooked by the Stalinists into joining their mischievous "second front" clamor and then promoting a credulous kind of internationalism that, if it has not been the direct cause of any damage in this badly damaged world, has been of little help in advancing the hour of reason's triumph. Barnes rescues Willkie from this sour and mistaken judgment. He does not claim much for the "One World" phase—the phase, incidentally, in which Barnes was most closely associated with Willkie, having made the global trip with him in an Air Force plane and having lent a hand in the composition of *One World*—but he does consider it, as indeed he should, evidence that Willkie could respond to the largest and most humane visions of his time and do it, despite all his surface infelicities, with gallantry and grace. The One World mission and Willkie's discourses on world politics may have been defective in ideology, but they were *beaux gestes* of a sort that no one else was then capable of making. (Mrs. Roosevelt was his only rival in the field; her husband was much too canny, too aware of political consequences, to do or say anything he could not defend in terms of immediate interests, of either his party or his nation. It is impossible to imagine Roosevelt undertaking the legal defense of William Schneiderman, the California Com-

192

munist boss whose right to citizenship Willkie gallantly upheld before the Supreme Court.) What was appealing about Willkie, what set him apart in his period, was not any doctrine or mode of action he stood for but the fact that there was never any meagerness about him. The earlier spokesmen of American conservatism—Coolidge, Hoover, Landon, and the rest—were shrewd, honest, and, in varying degrees, competent men, but the truths they perceived were mostly in the cautionary line, a series of "don'ts" and "bewares." Their views of life were invariably reductive and depreciatory; when their language showed any character at all, it was astringency. On most matters of substance, particularly the structure of American society, Willkie's outlook was about the same as theirs, but his gave the impression of being surrounded by plenty of light, air, and good nature. He was immensely likable.

He was not a great man, but he might, if things had worked out a bit differently, have become one. He had courage, hope, energy, curiosity, gregariousness, and flexibility. These were things that Franklin Roosevelt had, but Willkie had, in addition, a mind that was, if not of the first order, quicker than Roosevelt's and better stocked; far from being intellectually lazy, as Roosevelt was, he had a massive hunger for knowledge and ideas and for the company of intellectuals. Roosevelt was the craftier politician and the more experienced one, but Willkie might in time have caught up with him. If he had had more seasoning in the thirties, he might very well have won the election of 1940 and led the country through the war with Germany and Japan. A number of people have recently expressed the view that it might have been better all around if the political pendulum had made shorter strokes, so that the conflict with fascism could have been managed by an antifascist government of the Right and the developing conflict with Communism led by an anti-Communist government of the left. But Willkie emerged too late and died too early for any real fulfillment. His career in public life lasted only four years. He will probably be remembered only for the freakishness of his career—because although he was doubly a Beelzebub in our political demonology, being both a Wall Streeter and a power czar, he was looked upon by millions as a great democratic leader; because he was a registered voter in one major political party only eighteen months before he became the Presidential candidate of the other; and for a few more such peculiarities. The late Harold Laski said that if a man like Willkie turned up in European politics, it would be a sure sign that the social system was about to collapse. Laski claimed that the entire case for the viability of our political system could be deduced from the facts of Willkie's career. Laski had a weakness for large claims.

Still, Willkie should be remembered as more than an oddity. It takes no labored analysis of recent events to make clear his relevance to them. In thought and temperament, Eisenhower has no more in common with Willkie than any middle-aged Kansan has with any middle-aged Indianian, but Eisenhower's nomination and, even more, his election can be read as a vindication of Willkie's view of Republicanism and as a triumph for many people whose imagination Willkie was the first to fire. Except that Governor Dewey was a Warwick rather than a hopeful prince, the 1952 Republican Convention was a repeat of the 1940 one, of which William Allen White wrote, "Taft has most of the kingmakers, and Willkie has most of the enthusiasm." Enthusiasm carried the day not because it captured the delegates but because, as happened in 1952, the delegates believed it might capture the country. And the course of the campaign was strikingly like Eisenhower's. "This is not a campaign," Willkie said at the outset. "It's a crusade." The crusade ended rather squalidly. Willkie began as the antagonist of the party regulars and as the candidate who would steal the enemy's thunder. He held that Roosevelt was, if anything, too little of an interventionist, though he expressed approval of most of the things Roosevelt was doing. Candor and moderation were to be the hallmarks of the campaign. There would be no concessions to expediency. "I will not talk in quibbling language," he announced. No huckstering was to be tolerated—"I am purely a conversational farmer," he said in Rushville the day after his acceptance speech. "I have never done a stroke of work on a Rush County farm in my life, and I hope I never have to." But he was visited on the farm where "Louis Berkemier and

Joe Kramer do the work," by some people who had a few things to explain to him, among them the fact that there was another man running for President. Willkie listened and was persuaded that he might do well to alter his strategy. Roosevelt's destroyers-for-bases deal with Churchill, which Willkie had endorsed, became "the most dictatorial and arbitrary act of any President in the history of the United States." By the time the campaign was over, Willkie was as much in opposition to the man he had been a few months earlier (and was once more to be a few months later) as he was to his opponent. He reversed his field wherever it seemed profitable to do so, collaborated in just about every form of humbug that promised a vote ("I have never lost touch with the farm," he began to say), and sought and made alliances with the people for whom he had the greatest contempt.

All this, of course, enabled the Democrats to say, as they have lately been saying of Eisenhower, that the candidate had given himself to his enemies in the party. Having become the piper for this set, he would have to pipe the tunes they called. The argument is an old but spurious one, and Willkie's experience is only one instance of its falseness. After the campaign his dislike of those he had denied his own instincts to satisfy was greater by far than it had been before and greater, surely, than it would have been if they had left him alone. It mounted steadily over the years, so in the end he found it impossible to choose between the politicians in his party and those in Roosevelt's, and he died without having decided whether he would support Roosevelt in 1944 or would take a walk.

He died in full vigor and at the onset of what might have been the most productive of his several careers. Had he lived, I think he might have been one of the large figures of the postwar period. I doubt if he would have sought a Presidential nomination again (though it is barely conceivable that the Republicans would have pitted him against Truman in 1948), but he would surely have had a lot to say about American politics, and he would have been heard, for his partisans were as numerous and as dedicated as, say, those of Adlai Stevenson. I got to know him rather well in the last months of his life and to like him enormously. I was a young political journalist, and he had a lot of ideas he wished to see in print. I spent a good many amusing and instructive hours in his Broad Street office drawing him out (it was anything but difficult to do) on his views of men and events. In those last months and weeks, he was filled with resentment and scorn of Thomas E. Dewey, who had just beaten him hands down for the Republican nomination, but, strangely, he blamed his luck not on Dewey or fate but on, of all people, John Foster Dulles. It pleased Willkie to think of Dewey as a person of no consequence whatever—as, in fact, a product of Dulles' imagination. This conceit possessed him so that he elaborated it into a theory of history that made John Foster, Benjamin Harrison's Secretary of State and Dulles' grandfather, the author of the original sin. Foster had inflamed his grandson with the desire to be Secretary of State. To satisfy this desire, Dulles had first to create a President. He settled on Dewey, became Dewey's leading patron, financed the early Dewey campaigns. In the summer and early fall of 1944, Willkie could believe that the worst consequences of John Foster and his grandson were about to be realized. (One can imagine him opposing Eisenhower eight years later and elaborating still further his eccentric theory of modern American history.)

I often wish that Willkie had lived into the world of Eisenhower, the durable Dulles, Joseph R. McCarthy, Adlai Stevenson, and Richard M. Nixon. Defeat had liberated him from the worst of his political passions—as politics had earlier liberated him from his business past. He was growing in eloquence and sophistication. He was enjoying life immensely. He had organized a brilliant staff, and he had, of course, the money to finance any activity he chose to undertake. His essential liberalism was being strengthened—I do not think he would have been a quixotic one-worlder in the late forties and early fifties, but neither do I think he would have bought the rival brand of bologna, which was being peddled by dat old debbil Dulles. Whatever role he might have played, he would have played it with charm and verve and candor and generosity and a high sense of decency.

* The Interior Ickes

1 9 5 4

THE THREE PUBLISHED VOLUMES of Harold L. Ickes' *Secret Diary* make the fullest and most instructive of all inside accounts of the Roosevelt administration. Ickes is not just one more political diarist, interesting because strategically placed; he is one of the great journal-keepers, in at least some respects the peer of another narcissistic bureaucrat, Samuel Pepys. As often as not, Ickes deals with matters about which most of us nowadays could not care less—the late Ebert Burlew's opinion of the late James Scrugham; the politics of public housing in Lackawanna, Pennsylvania; the Senate vote on confirmation of a certain Harry Slattery as Under-Secretary of the Interior. Frequently, of course, he gives us his version of some large and still meaningful event —the recognition of the U.S.S.R., or Roosevelt's fight over the Supreme Court—but the remote and trifling affairs far outnumber the others. Ickes, however, generates an interest in whatever he is writing about. He has fashioned a work that has some of the attributes of creativeness. His Washington, like Dickens' London, Balzac's Paris, and Faulkner's Jefferson, is a community in which one can settle down and lead a life of one's own.

It is hard to say what makes Ickes so good. As a writer, he lacked distinction. He had a commonplace mind, full of firmly held, meritorious, wholly unoriginal views. Of sensibility, he had none. "To contemplate nature," he says in a passage that takes him as close as he ever gets to reflectiveness, "magnificently garbed as it is in this country, is to restore peace to the mind, even if it does not make one realize how small and petty and futile the human individual really is." He was celebrated as a wit, but his mots were coarse, hoked-up stuff. What is so funny about calling Wendell Willkie a "simple barefoot Wall Street boy"? This gamy line was his most admired one—and, as it turns out, it was not even his. He got it from the newspaper columnist Jay Franklin. But it could have been his. Other admired observations were that Huey Long had "halitosis of the intellect" and that Thomas E. Dewey had "thrown his diaper in the ring." This sort of thing had doubled up his New Deal colleagues and got under the opposition's skin, but politicians are notorious for their puerile judgment and jejune tastes in such matters. Ickes was a gagman, and not a very good one, even by television standards. It is a negative virtue of the diary that it is very nearly jokeless. Contrived humor takes contriving, and Ickes, dictating these entries at what must have been breakneck speed, did not have the time for it, thanks be.

Ickes was not much of a writer, and he certainly was not much of a human being. Indeed, the character one encounters here is so contemptible that one is forced to conclude that he could not possibly have been as bad as he seems. Either that, or he could not have seemed as bad as he was. Had he been as disagreeable in the flesh as he is in the diary, no one could have stood having him around. He was, by the testimony of these pages, selfish, vindictive, suspicious, servile, and disloyal. Lust for power ruled him. He loved no one and admired only those who regularly bathed him in flattery or conferred on him some portion of their authority. He wanted a large chunk of Henry Wallace's power and all he could get of Harry Hopkins', and he alternately praised and vilified both of them, praising when their resistance was low, vilifying when it was high. Since no one could make a career of gratifying Ickes, Ickes turned in the end against everyone. By 1936, his only remaining friend is Cissy Patterson, the newspaper publisher. In the second volume, he breaks with her. In 1933, he wrote, "I have a feeling of loyalty and real affection for the President that I have never felt for any other man." In 1936, after Roosevelt had declined to yield to Ickes' latest plan for expanding the Department of the Interior,

Ickes saw Roosevelt as a scoundrel. "Here is a plain case of being 'sold down the river' by the President," he wrote. Ickes could rise ignobly above his feeling of betrayal. Ten days later, Roosevelt gave him a chance to deliver an important speech. "I told him that I was willing to do anything that he wanted me to do," he wrote. He made the speech and then began to feel sorry for himself because he had not abandoned the administration and run against the President on the Republican ticket. "As I see the thing now," he wrote on July 21, 1936, "in all probability I could have won in November." What utter madness! Some self-seeking romancer had told him that he would make a fine candidate and that the Republicans would leap at the chance to get him. But he was always one to adjust and readjust his ambitions to the possibilities of the moment. By September, when it was clear that Roosevelt was no flash in the pan, Ickes was ready to settle down to another four years of sycophancy. He liked winners, and besides, J. David Stern, a White House emissary, had told him that "I was the outstanding man in the administration and a tower of strength to the President."

He was over the most virulent form of Potomac fever after the Democratic convention of 1936, but a lower-grade infection struck in 1940, the year in which Roosevelt insisted upon the Vice-Presidential nomination for Henry Wallace. A few weeks before the convention he started a Vice-Presidential boom for himself. He tells how on July 16, 1940 a group of Connecticut Democrats had called upon him to discuss matters in his Chicago hotel room early in the convention.

. . . They came in to discuss the Vice-Presidential situation. I told them all that I knew, which was nothing. They suggested that Henry Wallace would be a good candidate, and I agreed with them, although I did remark that he wasn't a particularly good campaigner and that, with the President tied up in Washington during the coming campaign, it would be necessary for our Vice-Presidential candidate to take Willkie on. Then [Representative William] Citron said, "I think that you would make a good Vice-President." I thanked him. The others seemed to fall in with the idea and said they could deliver Connecticut to me. All of them demanded my autographed photograph, which I promised to send them from Washington.

Some of his friends sounded out the California delegation, which was, according to Ickes, solidly for him, excepting only Representative Jerry Voorhis, the man who in 1946 was retired from politics by Richard M. Nixon. Voorhis was a dedicated liberal and one of the most intelligent men in Washington. But he opposed Ickes, who wrote: "Voorhis can always be depended upon to develop some half-baked idea. I have long held his judgment in contempt." Meanwhile, Roosevelt let it be known that he wanted Wallace, and he said he would not run if anyone else were nominated. The Ickes bubble burst. Governor Culbert L. Olson, of California, whom Ickes supposed to be the leading Ickes man in the convention, nominated Henry Wallace. But Ickes can still write, "If . . . early in the balloting a big block of votes had been cast for me, it is to be doubted whether Henry could have been nominated even with the President's support." And then an absolutely extraordinary thought struck the diarist:

It occurred to me that he [the President] might purposely be allowing a situation to develop in which he could with good grace decline the nomination. . . . Who knows but that the President could have welcomed this? Who can say that he forced the bitter pill of Wallace in the final hope that the convention would not swallow it . . . ? No? The whole thing is very obscure and confusing. . . . I am reminded that Jim Farley said to me over the telephone on Thursday that he would listen with interest to my speeches during the campaign lauding Wallace.

There was simply no end to his pettiness and vindictiveness. He says of his part in a controversy with General Hugh Johnson, "When I did get back at him, I tried to hurt as much as I could." Yet his very disagreeableness throws some sharp light on affairs of state:

Yesterday I got my bill from Mrs. [Cordell] Hull for my share of the Cabinet dinner to the President and Mrs. Roosevelt and it was $78.75. . . . I suppose that I resent it particularly because part of this money was to help feed the Vice-President and the Speaker of the House with their respective spouses. Next year I do not intend, at least without protest, to permit the Hulls or anyone else to invite guests without my consent to a dinner at which I am a joint host. Not only was the dinner this year the most expensive that we have had, it was the poorest.

And he relates the unpleasant with a candor possessed by no other New Deal memoirist:

> The President told Miss [Frances] Perkins that he would be happy if she could discover that Boake Carter, the columnist and radio commentator, who has been so unfair and pestiferous, was not entitled to be in this country. It appears that an investigation of his record is being made.

On May 6, 1939, Ickes wrote, "As I told Tom Corcoran, yesterday, the chances are today eighty out of one hundred that I will be resigning shortly. My morale is . . . at such a low ebb. . . . For the President arbitrarily and without even discussing the matter with me, to deprive me of so many of the powers that I have exercised is bad enough but what has cut me deeply is the manner of his proceeding." Ickes, who was of course the one man to last through all the Roosevelt administrations and into Truman's first, was piqued because Roosevelt had dictated some appointments to him. Exactly a week later, Ickes wrote:

> I lunched with the President on Thursday, and I kidded him a good deal about Forestry and Agriculture. Just what he will do with Forestry in the end I do not know, but I am going to keep after him, both directly and indirectly. Now that I have Fisheries and Biological Survey, it ought to make Forestry easier. I told him that he had made one great mistake; that coal was decayed vegetable matter, that it represented a chemical change in fallen trees and that trees were growing crops. . . . [And] I told him that in my judgement sending Rural Electrification to Agriculture was the same kind of mistake that had been made originally when the Bureau of Public Roads was set up in Agriculture. I pointed out that Rural Electrification involved the building of transmission lines and the selling of electric current. . . . I think I won him pretty far over to my theory that all of the agencies having to do with public power, including the TVA, ought to be set up in one strong agency in Interior.

It seems never to have occurred to Ickes that there was anything unwholesome about his appetite for power or flattery.

Nor, though he was ordinarily suspicious of the entire human race, did it ever occur to him that flatterers might be ignobly motivated. When Frederic A. Delano, the President's uncle, told him "how much he admired my ability, integrity, and intellectual honesty," Ickes set it down as though it were a report on weather conditions, a statement of plainly observable fact that no one could have any possible interest in misrepresenting. And again: "Felix [Mr. Justice Frankfurter] told me that next to the President I was the one man in the country who stood for a better civilization and whose voice carried farthest in behalf of a civilized way of living." It may be that the very grossness of his nature is one of the things that made him an exciting diarist. It helped him, perhaps, to order his world and bring his characters into a single, clear focus. The amassing of grievances, the slow spreading of his hatreds, give point and a kind of plot to this portrait of a sprawling agglomeration of people in most of whom, as individuals, our interest cannot be great. Each Burlew and each Scrugham is involved in either furthering Ickes' ambition or in blocking it, and we have a continuing interest in seeing when and for what reason they will become characters in the Ickes demonology. For while Ickes could bear frustration in great quantities, he did suffer as a result of his need to hate. He solicited praise and power with the brazen, businesslike air of a streetwalker on the prowl for clients, but he did develop a bad conscience about the number of people it was becoming necessary to despise. He stayed awake nights thinking how terrible it was that there were so many ranged against him: "A heavy barrage is being laid down to break my morale. . . . I am thoroughly persuaded that there is an active cabal working against me." He became addicted to soporifics, massive nightcaps, and driving through the countryside at ninety miles an hour. "Life simply can't go on on the basis of continued and implacable resentments," he wrote. But it did go on.

In his apparent innocence of the nature of corruption, Ickes calmly bequeathed us a self-portrait of a man corrupt in the deepest sense. But it is not the likeness of the portrait that makes it so striking; it is, on the contrary, its almost total lack of correspondence to reality. Ickes was the embodiment of a stunning paradox; he was corrupt on the inside and pure as the driven snow on the outside. His outer purity was no pose; it was a fact, a condition, and if it were not for this diary the evil that he did would not have lived after him. But there is no proof that he *did* any evil. None of the countless post-mortems on the Roosevelt administration have brought to light a single instance of Ickes abandoning the public interest. (The diary reveals only one. He mentions his support of a federal grant for the Queens Midtown Tunnel and says, "The reason I was so strongly in favor of this is because Senator [Robert F.] Wagner wants it badly.") Generally speaking, he was, in matters bearing on the common welfare, as straight as a die. The President's uncle may or may not have been speaking from the heart when he commended Ickes for his "ability, integrity, and intellectual honesty," but it was a judgment any reasonable man could have made if he had gone solely by the record. No scandal ever touched Ickes, and he was perhaps the best administrator Roosevelt had. The only clouds that darken his memory are those he sketched in himself in this remarkable diary.

Those volumes will stand as his most imposing monument. The self-portrait is repellent, but it is vivid and memorable. In fact, almost every virtue of the book seems attributable to some defect in its author's character. His candor was the product of his indelicacy. Being a schemer, he had need for information on those around him. Literal-minded, uninterested in ideas for their own sake, he found self-expression in a simple transcription of the intelligence he received—what was said at this dinner party, what was done at this conference, this Cabinet meeting, this poker game. The *Secret Diary* brings to life a Washington in which a social revolution is being engineered, but it would, one imagines, be hardly less absorbing if it dealt with the administration of Millard Fillmore.

* The Contrarieties of Ezra Pound

In the spring of 1957, the editors of Esquire *asked me to write an article on Ezra Pound. In the back of their minds, and of mine, was the idea of saying something that might create a new interest in the case and perhaps help get him out of St. Elizabeths Hospital. It has been said that the article, which appeared in September 1957, did play a part, and I like to think this is so. What was more important, however, was the initiative of the magazine's editors in soliciting letters commenting on the article and on the "case" from a large number of other writers—among them Marianne Moore, Van Wyck Brooks, Osbert Sitwell, John Dos Passos, William Carlos Williams, Richard Wilbur, Robert Graves, Norman Mailer, Mark Schorer, and Babette Deutsch. Their letters were published in* Esquire *over a period of three months and were used, as was my piece, by Pound's counsel, Thurman Arnold, who is perhaps the only lawyer ever to have a brief (the Pound one) rewritten by Robert Frost. A circumstance that helped greatly in getting Pound sprung was a change in the federal rule on insanity defenses; the old McNaghten's Rule, which held that a man could not plead insanity if he had been aware of the legal and moral consequences of his acts at the time of their commission, was replaced in federal courts by the doctrine that, to summarize briefly, a man could not be convicted of a crime if the crime was the product of his aberrations. For so long as this doctrine held, it would almost certainly have been impossible to prove Pound guilty. Anyway, on April 18, 1958, the charges against Pound were dismissed by Chief Judge Bolitha J. Laws of the Federal District Court in Washington. The Depart-*

204

ment of Justice had requested their dismissal after, its representatives said, being advised by psychiatrists that Pound would never be competent to stand trial and would be harmless if released.

Pound had refused to see me while I was doing the article. I suppose he assumed it would be hostile. After he saw an advance copy, however, he sent me a paperback Selected Poems *with an inscription scrawled over the first three pages. I deciphered it as follows:*

> *No bloke with a papal name shows benevolence for which my thanks. He neglected a few bits of homework, vide p. VIII (not p. 8.) One quote without context could be correlated with senate investigation of labor racketeering and European efforts to deal with that problem.*
>
>

R.H.R.
from
E.P., Ag 16 '57

IT WOULD BE HARD to name a living man who embodies more polarities of mind, temperament, and function than Ezra Pound, the poet, scholar, and sometime reformer who has spent the last twelve of his seventy-two years confined, as certifiably insane, in St. Elizabeths Hospital, the huge asylum maintained by the federal government on a rise of land in the southeast corner of Washington.

This inmate is one of the great champions and liberators of the modern spirit; he is also a crackpot poisoner of the well of opinion—a political crank who has proceeded from funny-money theories to a full-blown chauvinism. This xenophobe Pound is one of the truly cosmopolitan figures of the century—as the pre-eminent translator of his time, he has been a heroic builder of bridges to other civilizations; there is, however, a chamber of his poet's soul in which a yahoo dwells—a buckwheat oaf sounding off like a Kleagle of the Klavern or a New York street-brawler back in the days of the Christian Front. This cosmopolitan Pound is a true patriot—he has a love for the United States that is genuine and affecting and that has had a great deal to do with the making of American culture over the last fifty years; yet he has been, since November 26, 1945, under indictment for nineteen

separate counts of treason—the charge growing out of the un-
contested fact that he made propaganda broadcasts for the fascist
enemy from the enemy's camp in wartime.

In Ezra Pound's extraordinary person, the antipodal qualities
clang and clatter, the denial crowds the affirmation, antithesis is
always on the heels of thesis. Throughout his life, he has esteemed
the Confucian ideal of order, and much of his work reflects it;
yet his life and his work, taken as a whole, are sheer chaos—
though sometimes a glorious chaos, as in what William Butler
Yeats called the "stammering confusion" of the *Cantos*, the most
imposing of all his work. This great man has stood at once for
love and for hate, for friendship and for misanthropy, for reason
and for befuddlement, for unexampled purity and for pure
muck, for luminous spirits like Yeats and Robert Frost and for
deranged ones like Benito Mussolini and for fanatics like John
Kasper, the muddled youth who recently was denied appeal of a
one-year sentence for contempt of court committed in the after-
math of his efforts, undertaken a year or so ago—largely, he says,
at Ezra Pound's encouragement—to stir the lily-white animals
to riot and bloodshed in defense of segregation in the South.

In the world as Pound, in his better moments, wants it, first
things would be first, and the first thing about him is that he is
a great poet. It is by no means certain, though, that he or we can
have it that way. The object of public interest today, of syndicated newspaper articles and comment in the mass-circulation
magazines, is Pound the crazy writer who appears in relationship
to the White Citizens Councils and the general revival of Kluxery
to be somewhat as Lenin was to the Bolsheviks before 1917. The
comparison is, of course, absurd, and probably the connection
between Pound and Kasper is not everything that young Mr.
Kasper, hungering for a god and perhaps for a father, claims it to
be. The White Citizens Councils should not be hung around
Pound's neck simply on John Kasper's say-so. The records of
St. Elizabeths Hospital reveal no more than a half-dozen visits by
Kasper to Pound, and though there may have been more, no
number of visits would constitute acceptable evidence of Pound's
direct responsibility. The shrine is not to be blamed for everything the pilgrim does and is. There is bigotry in Ezra Pound,

and that is bad enough, but in justice it has to be acknowledged that he has never been known to address himself to the question of public-school integration. Still, the world does have a way, sometimes, of putting last, or secondary, things first, and to the world at the moment Pound *is* the inmate, the mental patient, the poet-writer who once committed treason or something and who now appears to be tied up with Kasper, the race agitator.

The world's way is to be noted but not in all cases, and certainly not in such cases as this, followed. The main thing about Ezra Pound is that he is a poet of towering gifts and attainments. Poetry is not a horse race or any other sort of competition, and it is silly to argue over which poet runs the fastest, jumps the highest, or dives the deepest. Still, a respectable case could be made out to the effect that the century has produced no talent larger or more fecund than Pound's. Certainly the fit comparisons would be with no more than half a dozen other men who write in English. These, as the reigning critics see the matter today, would be T. S. Eliot, Yeats, Frost (some dissent here, probably), W. H. Auden, and Dylan Thomas; later on, some of these names may be removed and replaced by some from the second rank, such as Wallace Stevens, Robert Graves, Walter de la Mare, Marianne Moore, William Carlos Williams, E. E. Cummings, and Robert Lowell.

Pound's position is secure, not only because of the power of his own work but because of his service as a midwife to genius and as an influence on other poets. Not long ago, the government which detains Pound in St. Elizabeths circulated abroad, as part of its effort to persuade the world that we Americans really care about the finer things, a flossy periodical in which it was asserted that Ezra Pound "has done more to serve the cause of English poetry than anyone else alive." (The article, by Hayden Carruth, a gifted critic, also said, "It is hard to think of a good reason why Pound should not have his freedom immediately.") The statement on his service is broad but difficult to gainsay. Of the poets of comparable stature, at least half have at one time or another been Pound's disciples; others were greatly aided by him. The best-known and most influential poem of our time, Eliot's *The Waste Land,* took the shape in which the world knows it under his expert hand. Eliot submitted it to Pound at many stages, and in its penultimate stage it was, according to Eliot, "a sprawling, chaotic poem . . . which left Pound's hands, reduced to about half its size, in the form in which it appears in print." The dedication of *The Waste Land* reads, "For Ezra Pound—*il miglior fabbro.*" Pound deeply influenced Yeats in the later phases of Yeats' career. But for Pound, the recognition of Robert Frost would have come more belatedly than it did. It was Pound who first got Frost published in the United States and Pound also who found a London publisher for James Joyce. Amy Lowell, E. E. Cummings, and William Carlos Williams sat, often in extreme discomfort, at his feet. W. H. Auden is of a later generation, but he has asserted that "there are few living poets . . . who could say, 'My work would be exactly the same if Mr. Pound had never lived.' "

And all of this influencing and literary politicking in addition to his own work: it is now just short of fifty years since the publication of his first book, *A Lume Spento,* and the flame is still bright and hot. He began with a rage to "purify the language of the tribe" and to make that purified language part of the stuff of life itself. Poetry was to *be* existence, not *about* existence. "Poetry is . . . as much 'criticism of life' as red-hot iron is a criticism of fire." The age, he said, in one of his most famous poems:

> . . . demanded an image
> Of its accelerated grimace,
> Something for the modern stage,
> Not, at any rate, an Attic grace;
>
> Not, not certainly, the obscure reveries
> Of the inward gaze;
> Better mendacities
> Than the classics in paraphrase!
> . . .
> A prose kinema, not, not assuredly, alabaster
> Or the "sculpture" of rhyme.

He provided for the age what he thought it demanded—volume upon volume of poetry, some of incomparable loveliness, some of unexcelled ugliness, and much besides. And he still does. In these last few melancholy years, many magical and magnificent things have gone out to the world from his bedlam in Washington. He has pressed forward with his *Cantos*, with his criticism, and with his indefatigable labors of translation, the latest fruit of which is a stunning version of Sophocles' *Trachiniae*. If the New York *Herald Tribune* now sees his wretched quarters in Anacostia as the place where young men like John Kasper are corrupted, others may some day compare them with the cells in which Cervantes wrote *Don Quixote* or Bunyan *Pilgrim's Progress*.

But Pound is alive and controversial in our world and much too thorny a subject to be dealt with only in terms of his major work. His madness, if it exists, will not be exorcised by his verses —any more than his verses can be hidden under his madness. Poetry, one can begin by saying, is, among other things, an act of the controlled intelligence. This is particularly true in the case of Pound, who has never failed to demand of himself and of his work cool, hard, purposeful thought, and who has, additionally, an analytical mind of immense power. However, a controlled and discriminating intelligence is not a sure defense against insanity. Both madness and genius can be spasmodic or simultaneous in a compartmented being like Pound.

The question of whether Pound is insane by any acceptable legal or psychiatric definition is a vexed one. Reputable authorities disagree. Four psychiatrists, one of them appointed by Pound's counsel, filed a unanimous report which led to his commitment to St. Elizabeths, sparing the defendant and the country the pain of a trial for a capital offense. But some doctors have maintained that Pound is quite a long way from being insane by the standards that court examiners are compelled to use and that justice was jobbed when Pound went to the hospital rather than to the gallows. From the layman's point of view, the matter is a good deal simpler. Whether Pound meets the legal and institutional tests for a criminally inculpable and confinable psychotic —and it seems highly doubtful that he does—he is a pathological personality who has, by the reasonable standards of most reasonable men, lost contact with reality at many crucial points. In the vernacular, he is off his rocker—or if he isn't, the rest of us are off ours. The paranoid's delusions, his morbid suspicions, his view of life as a conspiracy are all apparent, even in the fine poetry, which more and more over the last twenty-five years has dealt with Pound's political and economic obsessions. In Pound, those suspicions and delusions are evidence of mania. For a village eccentric to assert that Franklin Roosevelt was a tool of international Jewry, that we got into World War II because of a crooked financial deal pulled off by Roosevelt and Henry Morgenthau, that all world history would be changed if Martin Van Buren's autobiography had been published a few years sooner than it was—all this would not be conclusive proof of insanity. Such beliefs may merely show misguidance. But it is quite another thing for a man of Pound's cultivation to believe them and to make them the stuff of his poetry.

Since the onset of the great depression, Pound has been making silk purses from sows' ears. His major theme—as distinct from the secondary and supporting themes involving Roosevelt and Morgenthau and Van Buren—has been that mankind's troubles, all of them, are traceable to the hiring out of money at interest ("the beast with a hundred legs, USURA") by commercial lenders ("every bank of discount is downright corruption/every bank of discount is downright iniquity") and that life on earth would be sweet and noble and aesthetically rich if we had the wisdom to adopt the fiscal reforms advocated by Silvio Gesell, Major C. H. Douglas, and other hopeful currency tinkerers. These are his political convictions as well as the meat of his poetry, and since when, asks Dr. Frederic Wertham, one of the dissenting psychiatrists, has a political conviction, however aberrant, been regarded as proof of paranoia? The answer the layman can give, without attempting to satisfy either psychiatry or law, is that a political conviction is lunatic when it leads a man to tell a friend, as Pound once told William Carlos Williams, that at a given moment he preferred the sanctuary of St. Elizabeths to the world beyond its Nichols Avenue gates, where he believed he would be shot by agents of the "international crew."

The obsessions make him see the surface of life in a world that endures usury as "infinite pus flakes, scabs of a lasting pox," and the flux of life in this motion:

        as the earth moves, the centre
          passes over all parts in succession
        a continual bum-belch
          distributing its production

Still, the purses are silk beyond all cavil or dispute:

        The ant's a centaur in his dragon world.
        Pull down thy vanity, it is not man
        Made courage or made order, or made grace
          Pull down thy vanity, I say pull down.
        Learn of the green world what can be thy place
        In scaled invention or true artistry
        Pull down thy vanity,
                      Paquin pull down!
        The green casque has outdone your elegance.

It is characteristic of the great egotists to have little traffic with
their own years of innocence and learning. When they deal with
the period at all, they are likely to follow the example of Rousseau
and foreshorten and revise experience in such a way as to make
worldliness follow directly upon infancy. Pound is of the classic
breed—though not, as it happens, in any other way a brother to
Rousseau. One cannot accuse him of selfishness or of excessive
self-portraiture; his ego has asserted itself massively, in cock-
sureness, in literary and political arrogance, in conceits of dress
such as red velvet robes and conceits of leadership such as walking one pace ahead of his followers in every procession, and, in
these later years, in his paranoid delusions about the malign
sources of the world's resistance to his remedies. This kind of
self-concern has led him to consider himself and his life at great
length, to record his own comings and goings, to preserve the
least of his obiter dicta, and to reflect in hundreds of thousands
of words on the meaning of his own strange journey.

    Yet the shaping years are nowhere dealt with. In every auto-
biographical statement, the infant born in Hailey, Idaho, in
1885, the son of Homer and Isabel Weston Pound, becomes in a
sentence or two a central figure in American letters. Idaho could
have influenced him not at all, for in 1887 the family moved to
Wyncotte, Pennsylvania, and Pound's father took up his duties

as assayer of the United States Mint at Philadelphia. It is clear
from a handful of letters to his parents, published a few years
ago in his collected correspondence, that they were bookish,
serious-minded people. His mother, who was somehow related to
Henry Wadsworth Longfellow, was a musician of sorts, and his
father had a lively and informed interest in contemporary literature. Does the fact that Pound's father had a professional concern
with the value of currency explain Pound's obsession to any
degree? This has been rumored, but Pound himself has cast no
light upon it. All that is really known of him in the early years
is that he survived.

He was a gifted child and entered the University of Pennsylvania at fifteen. From this point on, he is not reticent in dealing with experience, but neither, one suspects, is he particularly
reliable. He paints himself as an enormously learned young man,
which he no doubt was, and as an enormously sophisticated one,
which he evidently was not. He did not enroll as a regular
undergraduate at Pennsylvania. He wanted no truck with most
of what they had to teach, so he was a "special student," working
mostly in languages. He claims to have had contempt for most of
his teachers and for most of his fellow students. Yet there are
contemporaries who remember him as a boy, gangling and shy
and humiliated by his life under a carpet of bright red hair, who
was terribly eager for acceptance and who, indeed, was so eager
to be pledged to a fraternity that, when he was finally rebuffed,
he transferred to Hamilton College. The story may be untrue;
it all happened in another world anyway, and memories are not
all they might be. But the quality of memories counts. William
Carlos Williams, a medical student at Pennsylvania at the time,
has the recollection that when Pound thought the moment had
at last arrived to try his luck at picking up a girl, he implored
Williams to come along for protection.

At all odds, Pound did transfer to Hamilton, where he took
prescribed courses and in 1905 was awarded a degree. After
Hamilton, he went back to Pennsylvania and got a master's
degree. (It is curious that in a one-page autobiography prepared
for his *Selected Poems* in 1949, Pound, while skipping over some
of the principal episodes in his life, should have listed three

academic degrees, two earned, from Hamilton and Pennsylvania, and an honorary Litt. D. from Hamilton in 1939. Before 1939, he had been writing of American universities as nothing but fancy beaneries. In April 1929, he advised the Alumni Secretary of the University of Pennsylvania that "All the U. of P. or your god damn college or any other god damn American college does or will do for a man of letters is to ask him to go away without breaking the silence." It was a different story when Hamilton asked the man of letters to accept its recognition. Among his many dualities are a contempt for authority and an almost sickening respect for it. When he lived in Italy, he had embossed on his stationery a gamy platitude from Mussolini—"Liberty is not a right but a duty.") In those student years, he wrote some of the poems that were to appear in his first book in 1908. It would be interesting, at least from the viewpoint of the gossip that lurks in each of us, to know how close he was to the trembling adolescent recalled by Williams and how far from this, which is from the period:

> For I was a gaunt, grave councillor
> Being in all things wise, and very old,
> But I have put aside this folly and the cold
> That old age weareth for a cloak.
>
> .   .   .
>
> I was quite strong—at least they said so—
> The young men at the sword-play. . . .

Pound had tried out for the fencing team at Pennsylvania.

Poems are born of hopes and imaginings, and so long as Pound had these within him, as he did in wild abundance, it should matter little to anyone—save those in a position to offer therapy —what else he was in that faraway time. After Philadelphia, he traveled abroad for a year, in Italy, Spain, and Provence, and then accepted an instructorship at Wabash College, in Indiana. Within a few months of his appointment, he was asked to resign, which he did. His story is that he had invited to his lodgings a penniless girl, stranded from a burlesque show, whom he had found on the streets of the town while going out in a raging blizzard to mail a letter. He claimed that he had been stirred by nothing more than an impulse to hospitality, and in the centennial history of the college, the authorities, eager to reclaim a genius, explained that the girl slept chastely in Pound's bed and Pound on the floor. It sounds plausible, but it scarcely matters. Pound's landlady discovered her. The college providentially booted him, and he returned to Europe, there to remain, except when he returned for his honorary Litt. D., until he was flown to Washington as a prisoner under armed guard on November 18, 1945.

"London, deah old Lundon, is the place for poesy"—thus Pound, to a stay-at-home friend on February 3, 1909. London was the place for Pound—or, at any rate, *a* place. It is difficult to believe that his awesome energies were greatly dependent on environment. At all odds, he pursued poesy; he gave it chase like a Nimrod being shot at from the rear. It is doubtful if any other American writer ever knew a period as fertile as the decade that followed Pound's move to London. He produced his finest half-dozen volumes of poetry, quite enough to sustain his reputation. ("Thirty pages are enough for any of us to leave," he once wrote. "There is scarce more of Catullus or Villon." There are perhaps a thousand pages of Pound's own poetry, with more coming all the time.) He translated: from medieval French, from Latin, from Greek, and from Chinese and Japanese, which he could not read but which he nevertheless rendered from the literal translations of Ernest Francisco Fenollosa, an American Orientalist who had taught philosophy at the Imperial Normal School in Tokyo and who made Pound his executor. He was the European editor of *Poetry,* the Chicago magazine which Harriet Monroe, a noble dilettante lady, offered this Philistine republic as "a place of refuge, a green isle in the sea, where Beauty may plant her gardens." He dug up Frost and Eliot for the magazine; he pestered established British writers for manuscripts. He got Wyndham Lewis, John Masefield, Ford Madox Ford, Rabindranath Tagore. He and Amy Lowell put their heads together, a consummation blessed by T. E. Hulme, a British philosopher with poetic leanings, and produced Imagism, a school. The doctrine was that poetic images should not be adornments but the guts of the work itself. The language, in

Hulme's words, was to be "cheerful, dry and sophisticated," or, in Pound's single word, "perfect." "It stands," he said, amplifying, "for hard, clear edges." And the best of it did have hard, clear edges; sometimes, though, the quest for perfection was destructive; the individual poem was lightened and hardened to the point where it was fleshless and boneless. Once Pound had the thought of describing some faces he had looked upon in the Paris Métro. He wrote a poem of thirty lines. It seemed rather fatty to him, so he put it aside, while he awaited further light on the problem. After a time, he went over it and cut it to fifteen lines. Still imperfect. He put it away again for a year or so, and then did some drastic surgery, so that the poem, called *In a Station of the Metro,* now reads, in its entirety:

> The apparition of these faces in the crowd:
> Petals on a wet, black bough.

Pound soon abandoned the school in favor of one he called Vorticism, which he proclaimed as vastly superior. He was alone in grasping the distinction; if there was one, it did not show in his work, in which he continued to make breath-taking approaches to perfection.

"Dear Miss Lowell," Pound wrote in November 1913, "I agree with you . . . that 'Harriet' is a bloody fool. Also I've resigned from *Poetry* in Hueffer's (Ford Madox Ford's) favor, but I believe he has resigned in mine. . . ." It was this sort of thing down through the years. Imagism to Vorticism and on along to Social Credit and Gesellism, thence to fascism. And from *Poetry* to *BLAST,* the official Vorticist organ, which had no bang at all and petered out in two issues, and back to *Poetry* and on to *The Egoist* and *The Little Review.* In between and amongst these, there were side enthusiasms—the music of George Antheil and Arnold Dolmetsch, the sculpture of Henri Gaudier-Brzeska. Pound learned to play the bassoon and for a time fancied himself a composer. He was everlastingly transient. It was not for long that London was good for poesy. By 1913, England was "this stupid little island . . . dead as mutton." After the war, he moved to Paris—accompanied by the wife he had acquired in London, Dorothy Shakespear, who lives today in the wastes of southeast Washington and never misses a visiting period at St. Elizabeths. And a few years after that to Rapallo, on the Italian Riviera.

"One has to keep going East," he told Mary Colum, "to keep one's mind alive." Any direction would have done, for it was really a matter of the restlessness of the literary plotter and organizer of movements. As Robert Graves saw it, "Slowly the frustrated Pound went mad-dog and bit the other dogs of his day; he even fastened his teeth in Yeats' hand, the hand that had fed him." This is too dour a picture of it. Pound was not, at bottom, disloyal. Indeed, even in his present madness, he remains fast to many of his oldest friends and his oldest principles. The cream of the ugly jest is that he remains intensely loyal to some of the principles he has been accused of betraying and, in fact, in his fashion did betray. When he insists, as he always does nowadays, that everything he did and was in politics had as its object the "saving of the United States Constitution," he is representing himself as honestly as he can. Even in the zaniest of the *Cantos*, in the mad, ranting passages about Adams and Jefferson and poor old Van Buren, one has a sense of him as a genuine American reformer, a zealous improver, the perpetual liberal optimist of American letters carrying on in the spirit of 1912. "Any agonizing," he wrote in that year, "that tends to hurry what I believe in the end to be inevitable, our American Risorgimento, is dear to me. That awakening will make the Italian Renaissance look like a tempest in a teapot."

If there is any one unbroken strand in Pound's experience, it is the one that begins with this statement and continues on to what is durable in his work today. Of all the contrarieties and polarities in Pound, none is more striking than that of the enemy broadcaster, the partisan of Mussolini, as American patriot. The courts may never be able to see this; it is perhaps proper that they should not. To be betrayed by a daft patriot is not much better than to be betrayed by a sanely calculating Iscariot. Nevertheless, the fact cannot be denied that Pound, as a writer and as a man, has had an immense and touching faith in the culture he appeared to be ready to abandon as a youth. He believed with

Whitman that American experience was fit and even glorious
material for poetry, and what he was at war with when he left
this country was the spirit that denied this and tried only for
"Attic grace" and the "classics in paraphrase." "Make it new,"
Pound kept saying, from his colloquial rendering of Confucius,
and "Make it American," as if he were a booster of home manu-
factures at a trade fair. "Are you for American poetry or for
poetry," he wrote Miss Monroe, when she was setting up her
magazine. "The latter is more important, but it is important
that America should boost [*sic!*] the former, provided it don't
[*sic*] mean a blindness to the art. The glory of any nation is to
produce art that can be exported without disgrace to its origin.
. . . The force we have, and the impulse, but the guiding sense,
the discrimination in applying the force, we must wait and strive
for." He believed, and was to persuade many others to believe,
that the American language as well as the American experience
was fit for poetry: the speech of our people, the garment of their
consciousness, was vigorous and supple and tender enough "to be
spoken by the gods."

And this has been the point of his curious and often debated
work as a translator: he has made everything new and everything
American. Edwin Arlington Robinson, the last poet to work
effectively in the tradition Pound rejected and sought to crush,
once wrote of how Shakespeare

> . . . out of his
> Miraculous inviolable increase
> Fills Ilion, Rome, or any town you like
> Of olden time with timeless Englishmen.

Shakespeare sent his imagination traveling in time and space
and was never anything but English to the core. Pound ex-
patriated himself for four decades in Europe and went back over
the years to Cathay millenniums before Christ—and was never,
in any time or place, other than American to the marrow and
gristle. He filled Rome and Crete and the France of the trouba-
dors and China and Japan with timeless Americans. This is no
defense against treason. Yet it is a fact. In his version of

Trachiniae, or Women of Trachis, a product of his labors at St. Elizabeths, he has Hyllos say of Herakles

> They say he's in Euboea,
>   besieging Eurytusville
> or on the way to it.

Eurytus*ville,* indeed! It is as if Shakespeare had written *The Merchant of Veniceshire* or *Timon of Athensford.*

One must return, sooner or later, to the denial that always follows hard on the affirmation. It could, of course, be no more than a cheap trick to call Eurytus Eurytusville, whereas it was, for an American, a foul one to broadcast, as Ezra Pound did, on May 26, 1942, when our forces were beleaguered in almost every quarter of the globe, that every rare and occasional decency of the United States government, "every reform . . . is an act of homage toward Mussolini and Hitler. They are your leaders. . . ." Unless our monitors had faulty hearing, that is what the man said. In the nineteen presumably treasonable utterances cited in the indictment, that is the one that, on 'the face of it, is the clearest and most shameful. More often, the broadcasts were a loony garble—so much so that the Italians for a time thought he was broadcasting secrets in code. But there it stands —"Mussolini and Hitler. They are your leaders."

It is possible to take the psychiatrists' way out and say that by then Pound was a nut not to be held responsible. But the matter will not rest there. Some sort of accommodation must be reached between Pound the glorious American poet and Pound the loony ideologue. Various possibilities suggest themselves. It has often been argued that there is an affinity between American populism and brutal American reaction. But this will not do for Pound the sweet singer; except for his hatred of bankers and his funny money, he was never fetched by the Populist fallacies. Quite the contrary. "It is the function of the public to prevent the artist's expression, by hook or by crook," he wrote, a few years after his departure from England. And: "I know the man who translated *Jean Christophe,* and moreover it's a popular craze, so I suppose there must be something wrong with it." And: "I should like the name 'Imagism' to retain some sort of meaning. . . . I cannot

trust any democratized committee to maintain that standard."
He was armored against undue respect for the mass of mankind.

A more promising hypothesis is that he was beguiled—eventually into insanity—by a predilection for conspiracy theories of life and history. The man thus beguiled sees society as a kind of machine in which things are always going wrong. This machine is hurting him. He himself is not part of it. He feels he has no control over its workings, and therefore no responsibility for it. He sees a human comedy and a human tragedy, and he may be deeply moved by the spectacles, but they are *spectacles*—things to be seen, from somewhere offstage. Eventually, if he is clever, he discerns ways of improving the spectacles, removing their flaws. The spectacles resist improvement; the stupid players strike back. ("I've got a right to be severe," the young Pound wrote. "For one man I strike, there are ten to strike back at me. I stand exposed.") Going to work on the problem, the intellectual hunts out a general principle—a theory of society's malfunctioning. Young men who pursued this line of thought thirty years after Pound clutched, for obvious enough historic reasons, at the proposition that the fault lay in the fact that the means of production and distribution were in private hands, when in fact, for virtue's sake, they should be in public hands, as in the Soviet Union. Some of them, delighted to have got at the root of the problem, betrayed their heritage as foolishly and in many cases far more effectively than Pound did. And some, too, were driven out of their minds.

It was no doubt always in the cards that Pound would reach for the purely mechanical device—currency reform—for righting social wrongs. Loving America, as in truth plenty of the young Communists did, he saw "society" as something else altogether—something hateful and machine-like. There were not many social vogues in his day. Marxism was little heard of in the circles in which he moved. Somehow he was reached by the Social Credit people, who promised order in society. Then he came upon Silvio Gesell, an erratic German who had observed that interest rates bore no logical relation to economic expansion. Usurers set rates according to what the traffic would bear. Who were the usurers? The principal ones, obviously, were the great international bankers. From this point, Pound made the classic leap to anti-Semitism. Somewhat earlier, he had made the leap to the corporate state in Italy. Pound clearly liked the grandiosity of it—and he liked the most comical of Mussolini's thrashings about in the name of "order," or meaningful timetables; it appeared a genuine effort to take the frustrations out of life, to organize society according to a principle, as Pound was trying to organize poetry according to a principle.

We can never know when the cord at last snapped. Nothing we can find in Pound's poetry or his life prepares us for the excessiveness or the sheer franticness of his social concerns. An infatuation with Mussolini would be understandable; Pound was given to infatuations. But the mind boggles when this great critical spirit is heard claiming for Mussolini the perfection he never found in others and so seldom found even in himself. "The more one examines the Milan speech," he wrote apropos of a run-of-the-mine bit of rhetoric by Mussolini, "the more one is reminded of Brancusi, the stone blocks from which no error emerges, from whatever angle one looks at them." A quotation from *Jefferson and/or Mussolini*, published in 1935.

By then the cord was certainly badly frayed.

In his years in St. Elizabeths, Pound has steadily maintained that he had no wish to oppose this country during the war. He points out, in lucid moments, that he could have saved himself all his misery by the simple device of accepting Italian citizenship in 1939. He clung to his American passport. It is a matter of record that he tried in 1942 to get aboard the last diplomatic train that took Americans from Rome to Lisbon. He was refused permission to board it. He had no choice but to stay in Rapallo. After a while the Italians asked him to broadcast. He accepted. He has said that "no scripts were prepared for me by anybody, and I spoke only when I wanted to." And he goes on, not at all lucidly, "I was only trying to tell the people of Europe and America how they could avoid war by learning the facts about money." The war was itself then an unavoidable fact, and it was not about money—though it does happen to be true that most of Pound's broadcasts did deal with his currency obsessions. It also happens to be true that he lent himself, on whatever terms, to the enemy. He now forgets the terms: "I'd die for an idea all right, but to die for an idea I've forgotten is too much."

He lived out the war in Rapallo, writing and making his occasional broadcasts, and in November 1945, hearing that units of the American occupation forces were looking for him, he delivered himself to the proper military authorities. They placed him under arrest and kept him in an encampment—or Disciplinary Training Center—near Pisa. Someone in the Army goofed; the word went out that Pound was violent and also that the fascists thought so highly of him that armed bands might seek to free him. A special cage was built for him out of the heavy mesh steel used for temporary runways. "They thought I was a dangerous wild man and were scared of me. I had a guard night and day. . . . Soldiers used to come up to the cage and look at me. Some of them brought me food. Old Ez was a prize exhibit." For months he lived caged, sleeping on the ground, shielded from the sun and rain only by some tar paper a kindly G.I. found for him. In the cage, he wrote furiously, madly, poignantly. The fruit of the imprisonment was *The Pisan Cantos*, for which a distinguished group of American scholars, appointed by the Librarian of Congress, voted him the Bollingen–Library of Congress Award of $1,000 for "the highest achievement of American poetry" in the year they were published, 1948. (The howls that went up after this put an end to the committee and the award.) By 1948, he had transferred his residence to St. Elizabeths, had suffered out eighteen months in a "maximum-security ward, and was enjoying the limited freedom he now has—freedom to roam the asylum grounds as long as he stays in sight of the building in which he lives and freedom to chat with such as Kasper and freedom to write

> The States have passed thru a
> dam'd supercilious era
> Down, Derry-down
> Oh, let an old-man rest.

He will very likely die there. There has been a clamor of sorts for his release over the last few years, but nothing ever comes of it. The indictment still stands; there is no statute of limitations on treason. The psychiatrists' opinion that he is incompetent to take part in his own defense still stands. Since he is not dangerous and since he receives no therapy at the hospital, he might be released—still under indictment, still adjudged incompetent to state his own case—in the custody of his wife and his friends, who are numerous and long-suffering. Would this mean encouraging intrigues with the likes of young John Kasper? He is free for these intrigues now, and if they are to be taken seriously—if, that is, anyone is really to believe that Ezra Pound is a force in our political life—his status as martyr and prisoner gives an extra cutting edge of hate and resentment to him and to his frowzier associates. Actually, there is no reason to believe that he is any sort of a force. He made some broadcasts for the fascists years ago. They were reprehensible. But, as he asked, "Does anyone have the faintest idea what I said?" No one does, unless he looks it up in the indictment. In the language he might be admiring if his contact with American life was restored, we won the war and, anyway, no one ever listened to that crazy jazz. The government, if it wished, could act not on grounds of justice but on grounds of largesse. It has sat by while some pretty low characters have been sprung in Germany, Italy, and Japan —real war criminals, now given positions of trust. The war-criminal side of Pound is as trivial in terms of history as his poetry is great. As Hayden Carruth wrote in *Perspectives USA,* the publication distributed to the intelligentsia abroad in bundle lots, "It is hard to think of a good reason why Pound should not have his freedom immediately."

✳ Sidney Hillman, or the Doctrine
of Good Connections

1 9 5 3

MATTHEW JOSEPHSON'S LIFE of the late Sidney Hillman is a long, dull, piety-ridden book but a document nevertheless of considerable interest. It is, for one thing, the most ambitious study of a labor leader that any American writer has undertaken. This is in itself an odd and striking circumstance. For years now, American writers, the main body of them anyway, have felt and sometimes passionately expressed an affinity for organized labor. On numberless occasions they have made common cause with its leaders. But while whole posses of novelists, dramatists, biographers, have been taking out after businessmen, politicians, Army officers, juvenile delinquents, inventors, movie stars, clergymen, doctors, hucksters, educators, hoboes, and just about everything else that American life turns up, no man of letters has seriously confronted the labor leader.

There have, of course, been books by Ph.D. candidates and journalists (the economist George Soule did a short life of Hillman in 1939), but Josephson is the first certifiable literary type to pick up the challenge. And Josephson is literary, all right, all right—a veteran of the Left Bank and left wing, a former Dadaist and editor of *transition,* the author of an early discourse on alienation, *Portrait of the Artist as an American,* and of biographies of Rousseau, Zola, and Stendhal.

It is fitting in a way that the man celebrated in this pioneering work should be Sidney Hillman, the founder and for thirty years the president of the Amalgamated Clothing Workers of America, the only man ever called a Labor Statesman in the New York *Herald Tribune,* the favorite labor leader of Franklin D. and Eleanor Roosevelt, friend of Henry Wallace and Henry Morgenthau and even Henry Luce, labor adviser to the National Industrial Recovery Board and co-director of the Office of Production Management in World War II, and, of course, the "Sidney" of "Clear everything with Sidney" in the 1944 Presidential campaign. (Franklin Roosevelt was said to have said it, and he probably did, and surely no labor leader in history had had anything of the sort even rumored to have been said about him by a President of the United States.) From the outset of his long and astonishing career, Hillman held enormous fascination for the highly placed and the high-minded. He seemed spread with a kind of honey that fetched intellectuals as if they were so many brown bears. Indeed, it was really this that made his career possible, though Josephson would have us believe it was something else. He says that "something like a religion of humanity" had led Hillman to the labor movement and "showed in him to the last." He claims that Hillman invented "industrial arbitration." He calls him the "political leader par excellence of labor" and "perhaps the most creative of modern American labor leaders." He sees Hillman as a great and shining spirit loved by the workers because he "was very human and close to them always." Hillman has, Josephson says, "become a sort of legend for the multitudes of American workers . . . whom he served."

This is all pretty absurd. Hillman was in many ways admirable, but no man could have been more remote from the workers, and he is no sort of legend among them. A few years after his death, he is a dim figure in the imagination, and outside the garment centers of the country one would have a hard time finding any worker who recalled more about him than his name —or as much. This does not mean he was unimportant. It means simply that he did not function at the workers' level. He functioned among reformers, editors, executives, congressmen, clergymen, and the like. He had been an apprentice cutter at Hart, Schaffner & Marx in Chicago for about a year before becoming, at twenty-three, a full-time union functionary, and after that the rank and file saw precious little of him. "He worked at pants for a couple of months, and then he became right away a statesman," a veteran garment worker was quoted as saying in a somewhat less reverent account than Josephson's.

Hillman rose in the labor movement and in the world because he won and held the admiration of estimable people with high social ideals. Among his early friends and patrons were Jane Addams, Louis Brandeis, Lillian Wald, Clarence Darrow, William O. Thompson, Mrs. Raymond Robbins, and Newton D. Baker. It was Miss Addams and her Hull House friends, particularly Earl Howard, of Northwestern University, who, seeing in Hillman a young man who looked like a poet and talked like a sociologist, commended him to Joseph Schaffner, the head man of Hart, Schaffner, & Marx, and something of an intellectual himself. The operators in Schaffner's pants factory had been restive. When Hillman started telling his former employer about the wretchedness of their lives, Schnaffner's conscience developed severe aches and pains, and a new day dawned in men's clothing.

Hillman was catnip for every social worker, every writer, every liberal attorney, and just about every manufacturer he met. His leadership first in the old United Garment Workers and then in the Amalgamated Clothing Workers, of which he became, in 1914, the first president, was in a large part a triumph of the Doctrine of Good Connections. Now and then employers would yield to the sheer power of the union, but more often they yielded to Hillman's verbalizing. Josephson tells how, in the winter of 1915, Hillman went to Montreal, where a bitter strike was in progress. "In temperatures of twenty below zero the picket lines were filled mostly by young girls who came out at six in the morning, only to be ridden down by the Royal Mounted Police." The outlook was bleak. All the war powers of the Canadian government were being used against the workers. Hillman was undaunted. "[He] despatched many telegrams to friendly business leaders in New York. . . . Through the intercession of a certain New York philanthropist . . . one of Montreal's largest clothiers, at length, agreed to receive him." Hillman called on the man and the Amalgamated was in like Flynn.

It was a novel approach to the class struggle and a hugely successful one. There was the case of the A. Nash Tailoring Company in Cincinnati, an enormous sweatshop owned by a

Seventh-day Adventist minister who was known as "Golden Rule" Nash. This divine was for years the leader of the open-shop forces in the industry and their chief ideologist. He claimed that God was running an open shop Upstairs. Hillman got some liberal churchman to arrange a conference with the Reverend Nash. "We prayed together," Hillman said. After the meeting, "Golden Rule" signed up with the union and explained to his business associates, "Let me tell you something, brethren, Sidney Hillman, to my mind, stands only second to the carpenter of Galilee in his leadership of the people themselves."

From one point of view, Hillman was a highly effective labor leader. From another, he was not a labor leader at all, but a workers' ambassador to the employers. The Hart, Schaffner, & Marx management bargained with him for two years before learning that they had been doing business with the business agent for Chicago Local 39 of the United Garment Workers. Hillman had been representing the workers without troubling to mention that the workers were organized in a union. The employers had thought they were simply doing the decent thing at the urging of a nice young man and their own better natures.

And so they had been. Learning that Hillman was connected with the union, they were "disappointed in and even much vexed at [him]." But not for long. Hillman gave them "the quiet assurance that he could make a proposed union agreement *pay* for them. [Josephson's italics.] He spoke in the language they understood, the American language of practical business." Hundreds of employers were to hear the same assurances, the same easy-to-understand language down through the years. And they were to discover that Hillman, as a rule, a golden one, was right.

Nothing contributed more to Hillman's reputation as a Labor Statesman than the Amalgamated's efforts to serve as a laboratory of social improvement. Viewed strictly as a trade union, the Amalgamated was, and is, just so-so. Not bad, really, but not so hot either. It is hard to compare its wage scales with those of other unions, even of so closely related a one as Dubinsky's International Ladies' Garment Workers'. But it has certainly done no better by its members than the average union, and an impressive case can be made out to the effect that it has not done nearly as well. In any event, many unions have done more. Judged by the degree of internal democracy, the Amalgamated is probably a bit below par. It is not as bad as the International Longshoremen's Association, but it is not anywhere near as good as, say, the United Automobile Workers.

But as an assembly of gadgets for "enriching" the lives of its members in other than financial ways, nothing matches it. Hillman went in for enrichment right at the start. A lecturer on elevating topics named Dr. Max Goldfarb said that the new union should be "a temple within and a fortress without," and the phrase so pleased Hillman that he put Dr. Goldfarb on the payroll to sow seeds of culture in Amalgamated locals all over the country. After Dr. Goldfarb came a whole flood of devices for uplift, co-operative living, and the like. There were housing projects, workers' schools, labor colleges, insurance plans, choral groups, art classes, worker-owned plants, children's programs, and other such side shows. Some of these turned out well; others, like the worker-owned plants, fizzled. The best known today, no doubt, are the Amalgamated Banks in New York and Chicago, which, as the late Benjamin Stolberg once wrote, "do a small and safe commercial business and render the members of the union no service that they cannot get elsewhere."

In the large view, however, these ornaments paid off quite handsomely. For it was upon them rather than upon its accomplishments as a collective-bargaining agency that the Amalgamated's reputation rested. Without them, it would have been just another union; with them, it was "the New Unionism." It was with these gimmicks, along with such purely verbal tricks as a redefinition of collective bargaining as "industrial science," that made Hillman seem a towering figure to the editors of the *Survey Graphic* and the *New Republic* and to reformers like Louis Kirstein, Felix Frankfurter, and William Z. Ripley; that brought him invitations to address political-science academies and other learned groups; that led to the term "Labor Statesman"; that made him a court favorite in two liberal administrations; and that produced this devotional essay by Matthew Josephson.

One wonders why all these trained minds succumbed so readily to Sidney Hillman. Is there some quirk in the pragmatic mind that is always getting form and substance mixed up? The experience of American intellectuals with Communism suggests such a possibility. Or is it, perhaps, that American liberalism has such a profoundly middle-class base that liberals are offended by militancy in collective bargaining and feel most comfortable with leaders who, like Hillman, appear to subordinate this gross activity to the task of housebreaking the workers?

In any event, the gimmicks, quite apart from what they may have done for Hillman's ego, a sizable and intricate one, were of value to the union qua union. The Amalgamated began as a dual organization, and it won its most notable advantage over the United Garment Workers when Hillman's friends in the Wilson administration fixed things so that it should be the favored agency in firms getting military-uniform contracts. Between the New Freedom and the New Deal, the Amalgamated had a fairly rocky time of it, particularly toward the end, but then Felix Frankfurter became a power in Washington, Miss Perkins was appointed Secretary of Labor, and Hillman was called on to help draft N.R.A. codes and advise on labor legislation. Under the New Deal the union in time consolidated its power. There is no more United Garment Workers. The Amalgamated is now secure, thanks largely to the gadgets which wowed the gadget-minded who were in a position to make it secure.

Hillman had a healthy interest in power and throughout most of his long career dreamed of being head man not only of the *men's* clothing workers but of the *women's* as well. He regarded it as irrational that the needle trades should be divided according to the sex for which the cutters and stitchers cut and stitched. He believed that the Amalgamated and the International Ladies' Garment Workers' should consolidate under his leadership. Josephson mentions this ambition and says that the barrier to it was the presence in the ILGWU of one man "to whom the idea of amalgamation was anathema." He goes on to say: "David Dubinsky, on the other hand, was one of the ILGWU executives who then [circa 1926] favored a combination of forces under the seemingly invincible Hillman." He does not explain why, when

Dubinsky replaced Benjamin Schlesinger as head of the ILGWU, the combination of forces did not take place. As a matter of fact, it almost did, and thereby hangs a tale, which Dubinsky loves to relate. Hillman was still strong for a wedding of the unions in 1933, when he became a labor adviser to the N.R.A. "I told him," Dubinsky has said, "that if he would help us get a good NRA code, I'd step aside and let him be president." Before he gave a thought to the men's-clothing code, Hillman worked like a dog getting a model code for ladies' garments. He wheedled, he coaxed, he waxed eloquent, he used all his Good Connections. He succeeded remarkably well. "Then he went to work on men's," Dubinsky says. "His credit with his friends—it was all used up. They said, 'Please, Sidney, I did everything I could for you last week—more don't ask of me.'" Thanks to the way Hillman had drawn on his credit, the ILGWU got a much better code than the Amalgamated, and Hillman, now in a poorer power position vis-à-vis Dubinsky, was in no hurry for a merger.

Josephson makes no attempt to judge Hillman's career as a whole. It would be difficult for anyone to do. Hillman did a lot to improve conditions in one of our worst industries. The United Garment Workers would never have done anything; it was a racket for selling union labels to sew on workingmen's overalls. Some of the Amalgamated's contracts were bogus, too. Hillman often signed an agreement that won union recognition but nothing extra in the pay envelope. But sooner or later the money came, and, taken on the whole, things got a good deal better over the years.

Hillman was also important because he was the first American labor leader to form a close alliance with bourgeois reformers and liberal politicians. He was not a ranter like John L. Lewis or a reactionary like William Green. As labor grew in power, it needed a "statesman," and Hillman looked the part. He was effective in the Office of Production Management, but so was William Knudsen, and no one thought of calling *him* a statesman; even the liberals assumed that industry could give the country some good public servants. Hillman led the Political Action Committee of the C.I.O. in 1944, and this was one of labor's first really organized political ventures. It was not really much of a success. Hillman allowed it to be overrun with Communists and fellow travelers; the last time the P.A.C. was heard about was when a large batch of its former functionaries joined Henry Wallace's Progressives in 1948. Hillman was not, of course, pro-Communist. Indeed, he had allowed racketeers into the Amalgamated in the twenties to pitch the Communists out, and he later had quite a time pitching the goons out. But he was an opportunist and a man knowing enough about left-wing affairs to realize that when the Communists were with you, they could take care of a lot of the dirty work. Hillman allowed them to wreck the American Labor party in New York as well as the P.A.C. Hillman was, in short, a labor politician. He was no statesman.

✳ The Wicked Conspiracy Against General MacArthur

1 9 5 6

NO LIVING AMERICAN, no eminent American of recent times, has been so hopelessly addicted to the conspiracy theory of history as General of the Army Douglas MacArthur. Alongside this warrior-statesman, Vice-President Nixon and Senator McCarthy have been mere triflers. Each has done his share to make the doctrine fashionable and serviceable, but there is no reason to suppose that either takes it with any real seriousness. Neither seems an authentically dedicated spirit. Senator James Eastland, of Mississippi, belongs, in my view, with them rather than with MacArthur. He has, it is true, carried the theory to new heights with his assertions that the Supreme Court has been "brain-washed" by radicals and that "left-wing pressure groups are in control of the government of the United States." But the very scope and grandeur of his charges seem to reveal an essential frivolity about the conspiracy theory. I hope it will not be regarded as frivolity on *my* part if I add that Senator Eastland is rather fat and has the look of a man very satisfied with his lot in life, which is in many ways an enviable one. In my researches, I have yet to encounter a really serious adherent of the conspiracy theory who is portly. My judgments may be subject to revision, though, when and if Senator Eastland conducts an investigation of General MacArthur's claim that his recall by President Truman in 1951 was part of a global plot in which the British traitors Guy Burgess and Douglas Maclean were the central figures, but as of now Eastland appears to stand with those who use the conspiracy theory as a good thing—not as the key to history.

Of MacArthur's earnestness, though, there can be little doubt. He is a True Believer—and not a rank-and-file one, but a commander, egocentric, messianic, *entêté,* a True Believer in himself. Like others of the breed, he finds it necessary to ascribe his disappointments, which have been numerous, to base intrigue. In his melancholy and wayward universe, there is no purely personal guilt; evil always has its cabalistic aspect. There is no such thing as *pure* malice or spite; there is malice in abundance, but it can never be pure—it is eternally in the service of, or somehow compounded by, dark and terribly complex contrivances. Thus, when he describes his recall as a "vengeful reprisal," as he did in his recent rejoinder, in *Life* magazine for February 13, to Harry Truman's reminiscences of the Korean war, he cannot let the matter drop there, for with this characterization of the act he is only on the outer surface of the truth as he knows it. He had been aware from the start, he has advised us, that "the disease of power was coursing through [Truman's] veins," but this, for MacArthur was not enough to know. A "vengeful reprisal" by a power-mad President is not in and of itself a conspiracy. If it had been *only* the President whom the General had to deal with, there would have been no contest. Besides, there cannot be, in the nature of things, a one-man conspiracy. "Quite apart from what Mr. Truman has to say in his memoirs," General MacArthur writes, "I had searched in vain for some logical explanation of my abrupt relief from command in the Far East." A "logical explanation" must be one in which malevolent design is apparent. "It was not," he tells us, "until the recent exposure of the British spies, Burgess and Maclean, that the true facts began to unfold."

Senator Eastland has promised to unfold the facts, presumably before the Senate Internal Security Committee. One hopes he will get down to work right away.* Meanwhile, there is some fascinating material about earlier conspiracies against General MacArthur in *MacArthur: His Rendezvous with History,* by Major-General Courtney Whitney. Whitney is a former Manila lawyer with whom MacArthur formed an enduring friendship

* He never did.

almost twenty years ago; he has been at MacArthur's side in one capacity or another from the Lingayen Gulf to the Waldorf Towers, from Corregidor to Remington Rand, and in spite of what must have been resourceful competition from Major-General Charles Willoughby, MacArthur's intelligence chief for many years, he has never had to relinquish his position as first among the sycophants. Of him, MacArthur says:

I know of no one better qualified than he intelligently to discuss . . . my role in the stirring events which have encompassed the Far East since the start of World War II. . . . [His] actual participation in the events and his knowledge of the concepts underlying my actions cannot fail to ensure the historical accuracy and corresponding value of his work.

He might have added that Whitney is blessed with a humility that is rare among memoirists. Although it is, after all, his book, he says little of anything about his participation in the stirring events. He retires from the scene entirely whenever it is possible to let MacArthur tell his own story, which is much of the time. The book consists very largely of documents—reports, memoranda, letters, wise sayings, public speeches by the rendezvouser with history himself, and may be considered, as Hanson Baldwin has pointed out, as General MacArthur's valedictory and apologia. It is informed and illuminated from start to finish by the view that not only the Far East but the world in general since the mid-thirties has been the stage for a titanic conflict between Douglas MacArthur and Satan in manifold disguises, most of them thin. Some of the early developments may be briefly summarized as follows:

1932: MacArthur defeats Communists on Anacostia Flats. Communists shrewdly figure that MacArthur is their principal adversary. Hatch plot to have "public trial and hanging in front of the Capitol of high government officials. At the very top of the list was the name of Army Chief of Staff MacArthur." Plot does not work out, but Communists form close anti-MacArthur alliance with " 'Europe-first' cliques in the War and State Departments."

1935-36: MacArthur now in Philippines, getting ready for World War II. Washington conspirators turn out to have long reach. "Even in those early days when he had first started building the Philippines' defenses, U. S. officials had harassed him right in Manila. Frank Murphy, as High Commissioner of the Philippines, betrayed his jealousy of MacArthur's stature in the islands by initiating a personal campaign of pressure on President Roosevelt to cause the General's removal." Time not quite ripe. Campaign fails. MacArthur retires voluntarily and receives "accolade" from F.D.R., who says, "Your service in war and peace is a brilliant chapter in American history." True enough. "But accolades did not prevent MacArthur from being sniped at." Mephisto never sleeps. Plot goes on.

1936-41: MacArthur working for Philippine government, head of armed forces, Field Marshal in Army. Nevertheless, finds himself "facing a movement to supplant him even in this position. . . . The movement gained powerful support in Washington but failed. . . ." It failed, but it did not cease. Complications in Manila. "[The] Philippine Assembly delayed on appropriations; some politicians tried to cut down the amounts MacArthur needed." Reflecting on all this, MacArthur one day said to Whitney, "Destiny, by the grace of God, sometimes plays queer pranks with men's lives."

1941-45: United States at war in Europe and Far East. Anti-MacArthur campaign stepped up. Navy becomes involved. Also England, France, and, of course, Soviet Union. But especially Washington. "While MacArthur, alone of all commanders in the Pacific, was stopping the enemy in his tracks, he was being sacrificed in Washington." Roosevelt (he of the deceptive accolade), Marshall, Churchill, Admiral Ernest J. King—the whole crew "handed MacArthur the stewardship of a military disaster. And what made it one of the cruelest deceptions of the war was that they not only did not tell MacArthur but instead tried with every circumlocution possible to pretend the opposite of the truth." MacArthur turns out to be the only man who wants to

win the war. "MacArthur's plan for a breakthrough and continued resistance [in the Philippines] was vetoed by Marshall.
. . . Evidently the indomitable will no longer existed in Washington. . . . Defeatism [seemed] to be infecting the Pentagon."
MacArthur forced to leave Philippines. Vice-Admiral Herbert Fairfax Leary refuses to lend good planes to evacuate MacArthur party. Offers three crates, one of which cracks up, killing two of crew. MacArthur finally gets decent plane; goes to Australia, wins war against heavy odds. King, Mountbatten, and other dupes "trying to relegate MacArthur to . . . a minor holding action," but cannot manage it. MacArthur in end receives Japanese surrender in splendid ceremony. Goes to Tokyo, rehabilitates Japan, and awaits Armageddon.

In the end, the entire United States is made to seem an instrument for bringing misery into the life of Douglas MacArthur. At first it is only the politicians who frustrate his grand designs, but after a time the plot thickens, and in the end we are all of us, dear Brutus, held in some measure responsible for "the humiliation that seared his soul." There is some justice in this dreadful world, though; for this "foul and shocking blow," we are being suitably repaid in kind:

Ever since the removal of MacArthur from a position of influence in Asia, Communism has progressively strengthened and become an increasingly powerful threat to peace and freedom.

There is authentic tragedy here as well as comedy, for the truth is that there are elements of greatness in Douglas MacArthur. He has served this country as a valorous and resourceful captain in the field and as a gifted proconsul. He has at times borne himself with splendor and shown himself capable of commanding abiding loyalties. I know an officer who served under him in the Pacific and is now one of the most intelligent and imaginative of American diplomatic strategists. He shares none of MacArthur's views on matters of policy and at the same time hugely admires MacArthur the military campaigner. One gets a sense of greatness even from Whitney's preposterous book. A basically cloddish mind is moved to imagination ("This, I thought, must have been what it was like in a tent in Gaul with Caesar; on the approaches to Cannae with Hannibal; on the plains before Guagamela with Alexander the Great . . .") and to massive recrimination by the spectacle of his commander's triumphs and misfortunes. Great soldiers are not the less great for having jejune views of history. Napoleon had a Napoleonic complex.

Indeed, a distinction that one cannot take lightly is the very concern with policy that has led MacArthur into so many difficulties. Whether the man is sensible or not in his political avouchments, he has never been a time-server, he has never been indifferent to the aims of the governments he has served. He has always, at least, cared. Liberals who have applauded the independence and the concern with policy of officers like Billy Mitchell and Charles de Gaulle have been a good deal too facile in condemning MacArthur for insubordination which consisted in the main of taking his case to the public. What was wrong was not so much his public contentiousness as the case itself, the strategy he favored. Robert Clive was similarly mistaken, and so was Gordon of Khartoum, a man very much like MacArthur. There is in MacArthur, as there was in them, something of the "heaven-born general," to use Pitt's phrase for Clive, another prodigy, mystic, orator, and empire builder.

Yet MacArthur, principally through his commitment to the conspiracy theory, insists on making himself ridiculous. Now, on top of the Whitney book, with its abundance of plots, he has come up with the superplot, involving Burgess and Maclean, and such is his prestige and the hunger of our Bolsheviks of the Right for conspiracies that the story has become a matter for serious public debate. To David Lawrence and to his *U.S. News & World Report*, part of the matter is already beyond dispute. "It was these two men," *U.S. News* has said, "who helped to trigger the invasion by armies of Communist China at the moment of defeat for Soviet-armed North Koreans." This is MacArthur's basic contention in these later days—that the Chinese entered the war because they had been assured by Burgess and Maclean that we would engage them nowhere in Korea. His second proposition is that it was a reluctance on the part of the Truman administration to reveal the simple but ugly truth that led to his removal by President Truman on April 11, 1951. The editors of *Life* have regarded this as a plausible version of history, and the editors of the *National Review* find so much political promise in it that they wish to have it investigated not by a mere committee, such as Senator Eastland's, but by a "mixed commission . . . with members from Congress, the administration, and the public."

It is characteristic of the mind in the grip of the conspiracy theory that it marshals argument untidily. Those who credit the new MacArthur story must do so either by faith in MacArthur himself or through a shared addiction to the theory. MacArthur is the only man who has ever made a stab at finding logic in it or imposing logic upon it, and his facility with the syllogism is far from all it might be. To stay with him even part of the way, one must concede that the Peiping government in 1950 was by one means or another being made privy to the discussions of American policy in the National Security Council and elsewhere, as well as to the decisions emerging from those deliberations. MacArthur himself has no difficulty in making this assumption, for to him it is only reasonable to take it for granted that the Chinese Communists would never have been stupid enough to engage him in battle if they had not had "definite advance information that my hands would be tied."

Only [he writes] if he were certain that we would continue to protect his bases and supply lines would a commander have dared to throw the full weight of the Chinese army in Korea.

The Chinese could not have been serious (even in delusion) in calling us a "paper tiger," so long as they knew that MacArthur was in command and had a free hand. But the tying of his hands made us in fact vulnerable.

To some of us, it may appear that a Communist leader who took at face value "definite advance information" on American strategy, which has been so consistently subject to abrupt change, would be well along the road to madness. If anyone even contemplates making war against the United States, he should acknowledge that the beginning of wisdom is an acceptance of our unpredictability. There is no such thing as "definite advance information" in matters of this sort.

But MacArthur thinks otherwise, and so, taking for granted that the Chinese had received the necessary advance assurances, he thinks it necessary only to uncover the "links in the chain to our enemy in Korea through Peiping by way of Moscow." Why not, one wonders, direct to Peiping or perhaps, as some people believed a few weeks back, by way of London or New Delhi? This is not explained, but a firm conviction is stated:

I myself have long been convinced that Red China's decision to commit its forces to the Korean peninsula was predicated upon assurances previously given through Moscow that such intervention would not precipitate retaliation against its attack bases.

Now to get Burgess and Maclean into the act: MacArthur makes a breath-taking leap from the enemy's knowledge of what was happening in Washington to his knowledge of what was going to happen in Korea. In theory, of course, what was happening in Washington should have been a reliable guide to what the American forces were going to do in Korea. But in fact a number of Americans and practically all Europeans had the feeling that perhaps one decision would be taken by President Truman and his advisers and another by General MacArthur. MacArthur, though, thinks everyone should have known better —in the Whitney book, the notion that MacArthur was ever at any time insubordinate to civil authority is treated as too absurd to discuss—and that the Chinese certainly did know better. (It is curious that MacArthur and Whitney consistently attribute sounder judgment to the Communists than to their adversaries, himself, of course, excepted.) Someone, it follows, had tipped the Communists off. It now appears, according to MacArthur, to have been Guy Burgess and Donald Maclean. How does he know? MacArthur, in *Life,* has constructed what passes for a syllogism in the conspiracy school. "General [Walton] Walker," he says, "complained constantly to me that the enemy was receiving prior information of his movements." Plainly, if they had prior information, it had to come from behind United Nations lines in Korea. Ordinary people might assume that, since there were plenty of spies in South Korea, what information the Communists had was provided them by their own agents behind the U.N. lines. MacArthur says this was not so. "We could find no leaks in Korea or Japan." If MacArthur's intelligence and counter-intelligence directed by the redoubtable General Willoughby could not find any leaks, then there could not have been any.

In time there was light. "Then suddenly, one of my dispatches concerning the order of battle was published in a Washington paper within a few hours of its receipt." He does not identify either the dispatch or the newspaper that printed it. He merely says: "I insisted that those responsible be prosecuted." Presumably he identified the guilty for the benefit of those he expected to undertake the prosecution. Fortunately, for unauthorized persons and latecomers, the Whitney book throws some light. It identifies the offending newspaper as the Washington *Post* and explains that "on December 30, 1950 . . . one of MacArthur's top-secret dispatches on the order of battle was in part published verbatim . . . under the byline of a prominent columnist." A check of the Washington *Post* of that date reveals that the columnist was Drew Pearson, whose work appears in some six hundred newspapers here and abroad, and that Pearson that day published what purported to be a report from MacArthur's intelligence section dated December 6, 1950. MacArthur's "few hours" turn out to be 576 (give or take ten or twenty for time changes and publication schedules), and it was not precisely one of his "dispatches concerning the order of battle," but, on the contrary, a dispatch from General Willoughby on the *Chinese* order of battle.

Still, there was a leak, rather a slow one, but nevertheless deplorable. Drew Pearson should not have had access to Willoughby's cables. Someone was responsible. Who? Burgess and Maclean, MacArthur now tells us. How come? MacArthur does not withhold the answer, though he gives it in question form:

If they did not report to their Kremlin masters fully upon our secrets in the conduct of the war against the Communists in Korea, what then could have been their treasonable ,purpose?

What indeed? Any good Communist spy would report anything he knew about the Korean war. If he got hold of news about

United Nations troop movements, naturally he would pass it on, in glee and triumph. And he would also report what our side knew about his side. But would he report to Drew Pearson? Was Pearson one of Burgess and Maclean's "Kremlin masters"? This is not gone into—nor does MacArthur cast any light on what was going on in the White House, the Pentagon, or the National Security Council. Somebody must have leaked to Burgess and Maclean before Burgess and Maclean could leak to Pearson.

MacArthur, incidentally, writes as if Burgess and Maclean were both in Washington at the time of the Chinese intervention. Maclean was in the Foreign Office in London; he had become head of the American desk on November 6, 1950, and no doubt he was receiving some British intelligence and some highly educated guesses about American policy and plans. Burgess was in fact in Washington. But it is doubtful if he was getting transcripts of N.S.C. proceedings within a matter of hours. And it was manifestly impossible for him to have been told the outcome of discussions that had no outcome. The truth is that on December 6, 1950, we had no settled policy on what we would do on the Yalu. The issue was under discussion—not only in Washington but at the United Nations in New York. There may have been a tentative American position—a decision on what this country would do if agreement with other powers could be reached and if the military conditions were right. But there is always a great gulf between decisions of this sort and the policy that is in time pursued. After all, we once had a policy in which Korea was held to be outside our defense perimeter. Dean Acheson has taken the rap for making it public, but MacArthur accepted it and was not averse to discussing it with newspapermen.* In any case, when the Thirty-eighth Parallel was breached,

---

* As early as March 1949, he had told the British newspaperman G. Ward Price that "Our line of defense runs through the chain of islands fringing the coast of Asia. It starts from the Philippines and continues through the Ryukyu archipelago, which includes its main bastion, Okinawa. Then it bends back through Japan and the Aleutian Island chain to Alaska. Though the advance of the Red Armies in China places them on the flank of that position, this does not alter the fact that our only possible adversary on the Asiatic continent does not possess an industrial base near enough to supply an amphibious attacking force." By our "main adversary," he could only at that time have meant the Soviet Union.

we reversed the policy. That is how things go in the real world. Men say they will do one thing and then do another. If the Chinese Communists, having seen us throw one policy decision to the winds, placed complete confidence in another, their sense of reality could not have been as formidable as some of us assumed it to be. They might have found the reports from Burgess and Maclean interesting, provided there were any such reports, but they would have been mighty foolish Communists to have put any stock in them. But then—they are no more exempt from foolishness than we are.

The Pearson incident is the central one in MacArthur's rendering of the history of 1950 and 1951. It proves, retroactively, that Burgess and Maclean told the Chinese they would have a romp if they entered the war. Burgess and Maclean told Drew Pearson, *ergo* they told Mao Tse-tung. (It is hard to explain why he does not avail himself of almost infallible logic: They were Communists, *ergo* they told Mao Tse-tung.) MacArthur explains that when he could find "no leak" in his own theater, he promptly recommended that "a treason trial be initiated to break up [the] spy ring responsible for the purloining of my secret reports to Washington." (This is a beautiful example of how the mind obsessed by conspiracy works. He concedes that he did not know *who* "purloined" the reports until years later. He wanted a trial before there were suspects—a trial of a "ring." As it turned out, the putative defendants had diplomatic immunity.) And he goes on: "I believe that my demand that this situation [there is no antecedent for the "this"] be exposed, coming after the Alger Hiss and Harry Dexter White scandals caused the deepest resentment. [The] case was never processed, and I was shortly relieved of my command."

And after him, the deluge.

* PART FOUR

JUDGMENTS RESERVED

* Privacy and the Claims of Community

1 9 5 8

IT IS REPEATEDLY asserted by solicitous groups and individuals that the right of privacy—described once by Mr. Justice Brandeis as the "right to be let alone . . . the most comprehensive of rights and the right most valued by civilized men"—is in sorry shape in this Republic today. The evidence is impressive. Wire tapping is epidemic; even where it is illegal, it flourishes, and some authorities believe that the number of telephones being monitored on any given day runs into the hundreds of thousands. "Bugging," the use of concealed electronic devices by absentee eavesdroppers, is an almost universal practice among policemen, private detectives, and both public and private investigators. People describing themselves as "investigators" are as numerous and as pestiferous, it often seems, as flies in late September. Each day, more and more of us are required to tell agencies of government more and more about ourselves; and each melancholy day, government agencies are telling more and more about us. Someone in the F.B.I.—not J. Edgar Hoover, certainly, but someone —slips a "raw" file to a favored congressman; the President instructs the Bureau of Internal Revenue to turn over income-tax returns to an investigating committee; the Defense Department gives medical records to an insurance adjuster. The existence of the files, apart from their disclosure, may itself be regarded as a violation of privacy; we are compelled to leave bits and pieces of ourselves in many places where we would just as soon not be.

Broadly speaking, invasions of privacy are of two sorts, both on the increase. There are those, like wire tapping and bugging and disclosure of supposedly confidential documents, that could con-

245

ceivably be dealt with by changes in law or public policy. Then there are those that appear to be exercises of other rights—for example, freedom of speech, of the press, of inquiry. A newspaper reporter asks an impertinent personal question; the prospective employer of a friend wishes to know whether the friend has a happy sex life; a motivational researcher wishes to know what we have against Brand B deodorant; a magazine wishing to lure more advertisers asks us to fill out a questionnaire on our social, financial, and intellectual status. Brandeis' "right to be let alone" is unique in that it can be denied us by the powerless as well as by the powerful—by a teen-ager with a portable radio as well as by a servant of the law armed with a subpoena.

Most of those who publicly lament the decline of privacy talk as if they believe that the causes are essentially political; they seem to feel that enemies of individual rights are conspiring to destroy privacy just as certain of them have sought, in recent years, to destroy the right to avoid self-incrimination. Some also see privacy eroding as a consequence of a diminishing respect for it. I think there may be something in both points, although a good deal less in the first than in the second; but it seems to me that the really important causes lie elsewhere—in our advancing technology and in the growing size and complexity of our society. Until the early part of this century, the right of privacy was seldom invoked. Though its broadest and most binding guarantee is in the Fourth Amendment to the Constitution, which affirms "the right of the people to be secure in their persons, houses, papers and effects" and prohibits unreasonable searches and seizures, it was not until 1905 that a court squarely upheld the right of privacy. The jurisdiction was Georgia, and the court laid it down as a common-law proposition that "the right of privacy has its foundations in the instincts of nature." In a thinly populated land, with government touching only lightly on the everyday lives of citizens and with a technology so primitive that people had to depend on their own eyes and ears to know what others were up to, men armed with the Fourth Amendment and with the squirrel gun permitted them under the Second Amendment could pretty well attend to their own privacy. Mostly, one supposes, it was not thought of as a "right" to be protected but as a condition of life cherished by some and merely accepted by others.

But then came the camera, the telephone, the graduated income tax, and later the tape recorder, the behavioral scientist, television (now being used to follow us as we move about supermarkets and department stores as a kind of radar for the light-fingered), the professional social worker, "togetherness," and a host of other developments that are destructive of privacy as a right and as a condition. Soundproofing is the only technological contribution I can think of that has been an aid to the right to be let alone. The rest have lent themselves to invasions of privacy, and the end is not yet in sight. Wire tapping, for example, is now in the process of being fully automated; where formerly the number of phones that could be tapped was limited by the number of personnel that could be assigned to sitting around all day waiting for a conversation to intercept, today innumerable phones can be monitored entirely by machines. Someday, no doubt, we shall be spied upon from space platforms equipped with television cameras. And all this time the welfare state has been developing—in the main, of course, as a response to technology. It may be that a disrespect for privacy has been on the increase, too, but what is certain is that those of a trespassing inclination are infinitely better equipped today and have infinitely more excuses for their incursions. I rather think this is the essential thing, for I believe that if the Georgia court was correct in saying that the "instincts of nature" provided foundations for the right of privacy, the same thing may also be cited as a source of motive power for those who assume the right to violate privacy. Was it not the late Senator McCarthy who screamed bloody murder when the Post Office Department ran a "mail cover" on his correspondence? (In a mail cover, postal officials do not open mail but examine envelopes and wrappings with a view to learning the identity of a victim's correspondents.) No doubt his outrage was as genuine as it was noisy. There is a hermit spirit in each of us, and also a snooper, a census taker, a gossipmonger, and a brother's keeper.

Technology has forced the surrender of a measure of privacy

in many different ways. It may be a man's business whether he drinks or not, but if he wishes to drive a car or fly an airplane or perform brain operations, society's need to inquire into his drinking habits must surely override his right to privacy in this serious matter. Government is society's instrument in such affairs, and the more responsibilities we saddle it with, the more we require it to take a hand in our lives. If we wish it to protect us against quacks, frauds, swindlers, maniacs, and criminals, we must give it powers of prosecution, punishment, and licensing. We can be reasonably certain that its tendency will be to go too far (the American Civil Liberties Union reports with distress that in some places tile layers must now be licensed by public authority), but we may—indeed, it seems to me that most of us do—judge its excesses to be less dangerous than complete *laissez faire* or *laissez passer*. Technology has made us all a great deal more dependent upon one another than we ever were in the past and necessarily, therefore, less able to protect our own privacy. Once we could labor alone—now there is a division of labor which relates my work to yours. Once we traveled alone —now our mobility is collectivized, and while we have a legitimate concern over the habits of the man at the controls, whose private life we find it necessary to investigate, we also constitute ourselves a captive audience and a group of hostages to those in whom the instincts of nature that lead to compulsive trespassing are more powerful than those that make sometime recluses of us all.

In my view, it gains us nothing to denounce J. Edgar Hoover or those who descend to what Mr. Justice Holmes called the "dirty business" of wire tapping—or even to expend rhetoric on the death of solitude in our kind of civilization, as William Faulkner now and then does when he feels himself affronted by the attentions of the press and the public. If there is any way at all out of the fish bowl, it will be found only by facing some hard facts of life today. For one thing, there is no stopping the technology that extends our senses by wires and waves and electrical impulses. For another, it is difficult—if, indeed, it is possible—to distinguish, morally and practically, between the use of these devices and the use of the senses unaided. I think that wire tapping *is* a dirty business, but I am not sure that I can find much logic to support my belief so long as I am willing to countenance the older, unmechanized ways by which society apprehends criminals. What is the moral difference between tapping a telephone wire and straining one's ears to overhear a conversation believed by the participants to be private? What is the moral difference between putting an ear to a keyhole and bugging a room? Or between using any and all bugging devices and planting spies and informers in the underworld? Or between carrying a concealed tape recorder to an interview and carrying a concealed plan to commit to memory as much of the talk as the memory can retain? Society needs detectives, or so at least I believe, and the means they employ have never been lovely and have almost always involved the violation of privacy. Society does a lot of dirty business.

So far as morality is concerned, I doubt if a valid distinction can be made between primitive and advanced techniques. But a practical distinction can be made, and in fact has been made (wire tapping is either outlawed or restricted by law in every American jurisdiction), and the rationale is not very different from that which proscribes mechanical devices in most sports. Whether or not wire tapping is dirty business in the Holmesian sense, it is dirty pool, and this applies, or soon will, one suspects, to most other gadgets. It may be no more immoral than other means used for the same end—any more than killing with thermonuclear weapons is more immoral than killing with a club—but somehow the advantage it gives to the police side is offensive to sportsmanship, and the numbers that can be bagged by automated spying, like the numbers that can be killed by a hydrogen bomb, make it seem more offensive to our humanity. Against this, it can be argued that crime and subversion have also benefited by science and that their adversaries should not have to fight a horse cavalry war against them. But the fact of the matter is that it is not narcotics peddlers whose privacy has been more efficiently violated by the use of the new techniques; the net has not been drawn tighter against society's enemies—it has simply been spread for a larger catch. And here another practical distinction can be made, even though a moral one comes hard. It is one thing to deceive and trap a dope pusher by almost any means available, and quite another to tap the phone of, let us say, a philanthropic foundation on the chance of turning up a relationship between it and some citizen of a heretical turn of mind. To be sure, the underworld members of the Apalachin rally have every bit as much right to privacy as the president of, say, the Fund for the Republic. But the law in its wisdom has found a way to draw a line between the two without denying their equality; this is the doctrine of "probable cause," embodied as the condition for seizure and arrest in the same Fourth Amendment that keeps most of us out of the broad net of policemen merely fishing for evidence in our homes and among our papers and effects.

It seems to me that it is by no means too late for law and public policy to deal with violations of privacy that are undertaken by zealous guardians of the peace and the public order. In all probability, wire tapping and the many forms of bugging can never be wholly eliminated, even where they are outlawed and the penalties for their use are severe; they suit the police mentality too well, and they may be easily employed without fear of detection. Moreover, there are circumstances in which even the most ardent civil libertarians would be forced to approve their use. But the third degree and the rubber truncheon also suit the police mentality, and free societies have managed to reduce their use to a point where they are not regarded as essential characteristics of the machinery of law enforcement. Probable cause, with high standards for the determination of probability, would seem a basic safeguard against present excesses. Another would be an extension of the rule of the inadmissibility of wiretap evidence; this, of course, is the rule in the federal courts today, and it has not stopped the F.B.I. and God knows how many other government agencies from tapping wires in the hope of learning where admissible evidence may be turned up. But there is no reason why the rule of inadmissibility might not be strengthened in such a way as to give ordinary criminal defendants a chance at acquittals and reversals whenever the prosecution's case has been made by playing dirty pool. The police, like merchants, do not care for profitless ventures, and somewhere, no doubt, there is a point at which most of the profit can be taken out of the indiscriminate wire tapping and bugging that is being employed today. Mr. Justice Murphy used to say that there was no means of preserving the liberties of citizens so efficacious as making the denial of those liberties disadvantageous to the police power.

Nothing will be done, however, along this line unless a certain amount of public pressure builds up against a catch-as-catch-can view of law enforcement and in defense of the right of privacy. And even if abuses of the police power were checked, we would be left with all those invasions that are the work not of the police power, but of other public authorities and of a multitude of private ones. Here, as I see it, we encounter problems far knottier than those posed by technology in the service of law and order. We were willed a social order dedicated to the sovereignty of the individual but, again thanks mainly to technology, dependent for its functioning largely on the interdependence of lives. My behavior affects my neighbor in a hundred ways undreamed of a century ago. My home is joined to his by pipes and cables, by tax and insurance rates. If my labor is not immediately dependent on his, it is on that of other men down the street and across the continent. When I move about, my life is at my neighbor's mercy—and his, of course, at mine. I may build a high fence, bolt the doors, draw the blinds, and insist that my time to myself is mine alone, but his devices for intrusion are limitless. My privacy can be invaded by a ringing telephone as well as by a tapped one. It can be invaded by an insistent community that seeks to shame me into getting up off my haunches to do something for the P.-T.A. or town improvement or the American Civil Liberties Union— possibly, for this worthy organization, making a survey of invasions of privacy. My "right to be let alone" is a right I may cherish and from time to time invoke, but it is not a right favored by the conditions of the life I lead and am, by and large, pleased to be leading. If I were to think of it as any sort of absolute right, I would be as blind to the world about me as those who used to believe that the United States could assert and by itself defend its right to be let alone. No kind of sovereignty has ever been absolute, but in the last century or so the decline has been staggering.

The meaningful invasions that are a consequence of the condition of our lives are, to be sure, those undertaken more or less in the name of the whole community: by organs of government other than the police, by the press, by education, by business. Against them, the law can offer few defenses without denying other freedoms and committing new invasions of privacy. The press has a right to describe Nathan Leopold's release from prison; whether it will exercise that right in the face of eloquent pleas not to do so is a matter of conscience and taste. In general, our rule is that those who lead part of their lives in public—politicians, entertainers, writers, and others, including celebrated criminal defendants, who court the public favor in one way or another—have forfeited the right to invoke the common-law doctrine that "a person who unreasonably and seriously interferes with another's interest in not having his affairs known to others . . . is liable to the other." In England, Randolph Churchill may raise the roof because the press is, in his view, too nosey about the private life of Princess Margaret, but here there would be no one to defend the proposition that the press and public should be kept in the dark about the President's health, as the British public was once kept in the dark about the health of Randolph Churchill's father. And the same tests of public interest and relevance that apply in the community of the nation apply in every subcommunity. To a degree, we can control our privacy by controlling our mode of existence, and if we can never retain anything like complete mastery, we can at least attempt an approach to it. But the costs are heavy and to many, probably most, Americans excessive.

It is common for Europeans to say that privacy will die in America because we care nothing about it. "An American has no sense of privacy," Bernard Shaw wrote. "He does not know what it means. There is no such thing in the country." Foreigners frequently profess to be scandalized by American institutions that seem to them destructive of the very idea of privacy—the standard sleeping car, for instance, and the now ubiquitous portable radio. Alistair Cooke has said that while in England good manners consist in not intruding oneself upon others, here they consist in being tolerant of those who lead their private life in public and remaining a good sport about all noisy intrusions. I think the differences are real but insignificant. The British may piously talk of the royal family's right to privacy, but their gutter press makes more lives miserable than ours does. The French set great store by privacy, but they allow their police a license that Americans would never tolerate. (The French police operate on the theory that their work would be quite impossible if they were not allowed to run mail covers, ransack telegraph files, and tap wires.) We are perhaps the most gregarious and community-minded of people and have developed social and technological interdependence further than any other, but it is still, I think, universally acknowledged that the man who tells another to "mind your own business" has justice on his side and speaks the common law. We are all in the same fix, and we all have to strike the same balance between our need for others and our need for ourselves alone.

∗ The Interlocking Overlappers—and Some Further Thoughts on the "Power Situation"

1 9 5 6

C. WRIGHT MILLS is a distinguished American sociologist who finds American society as presently organized an inferior piece of work. In *The Power Elite,* he says that our political life is managed by "crackpot realists" who have "constructed a paranoid reality all their own." What these men do, at home and abroad, is crazy. Almost nothing about our civilization, a term he would find unwarranted, seems admirable to him. American democracy is form without substance. American culture is jejune, inane. American education? Nothing more or less than a racket to train, and/or condition, people for industry, commerce, or the state at public expense. He will not even praise our technology—he says they make better things in Germany and England. From bottom to top, as Mills sees it, American life is pretty much of a fraud. The American public is rapidly turning into a jellied American "mass." The people nowadays exist only to be manipulated. Mills is certain he knows who does the manipulating, and how, and why. The "power elite" runs the country. It is "an interlocking directorate" drawn from among the leading figures in three spheres: the corporate, the political, and the military. It is "an intricate set of overlapping cliques [who] share decisions having at least national consequences. In so far as national events are decided, the power elite are those who decide them." He is persuaded that all the really important "events" are "decided."

254

As a sociologist, Mills is scornful of ideology, which he regards as a minor function of "position" and "interest." He insists that he is not constructing an ideological system of his own but merely a method of analysis. Nevertheless, he may be thought of, at least in terms of one of his own functions, as a reviser of Marxism. Some men hunger for theory as for salt, and those who do and yet see the inadequacies of Marxism will find in Millsism a doctrine that satisfies many of their yearnings. Although Mills offers it not as an explanation of all historical reality but merely of the present reality in the United States, it imposes order on seeming chaos; it provides a key to the mysteries, a plot for the story, a dramatis personae. He nourishes the precious sense of victimization. His world, like Marx's, is riven. It consists of the shearers and the shorn, the exploiters and the exploited, those who have and those who are had. The slaves are pretty much the same, but the masters are different—or, at any rate, more varied in function and origin. Mills thinks the Marxist term "ruling class" won't do for our time. " 'Class' is an economic term; 'rule' a political one. The phrase . . . thus contains the theory that an economic class rules politically." He thinks the contained theory is two-thirds wrong for the United States at the present time. It leaves out the political and military orders, which are of roughly equal importance. Anyway, the members of his "interlocking directorate" are "commanders of power unequalled in human history."

Millsism offers no comforting dialectic. It offers explanation but no remedy, even through bloody revolution. Unlike Marx, Mills perceives no significant amount of social tension. If there ever was a "struggle," it is all over now. He thinks that the "mass" is intuitively and quite cynically aware of "the power situation," but it is not greatly troubled by its awareness. It is not in revolt. The conservative fears of de Tocqueville and Ortega y Gasset were unfounded. "The bottom of this society," he says, "is politically fragmented . . . and increasingly powerless. . . . [The] masses in their full development are sovereign only in some plebiscitarian moment of adulation to an elite as authoritative celebrity." I think that by this last sentence he means that the people are given the illusion of sovereignty by being allowed to vote for President Eisenhower every four years and by being kept up to date on the doings of Rita Hayworth and Grace Kelly. All this is demoralizing.

I believe that Mills' book is at its core mistaken. I also believe it is symptomatic and important. It has some solid merits, and these must be acknowledged. By far the greater part of *The Power Elite* is descriptive. There is, as Daniel Bell has pointed out, a Balzacian texture in Mills' accounts of the lives of representative Americans. When Mills is not choked with indignation and disgust, he commands a strong and vivid satirical style. Moreover, I think he is fairly close to being right in his judgments of where the power centers of our society are. He is on solid ground in arguing that there is an almost autonomous political directorate in this country today. It is not as unified as he seems to think, but on what he calls the "big decisions," the big men of rival factions hammer out agreements that give continuity to major foreign and domestic policies. (Less hostile critics sometimes point to this fact as a reflection of the "stability" of American society, an expression of "consensus.") I am not so sure that the military can be set apart from either the corporate or political elements as easily as Mills thinks they can, but there is no doubt that in the postwar years, the military establishment has played a huge and at least semiautonomous role in American life and government. I believe that the power elite has some important members Mills does not recognize—drawn in part from the "public" he believes has disappeared, in part from the intelligentsia he regards as powerless, in part from the technological and managerial classes. Still and all, Mills' view of the basic elements in the power structure is, I think, reasonably sound. What seem to me to be absurd and destructive are his assumptions and conclusions about what power is and how it is wielded. He devotes relatively little space to this, but it is a central matter, and when he does deal with it he is forthright. His view is summed up in this passage:

The course of events in our time depends more on a series of human decisions than on any inevitable fate. . . . As the circle of those who decide is narrowed, as the means of decision are centralized, and the consequences of decisions become enormous, then the course of great events often rests upon the decisions of determinable circles. . . . [The] pivotal moment does arrive, and at that moment small circles do decide or fail to decide. In either case, they are an elite of power. The dropping of A-bombs over Japan was such a moment; the decision on Korea was such a moment; the confusion about Quemoy and Matsu, as well as before Dien Bien Phu were such moments; the sequence of maneuvers which involved the United States in World War II was such a "moment." Is it not true that the history of our times is composed of such moments?

It is indeed true that the history of our time is quite largely composed of such "moments." They are not the whole story, of course; history is also the passage of time, the accumulation of knowledge and anxieties, the development of creeds and institutions, and everlasting change—some of it planned and intended and more or less directed, some of it wholly unforeseen and probably wholly unforeseeable. But the moments Mills mentions (all of them, interestingly, having to do with war) were important and they were pivotal. Is it reasonable, though, to believe, as Mills does, that "the warlords, the corporate chieftains, and [the] political directorate" determined the American responses? I think it is demonstrably unreasonable—except just possibly in the case of our entry into World War II, an "event" made of such an "uncountable totality" of other events (to use a phrase of Sir Isaiah Berlin's) that it would be as difficult to demonstrate that the "decision" was not made by a particular group as to determine that it was. The other instances reveal, I think, the essential inadequacy of Mills' doctrine, and I shall attempt to show how they do so:*

* The literature of these events has, of course, grown enormously in the five years since this piece was published in *The Progressive*. In the late fall of 1961, for example, we have had yet another account of the decision to use the atomic bomb—Robert C. Batchelder's *The Irreversible Decision*. A few months back, Sherman Adams' *First-Hand Report*, discussed elsewhere in this volume, appeared with some new material on Quemoy and Matsu and Dienbienphu. I have not read everything in the field, but I have read quite a bit, and I have come upon nothing that would cause me to alter the substance of my original comments on Mills' four "moments." In the passages dealing with them, I have not used any of the new material—either to qualify what I wrote in 1956 or to amplify it by documentation. For my purposes here, the original text suffices. The paragraph on Hiroshima and Nagasaki is based on my reading of the written history available at the time

HIROSHIMA AND NAGASAKI: In the first place, very few members of the power elite knew there was any atomic bomb to be dropped or not dropped. Harry Truman has taken full personal as well as Constitutional responsibility for the decision. Though it must have been about as solitary an act of mind and will as any in history, we can acknowledge that no man ever acts wholly on his own—wholly unaffected, that is, by his immediate environment and by all that has gone into the making of the human being he is. In this case, Truman received a certain amount of advice from an *ad hoc* committee organized by Henry L. Stimson, a certifiable member of the power elite. (Stimson was an "overlapping clique" within his own person, being part of the corporate power of the nation, part of the political directorate, and, as Secretary of War and a former officer, a high figure in the military command.) Also, Winston Churchill and Joseph Stalin, a pair of foreigners, were consulted and ratified the decision in advance. (It is not clear that Stalin knew what he was ratifying, though if we are to believe Senator McCarthy, he knew at least as much about the atomic bomb as Harry Truman.) Truman, however, reports in his memoirs that he was decisively influenced by the opinions of the nuclear physicists whom he consulted or who were consulted in his behalf by the Secretary of War. According to Mills, physicists as intellectuals are powerless in our society and physicists as technicians are mere servants of the corporations and the military establishment. It is possible, to be sure, that Truman is no more accurate an appraiser of the origins of his own behavior than Mills is. But he is surely a bit closer to the source, and in the absence of compelling evidence to the contrary, one must, it seems to me, accept his account. At all odds, the first atomic bombs were dropped on the authority of one man who was the beneficiary of very sketchy advice from a handful of other men, most of whom were not, in Mills' terms, "commanders of power." In the nature of the case, it was quite impossible for any "intricate set of overlapping cliques" to have had much to do with this huge decision.

I wrote. In discussing the other events, I have drawn mainly on information I acquired as a reporter in Washington when the "events" (I recoil from the word but use it for want of a better) occurred.

KOREA: The decision to intervene was made in the course of a few hours by a very few men, hastily assembled to meet an unanticipated crisis. Earlier, some of the same men had determined that the national interest did *not* call for the defense of Korea. Some of those involved in both decisions could be regarded as important agents of the power elite. (There were no representatives of corporate power whose advice was asked or who proffered it unasked.) Those members of the government* who met with President Truman on June 24, 1950 were not in the beginning agreed on what the American response should be. Some differences were overcome during the meeting, some were tabled. The President again exercised a good deal of independent judgment, which is what a President is paid to do. It is interesting to note that the "decision" could not really have been an effective one if it had not been for a circumstance which the power elite could not possibly have arranged—the providential boycott by the Soviet Union of the United Nations Security Council.

QUEMOY AND MATSU: Mills speaks of the "confusions" about Quemoy and Matsu as a "moment" of "decision." In another passage, he makes it clear that what he has in mind are the feeble commitments the Eisenhower administration made to the Chinese Nationalists early in 1955—in our treaty with the Republic of China and in Public Law 4, a Congressional resolution that authorized the President to take certain actions in the Formosa Straits which he was already empowered to take by the Constitution. The situation, briefly, was this: to honor campaign pledges and to appease the Asia-firsters, the administration had

---

* It is, I think, worth pointing out that they were agreed on the general framework of policy and strategy. The guidelines had been laid down in the late forties by the Policy Planning Commission, headed by George F. Kennan, whom Mills describes in *The Power Elite* as "a distinguished student of foreign affairs." Most members of Kennan's staff were public servants with highly acceptable credentials as intellectuals. They may, of course, have tailored their own thinking to that of the power elite. I am rather inclined to think that they, with the help of the President, forced their views upon the interlocking directorate. After General MacArthur's recall in 1951, there was a fearful brawl over the ends of American policy, and the power elite seemed split—and not split down the middle, for there was surely more corporate, political, and military power for General MacArthur than against him. He lost. The views developed by Kennan and his staff prevailed.

to put out some loud and lofty rhetoric affirming its undying solidarity with Chiang Kai-shek; to honor reason and to avoid outraging our allies, the rhetoric had to be gutted, and it was. The treaty and the resolution committed the United States to the defense of Formosa, as the home and habitation of the Republic of China, and pledged the Republic of China not to attempt the reconquest of its former home and habitation on the mainland. (In the treaty, Chiang agreed to "refrain from the threat or use of force in any manner inconsistent with the purposes of the United Nations.") As for Quemoy and Matsu, they would be defended by the United States only in the event, according to Public Law 4, that an attack on them had been determined, by the President of the United States, to be preliminary to an attack on Formosa.

Many members of the power elite, including all but one of the Joint Chiefs of Staff, tried to argue the President into a more militant position. They failed. The reality is quite different from what Mills supposes it to be. The basic decision taken by this government was to make an act of disengagement sound like a declaration of engagement. Once again, it was, or seemed to most people at the time to be, a victory of the political arm of the power elite over its military and corporate arms.

DIENBIENPHU: Here is perhaps the oddest case of all. There is not much doubt that the power elite, to the extent that it had a single will and a single voice, wished the United States to intervene in Indochina, at the time of this critical battle.* At one time or another, the President, the Vice-President, the Secretary of State, and, again, all but one of the Joint Chiefs favored an effort to rescue the French. Among influential people generally, only a few were opposed, openly at any rate. Yet the decision that really counted was the one taken against the better judgment of the Washington representatives of the power elite—to stay out of the war.

"It was no historical necessity," Mills writes, "but an argument within a small circle of men that defeated Admiral [Arthur

* I am speaking here of the political and military branches. On matters of strategy the corporate branch often seems to lack a position. I doubt if it had one on Dienbienphu.

W.] Radford's proposal to bomb troops before Dien Bien Phu."
"Historical necessity" is a term Mills constantly uses to cover any
determinism or antideterminism that may be opposed to his
own view. He uses it as a punching bag—the way certain ma-
terialist and positivist philosophers use "idealism" or "romanti-
cism." In this context, I suppose he means that it was not historically inevitable that things turned out as they did and that an
"argument" turning on calculations of power, logistics, the
strengths and weaknesses of alliances, and strategic priorities
settled the question. To those of us who tried to understand the
decisions and indecisions of the time, however, it appeared that
"public opinion," a force of negligible significance in the Millsian
system, was of decisive importance. At the start of the controversy,
not only the technicians of diplomacy and military power
within the administration, but a Congressional majority seemed
agreeable to the administration view. Some members supported
it publicly; hardly any opposed it. Then John Foster Dulles went
off to Europe to see what arrangements he could make with the
British and the French. During his absence, something that can,
for the purposes of the moment anyway, be described as "public
opinion" began to take shape. The House of Representatives
went into a brief recess. Congressmen returning from the prov-
inces began to report that the people were anything but keen on
saving Indochina from the Communists. Within a week or ten
days, it became almost impossible to find a congressman who
favored sending "American boys" to Indochina to smash Communism there. Admiral Radford was as much in favor of intervention as he had ever been, but now not even Senator William
F. Knowland, of California, could be induced to declare flatly
in favor of it. The affair began to take on some new dimensions
as a result of the difficulties Dulles met with in London and
Paris, but it is doubtful if these affected the basic American
decision. What did affect it, so far as one could gather in Washington, was the attitude of what Mills describes as the "atomized
and submissive" masses, who, Congressmen discovered while sniffing at the grass roots during the Easter holidays, were not at all
well disposed to the idea of a shooting war in Indochina. It was
recalled by shrewd Republican politicians that the Eisenhower

administration's one great popular triumph had been in negotiating an end to the Korean war. The same administration would lose the political advantage thus gained if it led the country into another bloody jungle war. The masses, it seemed, were on this occasion sovereign.

Mills anticipates his critics and dismisses most of them as obscurantists who see "the power situation . . . as a romantic confusion." Behind his use of "romantic," there seems to lie the implication that those who see "the power situation" as characterized by confusion rather want to see it that way and find history more entertaining and less demanding—intellectually and morally—when they can regard it as mysterious. He charges them with believing that "history goes on behind men's backs." For my own part, I find the power situation confusing but hardly romantic. It is confusing because it is obviously compounded of many elements which are difficult to isolate, classify, and weigh. I do not believe that history goes on behind men's backs—if "behind men's backs" means beyond their field of vision. History is the life of the community of men within the framework of time. It goes on all about us and among us, sometimes within our sight and comprehension, sometimes—especially when crucial "decisions" are being made by those with the power to make them—beyond them. The truth about it is not, I should think, undiscoverable. I believe with E. H. Carr that "human actions have causes which are in principle ascertainable." But I believe that the truth remains largely undiscovered, largely unascertained, and it seems to me no more obscurantist to say this than to say that the laws of the psyche continue to be somewhat mysterious. Whether they will remain that way forever or only for a short while longer is not the point. The point is that they are in large part mysterious today—and so is history, if for no other reason than that the causes of human action that "are in principle ascertainable" have yet to be fully ascertained.

It seems to me that it is the cocksure approach of people like Mills that is basically obscurantist and hostile to the spirit of objective inquiry and the traditions of the questing intellect. Mills takes a series of perceptions—some of them very sharp and useful—about American society and fashions them into a law of that society's operations. No attempt is made at an empirical testing of the law's soundness—of its value, that is to say, in accounting for observable developments. He does not examine the "decisions" he cites to show us how they reveal the decisive influence of the power elite. All that he tells us is that "a compact and powerful elite . . . does now prevail in America." If it "prevails," then, it follows, according to Mills' logic, that the "big decisions" are attributable to it. But of course it is by no means proved that it does "prevail" in this sense. The only possible way of determining whether it is what Mills says it is would be by examining the decisions themselves, which Mills never does. I would suppose that if a man working in any of the physical sciences offered a doctrine of cause and effect in this way, he would be hooted out of the academies.

Mills denies that he has come up with a "conspiracy theory," but I think that this is exactly what he has done. It is a more sophisticated conspiracy theory than most and has more elements of plausibility than most. Nevertheless, it begins as a search for the responsible, accountable parties in society (this only after Mills argues to his own satisfaction that in our time, if not in all others, "the course of events . . . depends on a series of human decisions"), and its mood is that of a highly intellectual lynching bee. It is interesting to note that practically all of the "events" and "decisions" Mills brings up in this book are ones of which he disapproves. Conspiracy theories are invariably the work of people concerned almost to the point of obsession with the "bad" developments in human history—those who seem to have, in Richard Hofstadter's words, "a commitment to hostility." So far as I know, no general theory of accountability has ever been developed to explain the achievements of a civilization.* And none is the work of people who have much sense of

* Marxism may be regarded as an exception, but Marxism is not in any meaningful sense a conspiracy theory. Marx's "classes" do not "decide" or plot or plan or do anything, but behave as the pressures of history compel them to behave. It has been interesting to note that when Mills, some years after writing *The Power Elite,* became enthusiastic about Fidel Castro's Cuba, he tended to lapse into traditional Marxism. He saw no "interlocking directorates" or "overlapping cliques" bring Castro to power or maintain him there. He described the Castro revolution not as a plot but as a move-

being themselves implicated in history—as Mills would be, for example, if my analysis of Dienbienphu is reasonably sound. There is in their work no acknowledgment of the possibility that, as Dr. Bruno Bettelheim has put it, "maybe it [is] not society that created all these difficulties in man but rather the hidden, inner, contradictory nature of man that created these difficulties for society." I do not, of course, suggest that this is a viable doctrine for a sociologist or historian seeking to understand the "power situation" in the United States. I do, however, think that it is exceedingly difficult to write very helpfully about any aspect of the human comedy or the human tragedy if one regards oneself not as part of it but merely as a member of a small captive audience.

Mills repeatedly speaks of the "irresponsibility" of the people who decide. He does not mean that they are as individuals capricious or flip or reckless when they are dealing with matters of life or death. He means, if I understand him, that they exercise power with little of value in the way of tradition or philosophy to guide them. "It is not," he says, "the barbarous irrationality of dour political primitives that is the American danger; it is the respected judgments of Secretaries of State, the earnest platitudes of Presidents, the fearful self-righteousness of sincere young American politicians from Sunny California. These men have replaced mind with platitude, and the dogmas by which they are legitimated are so widely accepted that no counterbalance of mind prevails against them. They have replaced the responsible interpretation of events with the disguise of events by a maze of public relations." He has John Foster Dulles, Dwight Eisenhower, and Richard M. Nixon clearly in mind, but he is as contemptuous of their immediate predecessors and would be as contemptuous of any imaginable successors.

Is he right in maintaining that they exercise their power within "the American system of organized irresponsibility"? I think he is very much in error. I believe that an examination of the crucial decisions reveals a high degree of responsibility in the

ment of restless, surging humanity struggling to fulfill its needs and aspirations. In fairness, though, he claimed no theoretical jurisdiction beyond the United States.

"interpretation of events." I do not exclude the decision to drop the first atomic bombs. That act may be one for which the future, if it gets the chance, may damn Harry Truman and all the soldiers and scientists around him and all of us who were part of a society which was not thoroughly outraged. Still, I do not think the act was irresponsible. The President knew, in the first place, that he was making a decision of considerable moral significance. He could not have measured its significance as clearly as some of us now do, for the decision was taken in the last days of the preatomic age. He made the decision as a military commander, responsible for the lives of millions of young Americans summoned to risk death in the greatest war in history. As commander in chief, it was his duty to seek estimates of the probable saving of American lives and the probable loss of Japanese lives. As a human being, it was his duty to weigh values of a different sort—the effect of this act of war on the nature of the peace it might bring, the effect of a victory achieved this way on his country's standing in the world after victory, even the problem of whether it was right at all to see the problem in these terms.

Nothing that I have read about Harry Truman's decision suggests that he was heedless of these considerations. He approached his awful dilemma soberly, or as soberly as it was possible for a man like Harry Truman to be at a time when the world was awash with blood. He consulted others. In the nature of this peculiar case, he could not avail himself of all the wisdom in the country or the world. But he did, with proper humility, consult men whose judgment he regarded as in many respects superior to his own. Of their number, only a very few, perhaps five per cent, counseled him not to use the bomb at all. A few suggested he give the Japanese a decent warning; others, however, thought that this might result in an even greater loss of life than an unannounced use of the weapon. In any case, he sought advice of this sort, and then he acted. I cannot see how he, or those around him, can be accused of "irresponsibility"—or of having constructed about themselves a "paranoid reality."

The Truman administration took us to war in Korea. The Eisenhower administration took us to "the brink of war" in the

Formosa Straits and in Indochina and then withdrew. It happens to be my personal view that both administrations exercised sound and mature judgment in these three affairs. I think, in short, that the government was "right," and I set this down because I realize that a man who regards a judgment as a sound one could hardly be expected to regard it as irresponsible. But I think that I also understand the case against all these decisions, and I think the issue can be limited to responsibility alone. Those who decided to intervene in Korea believed that intervention, if it were successful, would prevent similar aggressions and that nonintervention would encourage them. A good deal of the confusion about the Korean war exists because the factor of *time* is not given enough weight. It was true that American policy, before June 22, 1950, held the Republic of Korea to be outside our system of national security; that policy was abruptly reversed. But when the North Koreans attacked across the thirty-eighth parallel, it was the first aggression by a Communist army in the history of the cold war. Military pressure had been used before, as it was to be used again. Communist armies had fought non-Communist armies in wars of an essentially civil nature. Communist armies brought about the downfall of presumably sovereign governments by their mere presence as occupying forces. But this was the first assault against an international boundary. Thus, it was less Korea as a tract or even the Seoul government as the seat of a sovereign power to which policies and strategies did or did not apply—it was the Republic of Korea as the place where Communist power was seeking to determine whether it could succeed by armed conquest.

There were other considerations, to be sure. The "prestige" of the United Nations appeared to be involved. Though Korea was outside our "defense perimeter," the country was one for which we had shown a great deal of concern. I can well understand believing that none of those things justified our presence in Korea and that, in fact, it was not justified at all. Walter Lippmann is only one of many estimable people who have taken this view. But again, I cannot see the decision to intervene as anything but one taken with a high degree of responsibility.

Indeed, it seems to me that those members of the power elite who made the decision took a lofty and noble view of their responsibilities in this world. And a remarkably disinterested view as well. It is probable that on the night of June 22, 1950, they were not fully aware of the fact that they were leading the country into the most hated war in its history and that this might cost them and their party the control of the country. But all politicians and most statesmen know that all wars of even short duration are hated and that they were not marching down any highway to political success. If anything, their action was a bit too disinterested in this regard, for a large part of the case against the Korean war—seen from this perspective in time—was that it was so divisive and so productive of hatreds and bitterness that it might very well have been better never to have become involved in it. To a degree, these were the considerations that led to the Eisenhower administration's avoidance of commitments in Quemoy and Matsu and in Indochina. Other things were different as well: the Eisenhower administration, for all of Dulles's rhetoric, was more reluctant to assume initiatives of any sort than the Truman administration, and neither Formosa nor the French regime in Indochina could be regarded as having so clear a title to the disputed territories as the Seoul government, with its U.N. support, had in South Korea. But I am talking not about the problems but about the quality of responsibility in their eventual resolution. I am not an admirer of the general judgment of those in the Eisenhower administration who were charged with official responsibility in these matters, but I fail to see how they can be faulted for "irresponsible" decisions.

And, as a matter of fact, it seems to me that it is probably a general rule in our society—and perhaps in most societies—that what are thought of as the "big decisions"—those that are almost immediately crucial, those that involve the nation as a whole and are known to the world while they are being made or immediately afterward—are more often than not "responsible" and, within the limitations of the time and the men who seem to dominate the time, statesmanlike. There are exceptions, of course (Munich would come to mind and Eisenhower's determination of the adequacy of our scientific efforts), but if I were a C. Wright Mills and were seeking to show the unhappy influence of the interlocking directorate of corporate, political, and military leaders, I think I would look not to large decisions but to small ones and to the whole tone and temper of our society at the present time. But that is another story, and not the one his work compels us to deal with.

✳ Life and Death and Sentience

1 9 5 7

ARTHUR KOESTLER's *Reflections on Hanging* and Glanville Williams' *The Sanctity of Life* are notable works of the humane intelligence. Koestler's book is a tract against capital punishment. It has attained historic importance in England, where it was serialized in the London *Observer*. It was the leading abolitionist text in the public and Parliamentary debates that led to a two-year moratorium on hanging in England and came very close to ending it forever. Koestler pleads his case, which would be as pertinent in the forty-two of our states that allow capital penalties as it is in England, with force and fervor; the book has none of the mere cleverness one often finds in his novels and none of the slipperiness one finds in so much of his political writing. It is not, though, as interesting or as brilliant a piece of work as Williams'. In a sense, Williams' book runs counter to Koestler's. Koestler is opposed to killing by due process of law. Williams says nothing about capital punishment; his book is, among other things, a plea for modifications of Anglo-Saxon law that would lead to a more liberal view of a number of practices that are regarded by many as partaking of homicide—for example, euthanasia, suicide, contraception, abortion, and sterilization. The laws that deal with life-and-death matters only codify certain moral and religious attitudes—not necessarily the prevailing ones—toward these grave issues, and it is to these attitudes that Williams addresses himself. He brings to the task a great store of knowledge, a fastidious logic, and style of unfaltering clarity.

In his polemic, Koestler uses every argument but one against

269

capital punishment; he never invokes the Sixth Commandment or holds that the destruction of a human spirit is too great a responsibility for any temporal authority. He never says that killing is wrong in itself. What he does say is that hanging is barbarous and sickening; that electrocution and the gas chamber are no less brutal and repellent; that the death penalty is not a deterrent to crime; that guiltless men are sometimes put to death by law, and that execution degrades any society that tolerates it and every judge who orders it. In the case of murder, he says, it is a punishment that conspicuously fails to fit the crime; murder is almost always the work of the deranged and is almost never a planned pursuit—such as, say, larceny—of the criminally bent. (The United States may be an exception. We have had killers who were professional in every sense of the word.) It is in some ways remarkable that his book should have had so great an impact when it makes no use of the argument one would expect to weigh most heavily on people reared in the Judaeo-Christian tradition. Yet only once is it suggested that capital punishment is inherently wrong, a *malum in se,* regardless of the technique, regardless of the victim's guilt, regardless of social or penological considerations, and that suggestion occurs not in Koestler but in the introduction for American readers, by Professor Edmond Cahn, of the New York University Law School. Professor Cahn cites a statement by the late Judge Jerome Frank that the frequency of judicial error relieves the opponents of capital punishment of the need to fall back on the argument that "no man may morally play God." This argument might be adduced, Judge Frank said, if we could be sure that every man under sentence of death had committed the crime for which he was paying. "But such a thesis need not be considered," he remarked, with evident relief at having sidestepped an awkward dispute, "for it assumes the impossible. Experience teaches the fallibility of court decisions. . . . How dare any society take the chance of ordering the judicial homicide of an innocent man?"

The truth is that the modern mind would have a hard time arguing anything on the premise that human life is sacred. This is not because it disbelieves in sacredness or because it holds, with Mr. Justice Holmes, that the sanctity of life "is a purely municipal ideal of no validity outside the jurisdiction," which is a way of saying that the sanctity of life is simply a legal rather than an ethical concept. And it is not because life is held in low esteem; the secular mind, which may see death as an everlasting nothingness, can build a mystique of earthly existence in which far more value is placed on the privilege of inhaling and exhaling than most theologies have ever attached to it. But it would be almost fatuous, in the middle of the twentieth century, for even the most devout theologian to say that man cannot or should not play God—provided he means that man should not interfere with those processes that in earlier centuries were held to be reserved to Providence. Man must play God, for he has acquired certain Godlike powers, though not, because it is beyond the purview of the criminal law, with the most wonder-working of them all, atomic energy. Science has put into our hands—and politics has required us to grasp firmly—instruments that force a human judgment on whether or not the entire race is to be executed; even in benign employment, these instruments can affect the very image of man many millennia hence, and, for that matter, the duration of all life. In a less awesome—but awesome enough—way, modern medicine has been usurping prerogatives once held to be God's alone. It has learned to cheat death not merely by the prolongation of life but by calling men back to life after several hours on the other shore. The judge who orders an execution is no more guilty of playing God than the doctor who, having decided that a human being has been summoned to eternity too soon, restores him to the world of time and suffering and sin. Hanging may be more offensive, but it is not more presumptuous. We have control over creation, too, and are more and more in a position to determine not only who shall die and when but who shall be born and when. If it is Godlike to cut a life or a death short, it is hardly less Godlike to arrange for a woman innocent of adultery and even wholly chaste to nourish in her womb and bear a child of whom she is not the "natural" mother and of whom her husband, if she has one, is not in any sense the father. The "natural" father, in fact, could very well be a man who has died years before his transplanted and refrigerated sperm fertilized the ovum.

In making his argument, Williams accepts Bertrand Russell's assertion that moral progress consists of a widening of the boundaries of human sympathy. That definition leaves much undefined. Is sympathy to be forever widened, until there is no lack of it anywhere? Does sympathy mean toleration? "Moral progress" has a metallic ring, and it is doubtful that men as perceptive as Koestler and Williams could find much satisfaction in being described as "morally progressive." But Russell's concept does illustrate the basic distinction between Koestler and Williams. By a literal application of the concept, Koestler qualifies easily for a place in the moral vanguard; he is begging mercy, the active stage of sympathy, for murderers. Williams' plea would be more difficult to justify, for the world is full of people of unassailable morality who would say that he is really asking us to withhold sympathy from many human beings whom our laws now protect. He favors the compulsory sterilization of the feeble-minded, the epileptic, and persons with certain hereditary physical defects. He would permit the destruction of grievously malformed infants. He thinks it should be "permissible both morally and legally so to define a human being as to exclude the grosser sports of nature." While he may share Koestler's view that one murder does not justify another, he would have the criminal law make infanticide a lesser form of homicide—an attitude that plays hob with Russell's dictum, since it could be described as a denial of sympathy to the victim.

Koestler argues against hanging with a revolutionist's ardor and the arid logic of a mere reformer. Minus its rhetoric, which is sometimes quite splendid, his tract is a series of pragmatic propositions of the sort he might work up to oppose anything he chanced to regard as unsound public policy. It cannot, however, be this purely municipal spirit that accounts for the abolitionist passion that has become for him, at least in part, a moral substitute for the Bolshevism that fired his imagination in his youth. (In 1936, he acquired a certain concern with capital punishment when, as a young Communist, he spent three months under sentence of death in one of General Franco's jails.) For while the ending of capital punishment may commend itself to many of us, it is not the kind of crusade that justifies and supports the fervor that moves Koestler. As Koestler himself remarks, the only direct beneficiaries in England are the "thirteen wretches a year" normally sentenced to death. This is but one inhabitant in three million, which is not very much, particularly if one believes that murderers, on the whole, are a poor lot. What, after all, is so important about ending capital punishment? Stricter traffic controls or increased appropriations for cancer research would save many, many more lives, and it seems nonsensical to imply, as Koestler does, that the death penalty compromises before the rest of the world the moral positions of the countries that impose it. (Oddly, the three most humane of modern Western societies—Britain, France, and the United States—are almost the only ones of those societies who still keep the category of capital crime on their books.) Actually, the Sixth Commandment is at the bottom of Koestler's case. The unstated assumption of this worldling's argument is that there is something profane, something supremely wicked about the taking of any human life. Though he advances only the standard municipal claims in support of abolition, one feels that his position would be the same in the face of incontrovertible evidence that hanging is an effective deterrent to murder. Koestler may be a worldling, but his passion has a transcendental base. This situation, as Glanville Williams points out, is not at all uncommon. "Even the modern infidel," he says, "tends to give his full support to the belief that it is our duty to regard all human life as sacred, however disabled or worthless or repellent the individual may be."

Williams, however, does not give his full support to the opposite belief. He, too, may oppose hanging, but he could not do it with Koestler's zeal, for he thinks it is urgent common sense to measure the value of life both qualitatively and quantitatively. Life is feeling and awareness, not mere animation, and the more highly developed the feeling and awareness, the more deserving a particular life is of respect and protection. Life is also the community of the presently living, to whom the problem of numbers—the size of families, for example, or the relation of population to resources—can be of crucial importance. In a general way, Western man acts on these views even when his religions and his criminal laws run contrary to them. We reserve our severest penalties, such as hanging, for those who destroy or tamper with a life that is highly sentient and do not apply them in cases of low degree of sentience. Infanticide has seldom been looked upon as murder; in some societies it has been encouraged, in others it has been tolerated. The destruction of a life in a declining state of sentience is also given a large degree of tolerance. In no Western jurisprudence is it conceivable that a doctor who relieves a dying patient's pain by a dose of anodyne that ends pain forever will suffer the *full* vengeance of the law.

Williams' book is in part an analysis of religious and legal estimates of the value of human life and in part a plea for the frank acceptance of municipal standards. The community of the living is obliged to be concerned with community problems. If life is sentience, then sentience must be respected. Williams would establish a man's right to put an end to what he chooses to regard as his own agony by suicide—the unsuccessful attempt at which is now, preposterously, a crime in most Anglo-Saxon jurisdictions—or by requesting euthanasia. Williams would also preserve the right of the community of the living to limit its numbers and to regulate, as far as possible, its quality by birth control, by sterilization, and by artificial insemination. According to statisticians in whom he has confidence, a *laissez-faire* eugenic, or perhaps even dysgenic, policy is almost bound to lead (through the tendency of the less sentient to be more prolific) to a decline in average intelligence as high as one per cent a generation—and this in a society that is already putting an enormous strain on its reserves of intelligence. In a way, the prospect of a society that took matters of life and death into its own hands as coldly as Williams would have it do is a terrifying one; reading him, one often has the feeling that it would be better and safer if we clung blindly to the simple precepts embodied in our law than if we settled coldly upon the idea that we ourselves are the makers of values. What Williams demonstrates, though, and what the worldling Koestler illustrates, is that the best of our secular minds have treasured life fully as much as the best of our transcendental minds. Who wrote a tract that helped bring an end to hanging in England? Arthur Koestler. A little over a century ago, English children were being hanged for petty thefts, and today there is mercy even for the merciless. And the burden of Glanville Williams' book is that the boundaries of our sympathies for all those who share our state of being should be immensely widened.

✳ The Conscience of Arthur Miller

1 9 5 7

"I WILL PROTECT my sense of myself," Arthur Miller told the House Committee on Un-American Activities when he declined to name some people, mainly writers, he had met at various gatherings presumed by the Committee and by Miller to have been arranged by Communists. He did not invoke the Fifth Amendment. Had he done so, he would probably have escaped any difficulties with the law—though sharp questioning on the possibility of self-incrimination might have denied him this refuge. (Merely to have encountered Communists in the thirties and forties was never held to be incriminating, even in McCarthy's fifties. And Miller had already talked a great deal about his own political past.) Instead, he invoked, in defense of what he claimed was his right to be unresponsive, the First Amendment, which protects freedom of speech and in recent years has also been held to protect the necessary corollary of free speech, free non-speech. "I could not use the name of another person and bring trouble on him," Miller said. The refusal led to a conviction for contempt of Congress. The presiding judge found Miller's motives "commendable" but felt constrained to hold his action legally indefensible.

"I will protect my sense of myself"—legalities aside, this was Miller's basic statement of his own case, as he evidently viewed the matter. As a rule, a writer's sense of himself is to be projected as well as protected. It becomes, through publication (or, in his case, production), a rather public affair. In fact, I think, it was only in a rather narrow meaning of the term that he was protecting any "sense of himself." He was defending, under the

276

threat of a year in jail and a fine of a thousand dollars, his view that it is unmanly and irresponsible and undemocratic and even unpatriotic to be an "informer." Actually, what he saw as the testing of his integrity—the challenge to his "sense of himself"—was a question involving not himself but others. ("I could not use the name of another person . . .") Of himself, of Arthur Miller, noted playwright, he talked freely, not to say garrulously. He chatted, almost gaily, about his views before the war; his views during the war; his views after the war; about the case of Ezra Pound; about Elia Kazan, his collaborator both in left-wing politics and in the theater, who, unlike Miller, had provided the Committee with the "names" by which it sets such great store. He confided his views of Congressional investigations, of the Smith Act, and of just about anything in which the Congressmen showed any interest. When he was asked why he wrote "so morbidly, so sadly," the author of *Death of a Salesman* responded courteously and patiently—rather as if it were the question period following a paid lecture before a ladies' club. His self-esteem was offended only when he was asked to identify others.

Thus, one might say, it was really a social or political ethic that he was protecting, while of his sense of himself he gave freely. In legal terms, this might be a quibble, for there is no reason why a man should not have a right to his own definition of self-respect. In a literary sense, it is not a quibble, for Miller is a writer of a particular sort, and it was in character for him to see things this way. He is, basically, a political, or "socially conscious" writer. He is a fortunate survivor of the thirties, and his values derive mostly from that decade. He is not much of a hand at exploring or exploiting his own consciousness. He is not inward. He is more Ibsen than Strindberg. He writes at times with great power, but not with a style of his own, and those who see his plays can leave them with little or no sense of the author as a man. He is not, in fact, much concerned with individuality of any sort. This is not an adverse judgment; it is a distinction, or an attempt at one. What interests Miller and what he can often convey with force is the crushing impact of society upon its members. His human beings are always on the anvil, awaiting the hammer, and the act that landed him in his present trouble was the attempt to shield two or three of them from the hammer's blow. (It was, of course, a symbolic act, a gesture, for Miller knew very well that the Committee knew all about the men he was asked to identify. It already had their names and didn't need them from him. He could not really shield; he could only assert the shielding principle.) What he was protecting was, in any case, a self-esteem that rested upon a social rule or principle or ethic.

One could almost say that Miller's sense of himself is the fashionable principle that holds "informing" to be the ultimate in human wickedness. It is certainly a recurrent theme in his writing. In *The Crucible,* his play about the Salem witchcraft trials, his own case is so strikingly paralleled as to lend color—though doubtless not truth—to the view that his performance in Washington was a case of life paying art the sincere flattery of imitation. To save his life, John Proctor, the hero, makes a compromise with the truth. He confesses, falsely, to having trafficked with Satan. "Did you see the Devil?" the prosecutor asks him. "I did," Proctor says. He recognizes the character of his act, but this affects him little. "Good, then—it is evil, and I do it," he says to his wife, who is shocked. He has reasoned that a few more years on earth are worth this betrayal of his sense of himself. (It is not to be concluded that Proctor's concession to the mad conformity of the time parallels Miller's testimony, so far as it went, for Proctor had never in fact seen the Devil, whereas Miller had in fact seen Communists, plenty of them. Moreover, Miller did not regard the Communists he had seen as devils.) The prosecutor will not let Proctor off with mere self-incrimination. He wants names; the names of those Proctor has seen with the Devil. Proctor refuses; he does not balk at a self-serving lie, but a self-serving lie that involves others will not cross his lips. He will speak of the Devil but not of the Devil's and his friends. "I speak my own sins," he says, either hyperbolically or hypocritically, since the sins in question are a fiction. "I cannot judge another. I have no tongue for it." He is hanged, a martyr.

In his latest play, *A View from the Bridge,* Miller returns to the theme, this time with immense wrath. He holds that conscience—indeed humanity itself—is put to the final test when a man is asked to "inform." Eddie, a longshoreman in the grip of a terrible passion for his teen-age niece, receives generous amounts of love and sympathy from those around him up to the moment he is beguiled into tipping off the Immigration officers to the illegal presence in his home of a pair of aliens. His lust for the child has had dreadful consequences for the girl herself, for the youth she wishes to marry, and for Eddie's wife. It has destroyed Eddie's sense of himself and made a brute of him. Yet up to the moment he "informs" he gets the therapy of affection and understanding from those he has hurt the most. But once he turns in the aliens, he is lost; he crosses the last threshold of iniquity upon becoming an informer. "In the garbage can he belongs," his wife says. "Nobody is gonna talk to him again if he lives to a hundred."

A View from the Bridge is not a very lucid play, and it may be that in it Miller, for all of his wrath, takes a somewhat less simple view of the problem of the informer than he does in *The Crucible.* There is a closing scene in which he appears to be saying that even this terrible transgression may be understood and dealt with in terms other than those employed by Murder, Incorporated. I think, though, that the basic principle for which Miller speaks is far commoner in Eddie's and our world than it could have been in John Proctor's. The morality that supports it is post-Darwinian. It is more available to those not bound by the Christian view of the soul's infinite preciousness or of the body as a temple than it could have been to pre-Darwinian society. Today, in most Western countries, ethics derive mainly from society and almost all values are social. What we do to and with ourselves is thought to be our own affair and thus not, in most circumstances, a matter that involves morality at all. People will be found to say that suicide, for a man or woman with few obligations to others, should not be judged harshly, while the old sanctions on murder remain. Masturbation, once known as "self-abuse," receives a tolerance that fornication does not quite receive. A man's person and his "sense of himself" are disposable assets, provided he chooses to see things that way; sin is only possible when we involve others. Thus, Arthur Miller's John Proctor was a modern man when, after lying about his relations with the Devil, he said, "God in heaven, what is John Proctor, what is John Proctor? I think it is honest, I think so. I am no saint." It is doubtful if anyone in the seventeenth century could have spoken that way. The real John Proctor surely thought he had an immortal soul, and if he had used the word "honest" at all, it would not have been in the sophisticated, relativistic way in which Miller had him use it. He might have weakened sufficiently to lie about himself and the Devil, but he would surely not have said it was "honest" to do so or reasoned that it didn't really matter because he was only a speck of dust. He was speaking for the social ethic which is Arthur Miller's—and he resisted just where Miller did, at "informing," at supplying "names."

It is, I think, useful to look rather closely at Miller's social ethic and at what he has been saying about the problems of conscience, for circumstances have conspired to make him a leading symbol of the militant, risk-taking conscience in this period. I do not wish to quarrel with the whole of his morality, for much of it I share—as do, I suppose, most people who have not found it possible to accept any of the revealed religions. Moreover, I believe, as Judge Charles F. McLaughlin did, that the action Miller took before the Committee was a courageous one. Nevertheless, I think that behind the action and behind Miller's defense of it there is a certain amount of moral and political confusion. If I am right, then we ought to set about examining it, lest conscience and political morality come to be seen entirely in terms of "naming names"—a simplification which the House Un-American Activities Committee seems eager to foist upon us and which Miller, too, evidently accepts.

A healthy conscience, Miller seems to be saying, can stand anything but "informing." On the one hand, this seems a meager view of conscience. On the other, it makes little political sense and not a great deal of moral sense. Not all "informing" is bad, and not all of it is despised by the people who frequently speak of it as despicable.* The question of guilt is relative. My wife and I, for example, instruct our children not to tattle on one another. But if either of us saw a hit-and-run driver knock over a child or even a dog, we would, if we could, take down the man's license number and turn him in to the police. Even in the case of children, we have found it necessary to modify the rule so that we may be quickly advised if anyone is in serious danger of hurting himself or another. (The social principle again.) Proctor, I think, was not stating a fact when he said, "I cannot judge another"—nor was Miller when he said substantially the same thing. For the decision not to inform *demands* the judging of others. "They think to go like saints," Proctor said in favorable judgment upon those he claimed he could not judge, and Miller must have had something of the sort in mind about the writers he refused to discuss. He reasoned, I have no doubt, that their impulses were noble and that they had sought to do good in the world. We refuse to inform, I believe, either when we decide that those whose names we are asked to reveal are guilty of no wrong or when we perceive that what they have done is no worse than what we ourselves have often done. Wherever their offenses are clearly worse—as in the case of a hit-and-run driver or a spy or a thief—we drop the ban.

If the position taken by Miller were in all cases right, then it would seem wise to supplement the Fifth Amendment with one holding that no man could be required to incriminate another. If this were done, the whole machinery of law enforcement would collapse; it would be simply impossible to determine the facts about a crime. Of course, Congressional committees are not courts, and it might be held that such a rule would be

---

* In the summer of 1961, some juvenile gangs in New York undertook a campaign of guerrilla warfare against the police. Concrete blocks were dropped from roofs and windows on prowl cars; packs of delinquents assaulted foot patrolmen on the streets. The New York *Post,* a liberal newspaper which had supported Arthur Miller in 1957 and which in general had urged that these difficult youths be treated with kindness and consideration, felt that things had gone much too far. It deplored the resistance to "informing" that made it impossible to identify and punish the guilty. "When witnesses," it said in an angry editorial, "who can identify the assailants refuse to cooperate in tracking them down, a serious sickness is in the air." Obviously, it all depends.

useful in their proceedings. It would be useful only if we wished to destroy the investigative power. For we live, after all, in a community, in the midst of other people, and all of our problems—certainly all of those with which Congress has a legitimate concern—involve others. It is rarely possible to conduct a serious inquiry of any sort without talking about other people and without running the risk of saying something that would hurt them. We can honor the conscience that says, "I speak my own sins. I cannot judge another." But those of us who accept any principle of social organization and certainly those of us who believe that our present social order, whatever changes it may stand in need of, is worth preserving cannot make a universal principle of refusing to inform. If any agency of the community is authorized to undertake a serious investigation of any of our common problems, then the identities of others—names—are of great importance. What would be the point of investigating, say, industrial espionage if the labor spies subpoenaed refused to identify their employer? What would be the point of investigating Teapot Dome or Dixon-Yates if it were impossible to learn the identity of the businessmen and government officials involved?

The joker, the source of much present confusion, lies in the matter of seriousness. Miller and his attorneys have argued that the names of the writers Miller had known were not relevant to the legislation on passports the Committee was supposed to be studying. This would certainly seem to be the case, and one may regret that Judge McLaughlin did not accept this argument and acquit Miller on the strength of it. Nevertheless, the argument really fudges the central issue, which is that the Committee wasn't really investigating passport abuses at all when it called Miller before it. It was only pretending to do so. The rambling talk of its members with Miller was basically frivolous, and the Un-American Activities Committee has almost always lacked seriousness. In this case, as Mary McCarthy has pointed out, the most that it wanted from Miller was to have him agree to its procedure of testing the good faith of witnesses by their willingness to produce names, names, names. It was on this ground that Miller was morally justified in his refusal.

Still, Miller's principle, the social ethic he was defending, cannot be made a universal rule or a political right. For it is one thing to say, as I am saying now, that the House Un-American Activities Committee is frivolous and mischievous and politically contemptible and another to assert before the law that such a judgment gives a witness the right to stand mute before the Committee without being held in contempt. As matters stand today, Miller was plainly in contempt. At one point in *The Crucible,* John Proctor is called upon to justify his failure to attend the church of the Rev. Mr. Parris and to have his children baptized by that divine. He replies that he disapproves of the clergyman. "I see no light of God in that man," he says. "That is not for you to decide," he is told. "The man is ordained, therefore the light of God is in him." And this, of course, is the way the world is. In a free society, any one of us may arrive at and freely express a judgment about the competence of duly constituted authority. But in an orderly society, no one of us can expect the protection of the law whenever we decide that a particular authority is unworthy of co-operation. We may stand by the decision, and we may seek the law's protection, but we cannot expect it as a matter of right. There are many courses of action that may have a sanction in morality and none whatever in law. Contempt of Congress is a punishable offense. It is also an attitude that reason and honor may demand of a man. But the fact that Congress or certain Congressmen may seem contemptible does not in itself deprive the institution of its power or its Constitutional function in the American scheme of things.

Yet the law is intended to be, among other things, a codification of morality and of common sense, and we cannot be pleased with the thought that a man should be penalized for an act of conscience—even when his conscience may seem not as fully informed by reason as it ought to be. In a much more serious matter, war, we excuse from participation those who say their consciences will permit them no part in it. One of the reasons the order of American society seems worth preserving is that it allows, on the whole, a free play to the individual's moral judgments. In recent years, Congressional committees have posed the largest single threat to this freedom. The issues have often been confused by the bad faith of witnesses on the one hand and committee members on the other. Still and all, the problem is a real one, as the Miller case shows. If there is not sufficient latitude for conscience in the law, then there ought to be. It would be irresponsible, I think, simply to permit anyone who chooses to withhold whatever information he decides he does not care to impart. The Fifth Amendment seems to go as far as is generally justified in this direction. Changes in committee procedures have often been urged, but it is doubtful if much clarification of a problem such as this can be written into rules and bylaws. The problem is essentially one of discretion and measurement; it is, in other words, the most difficult sort of problem and one of the kind that has, customarily, been dealt with by the establishment of broad and morally informed judicial doctrines.

On August 7, 1958, the Circuit Court of Appeals in Washington unanimously ordered Miller's acquittal. It proclaimed no doctrine on the rights or privileges of conscience. It held that the House Committee had not given the witness sufficient warning of the consequences of failure to respond. Miller was the better off by $500 (this and a suspended sentence of one year were the penalties that had been imposed by the Federal Court) and by a record that shows no conviction for contempt of Congress.

* Communists and Intellectuals

1 9 5 3

INTELLECTUALS seem to delight in blaming their own class or caste or callings for the malfunctionings of society and particularly for its political aberrations and tyrannies. Sometimes their guilt is held to be a product of their apathy and indifference (from Athens to the Weimar Republic), sometimes a product of their excessive or mistaken interventions (from Jacobin France* to the Paris of Julien Benda†). McCarthyism and the developments that have encouraged its lamentable rise and spread have brought on a new wave of intellectual self-reproach in this country. A number of intellectuals are angry at other intellectuals. One of the angriest is the poet and historian Peter Viereck. A couple of years ago, in a widely discussed article entitled "Bloody-Minded Professors" ‡ and more recently in his book *The Shame and Glory of the Intellectuals,* he has given his brethren in the arts, the academies, and the learned professions such a beating about the ears as they have not received in a generation. Viereck would have us believe that a direct cause of the death of freedom in many parts of the postwar world has been the affinity a certain number of Western intellectuals had for Communism in the early thirties and forties. "The misinter-

---

* *Je suis tombe a terre*
  La Nez dans le ruisseau
  C'est la faute a Voltaire,
  C'est la faute a Rousseau.
      (Anon. Circa 1792).
† *La Trahison des Clercs,* 1927.
‡ *Confluence,* September 1951. The title is by courtesy of Winston Churchill, who attributed the rise of Communism to "a gang of ruthless and bloody-minded professors."

pretation of Soviet world-conquest," he says, "by certain of the best educated non-oxen of the West did not merely affect the realm of abstract theory. It affected the course of actual history." Maybe. Since I tend to believe, with Tolstoy as my leading fellow traveler, that in all probability (a word I do not use lightly) everything affects everything in history, I cannot take the view that the "educated non-oxen" played no role at all. But I cannot go along with Viereck, who maintains that American resistance to Soviet aggression would have stiffened far earlier and thus have been far more effective if it had not been for the sapping of morale by intellectuals whose own morale had been sapped by Stalinism and other debilitating influences, many of these latter originating in Bohemia.

Viereck is one of the more passionate and hard-breathing of the modern school of *"C'est la faute a Voltaire,"* but he states the case pretty much as most of them are stating it nowadays, and he does recognize Senator McCarthy for the charlatan he is. I propose to deal critically with some of his contentions. It is probably to my advantage to say that I propose to offer no defense of the American intellectuals who embraced Communism in the thirties or forties or to argue that what they did had no bearing on the course of events. The American intellectuals who succumbed to Stalinism (if I qualify as an intellectual, then I was one of their number for a brief but inexcusably long period in the late thirties*) damaged this country and the idea of a free and open society. They did this, I believe, largely by damaging themselves and by pouring bilge into our culture. But I find it hard—indeed, almost impossible—to believe that they delayed the formulation of the Truman Doctrine or the North Atlantic Treaty, which is Viereck's astonishing and undocumented contention. I find what he says astonishing not because I underestimate the importance of ideas or their purveyors but, I think, because I estimate more highly than he does the world's great weariness at the end of the war and the lag in perception of any society of men—most conspicuously a democratic society. (I would think it worth pointing out that, judging from evidence

* I was an associate editor of the *New Masses*, a Communist weekly, from March 1938 to September 1939.

available at the moment, neither the Truman Doctrine nor
NATO came too late. Both seem to have *worked*.) In any case,
my hope is to set down a few things that may help keep the
record straight.

Viereck writes: "Totalitarianism has had an innate attraction
for an able minority of intellectuals as far back as Plato." And:
"Intellectuals are more susceptible to the totalitarian lure than
any group in America."

"As far back as Plato" is a bit further back than I see any need
to go. And if we are to take Miss Hannah Arendt's word for it,
"totalitarianism" belongs to our time, not Plato's. Viereck,
though, is insisting that there is some connection between what
he regards as the affinity of modern intellectuals for modern
totalitarian systems and the association of intellectuals of the
past with some of its less respectable power systems. No doubt
this is so. I would assume that there has never been a tyranny
that has failed to attract support as well as opposition from a
certain number of intellectuals. Every society, wicked or otherwise, has an organizing principle. Organizing principles are the
concern of intellectuals, wicked or otherwise. Both Voltaire and
Dr. Johnson said that there was no idea—*i.e.*, no organizing
principle—so ridiculous but that it could not find defenders
—*i.e.*, Viereck's "able minority." The notion, though, that there
is any binding tie between, let us say, the scholastics who took
part in the Inquisition and the American intellectuals who have
been Communists, is, in my view, pure scholasticism itself. And
if "totalitarianism" can be stretched to describe illiberal systems
that predate fascism and Communism, then I cannot think of a
time in American or Western history when even a significant
minority of genuine intellectuals have been on the totalitarian
side.

The second of Viereck's statements—that intellectuals of the
recent past have been "more susceptible to the totalitarian lure
than any other group in America"—seems to me somewhat less
than half true. Although a considerable number of American
intellectuals were fetched by Stalinism in the thirties and early
forties, there was a large difference between the quality of minds

attracted in those two periods. I think it is entirely reasonable to say that it was only in the earlier decade that any substantial number of really first-rate people—people, that is, fit to represent the intellectual community—were under Communist influence. And even then, the number who resisted Stalinism probably exceeded the number who succumbed. Those who remained in the Communist movement after the Moscow trials and the Soviet-Nazi pact or who entered it during the war years were for the most part intellectuals *manqué*—people whose intellectual pretensions outran their performances. The Stalinist fever assailed the literary and academic communities in the mid-thirties and had about run its course by 1940; after the Nazi attack on Russia in June 1941, it became mildly epidemic in Hollywood and in certain other centers of the lively arts. There was a small revival in academic and religious circles but nothing to be compared to the movement of the thirties. I can think of a dozen or so fairly serious contributions to American culture made by people under Communist influence in the thirties; I cannot think of one in the forties.

The distinction I have in mind is made by Eric Hoffer in *The True Believer.* "Whence come the fanatics?" Hoffer asks, answering, "Mostly from the ranks of the non-creative men of words. The most significant division of men of words is between those who can find fulfillment in creative work and those who cannot. The creative man of words, no matter how bitterly he may criticize and deride the existing order is actually attached to the present." And Hoffer goes on to point out that it is the uncreative sort who cling to their roles as true believers long after there is nothing left to believe in. It was men of this sort, barren and bitter, who continued to lend themselves to Communism in the forties and who, in considerably diminished numbers, do so today. They represent little apart from their own inadequacies.*

* I believe I overlooked another crucial distinction. The noncreative men of words did constitute a large manpower pool for the Communists, but dupes also came in large numbers from the ranks of intellectuals whose principal currency was something other than words. I am thinking, on the one hand, of scientists like Klaus Fuchs and Bruno Pontecorvo and, on the other, of artists like Pablo Picasso and David Siqueiros. It would be foolish to speak of such men as intellectuals *manqué*. They simply come from differ-

In the thirties, there were at least two totalitarian lures. The one that seemed to pose the greater threat to freedom and decency had no intellectual following at all in this country. On the contrary, American intellectuals, almost to a man, abhorred fascism, and if a number of them lent themselves to a tyranny quite as evil, it was in large measure their loathing of fascism that led them to do so. This did not justify or exonerate them. Many of our sins are functions of our virtues, and often these are the very worst kind. But the fact remains—and the present generation ought to have a clear understanding of it—that it was precisely when Communism appeared to be in militant opposition to totalitarianism that its attracting powers were greatest; and the point at which intellectuals in large numbers abandoned it was as a rule the point at which it became clear to them that Communism was itself totalitarian.*

Viereck says that American intellectuals, in 1953, "have still not rejected . . . the most successful Communist hoax ever perpetrated: the confusion of criminal deeds with free thought." And he speaks of "the literary defenders of [Alger] Hiss, [Judith] Coplon, and the eleven convicted Communist leaders" —as though there exists some school or sizable bloc of literary people that can thus be characterized.

So far as I know, Alger Hiss is the only one of those Viereck mentions who has had any defenders who could reasonably be described as "literary." Only the Communist press, which is not literary and often is not even literate, has defended the Communist leaders convicted under the Smith Act. (It has had little to say about Hiss and nothing to say, I believe, about Miss Coplon.) There is only one case I am aware of—that of Julius

ent intellectual realms. Their knowledge and gifts in dealing with social and political ideas may be as underdeveloped as those of the verbally noncreative of whom Hoffer spoke. There were more illustrious members of the group I overlooked abroad than in this country, but this country was not lacking in them in the forties.

* A history of defections would be told largely in terms of the events that revealed totalitarian drives: the Kronstadt Rebellion, the banishment of Leon Trotsky, the enforced famines of the early thirties, the Moscow trials, the Soviet-Nazi pact, the Stalinist pogroms of the early fifties, the crushing of the East German and Hungarian revolts.

and Ethel Rosenberg—in which it could be maintained that "the confusion of criminal deeds with free thought" had anything to do with sympathy for the accused. It is curious that Viereck overlooks it. To be sure, the demonstrations for the Rosenbergs took the form of protests against the death penalty. Some of those who wished the Rosenbergs spared may have had genuine doubts about their guilt or the fairness of their trial. But in a good many cases, one can be sure, the doubts as to guilt arose from the confusion of which Viereck speaks. And in some cases, of course, there was neither confusion nor doubt, but a conviction that the "criminal deed" was fathered by noble thoughts.

So far as the others are concerned, I know of no defense of them in their role as Communist agents. I think that Viereck himself is confusing disapproval of the Smith Act under which the Communist leaders were convicted with sympathy for the politics of those defendants. I happen myself to believe that they were convicted for what might best be described as a malevolent exercise of free thought and not for anything that in sound usage or American law deserves to be called a "conspiracy." But disapproval of the law need not breed sympathy for its victims.

It is a fact that a large part of the American intellectual community refused for some time to entertain seriously even the *possibility* that Alger Hiss could have been guilty as charged, and there are still people who cannot bring themselves to confront the formidable evidence the government brought forth. But Viereck confuses *disbelief* in Hiss's guilt with *sympathy* for the crime of which he was accused. (I am putting aside as a technicality the fact that he was indicted for perjury rather than, because of protection by the statute of limitations, espionage.) This, to be sure, does not invalidate Viereck's charge that many of Hiss's defenders were, as John Dos Passos put it, parties to the unlovely spectacle of "the moral lynching of Whittaker Chambers." Those people, most of whom knew Hiss not as a man but as a symbol of what they thought of as their own nicely ordered world, were smug and prideful in their own values, and those values got in the way of their understanding of evil.

But their inability to believe that Hiss had been a spy was a very different thing from defending him *as* a spy, and it is the kind of difference that one is distressed to see a serious historian not make. It was not because many people sympathized with Communist agents that they defended Hiss and reviled Chambers; it was because they thought Hiss had been unjustly accused of being so loathsome a thing as a spy—and accused, as it happened, by a man who owned up to having been one. They felt, most of them, that Hiss's virtue was as secure as their own because Hiss happened to be peculiarly one of their own. Most of them saw Chambers not as an anti-Communist but as a Communist apostate, and it was almost as much his having once been a Communist spy as his current state of apostasy that turned them against him before they had weighed his testimony. What worked in Hiss's favor, what bred incredulity about his guilt, was the gentility of his background and his associations: Harvard, Oliver Wendell Holmes, Jr., old-line law offices, John Foster Dulles, the Carnegie Endowment, and success. It was not the destructive, revolutionary instincts he appealed to but the deeply bourgeois ones.

Viereck is almost at one with the Yahoos in identifying Communism with the avant garde. American intellectuals, he says, "naturally know best the society they have studied best. . . . This is a society seen through the colored glasses of a literary (at first nonpolitical) anti-bourgeois crusade." He goes on to speak of the "familiar blend of an 'aristocratic' snob in art and a fellow-traveling 'progressive' in politics," and he associates the attitudes of T. S. Eliot, Ezra Pound, and Henry Miller with those of the Communist intellectual. Before he is through, he has managed to involve Joyce, Baudelaire, Flaubert, Spengler, Rimbaud as ancestors of his Bloody-Minded Professors.

Nothing, it would seem to me, could be wider of the mark. The American intellectuals who fell hardest for Communism were men not of avant-garde tastes but of tastes rather safe and conventional. Scratch a Communist today and you will find not an admirer of Rimbaud but of John Greenleaf Whittier, not a student of Eliot but of Carl Sandburg. (I imply here no political judgment of either American.) Communists do not read Joyce or

Flaubert but Jack London and Upton Sinclair. How Mr. Viereck can associate either mandarin or avant-garde literature with Communists or fellow travelers is beyond me, particularly when he seems to be well aware of the fact that the cultural tone they set in the thirties (and there can be little doubt that they *did* set a tone in that period) was deplorable because it was cheap and metallic and strident. Here, as in the Soviet Union, Communist writing and Communist painting and Communist thinking have been corny and vulgar and innocent of any subtlety.

Historically, the fact is that mandarin and avant-garde tastes were a protection against the Communist heresy—though one could hardly say that they strengthened sound political judgment. Pound admired Mussolini and Hitler. Yeats and Wyndham Lewis were fascist fellow travelers for a time, and Eliot's politics have always seemed to me less admirable than his poetry and criticism. Nevertheless, it was the writers who were under the kind of literary influences Viereck dislikes who had the least to do with Communism and who, when they did become involved, made the earliest departures—while those with the minds of accountants lingered on. Compare the political record of Edmund Wilson, Allen Tate, and Wallace Stevens with that of Howard Fast, Dalton Trumbo, and Michael Gold. It is difficult to find Communist names that do not look ludicrous alongside the others.

From a moralist's point of view, it matters hardly at all whether the Communist intellectuals achieved any of their political aims or "affected the course of actual history." Guilt is individual, and a man who is defeated by others in an attempt at crime has as much to answer for everywhere but before the law as the man who is successful. But moralists like Viereck have a yen to strengthen their case by imputing success wherever possible to the devils of their pieces. Viereck talks a lot about Communist infiltration of the New Deal and about the terrible presence of Alger Hiss at Yalta. There is no doubt that Communists did infiltrate the New Deal. It would be surprising indeed if they had not done so. They were part of a world-wide infiltrating movement, and some of them managed to get into

governments policed a great deal more carefully than ours—
Nazi Germany's, for example, and Imperial Japan's. Recent
Congressional investigations may have exaggerated the extent
of infiltration, but there was some, and there is no reason why a
sovereign state should have anywhere within its government
agents of a hostile state. Alger Hiss, Julian Wadleigh, and Carl
Marzani should not have been in the State Department. Lee
Pressman and John Abt should not have been in the Department
of Agriculture.

I have never seen, though, the slightest evidence that Communists in the government had any effect on policy. I have never
been able to think of a single major policy or decision that would
not have been taken if Washington had never let a Communist
past the District of Columbia line. This does not mean that
Communists had no influence at all; it simply means that I, in
common with Senator McCarthy, cannot come up with instances
of their influence. And it means that it is possible to conceive
of the history of the past twenty years as having been exactly
what it was without a trace of Communist influence. Viereck
speaks of Hiss at Yalta, of Hiss at San Francisco when the United
Nations was being organized, of Hiss in the State Department
throughout the war. And Hiss himself has spoken of his work on
the Yalta agreements and at the founding sessions of the U.N.
But the point about Yalta, surely, is not what papers Hiss may
have had a hand in drafting but in what agreements Roosevelt
and Stettinius signed. I cannot see what would have been
different if Hiss had been second secretary at Lima throughout
the conference. Quite conceivably some minor actions may have
been traceable to the presence of Communists and some decisions
affected to a degree by them; someone may have tucked in an
extra locomotive on a shipment to the Soviet Union or have
written a memorandum that influenced General George C.
Marshall's view of events in China. And it is even conceivable
that a balance was somewhere tipped by a Communist's exertion
of minute authority. Only the most cocksure of determinists
could categorically deny such possibilities. But reasonable men
do not spin theories around them.

Viereck prefaces his essay on the Bloody-Minded Professors

with the famous observation of the late Lord Keynes that "Madmen in authority, who hear voices in the air, are distilling their frenzy from some academic scribbler of a few years back." But Lord Keynes' remark applies to some demagogues and not to others and in varying senses and degrees to those of whom it is true. The Communist movement owes a clear and heavy debt to a few intellectuals, all of them long since dead, but how about the fascist movement? One could draw up a list of Hitler's and Mussolini's intellectual obligations, certain of which would be to Marx and Lenin, but I doubt very much if the prophets of fascism were in any sense necessary to the movement. Hitler and Mussolini were, like so many madmen in authority, scribblers themselves, and even if I am mistaken in suspecting that they distilled most of their own frenzies, their ideas were simple enough and rude enough to have been generated in their own rude minds in the event that this had been necessary.

And if a writer or professor stands at the shoulder of every demagogue, where are the mentors of a man like Senator McCarthy? Regrettably, this destroyer comes by a certain amount of the misinformation he spreads through people who qualify or once qualified as intellectuals, but what few ideas he has appear to be strictly his own. The case of Stalin is also instructive. Stalin has recently composed an essay—the eagerness of tyrants to *be* scribblers is quite a phenomenon in itself—that is full of political ideas and analyses, but these, apparently, do not grow out of any reasonable or even unreasonable reading of the sacred texts of Marxism. They seem to grow, on the contrary, directly from the strategic requirements of the situation in which he finds himself at the moment. And this, I think, is where tyrants get most of their ideas. They may plagiarize their betters out of vanity; they may conceal the evils they propose in the language of philosophy; they may indeed be greatly aided by ideas and may manipulate them to secure advantages of power. But, by and large, power has its own logic, which is well within the grasp of even the most sluggish of intellects, and it is a misreading of history to suppose that because some disasters have been abetted by *la trahison des clercs,* all disasters can be understood by some doctrine of *cherchez le clerc.*

* The Dead Red Decade

1 9 5 6

MURRAY KEMPTON's *Part of Our Time: Some Ruins and Monuments of the Thirties* is easily the best essay on American Communism and Communists that anyone has done, and it should rank high in the broader category of books about American life and politics. Kempton is a journalist of formidable talent and versatility. Every phase of life interests him, and he has a novelist's sense of character and change. His work is not without grave defects. He is a word-lover who sometimes lapses into mere wordiness. His insights can be brilliant but his logic can be ragged. He is an easy paradoxer and at times an outrageous generalizer. He is capable of schmalz, particularly when, after the current fashion, he stops writing about men and gets himself all worked up over Man—for example, "Man always hates his last blind alley." On the whole, though, he is a remarkably rewarding writer.

Kempton calls this book an account of "the myth of the nineteen-thirties." He has in mind two myths, one the ridiculous view of the world held by the Communists of the period, the other the ridiculous view of the Communists of the period held today in certain political circles in Washington and certain intellectual circles in New York. Kempton is not the sort to be trapped by his own schemes or held to his own agenda, and he soon finds better things to do than deal with these myths, both of which can be disposed of with a few light applications of reason. In the main, his book is a series of character studies. His "ruins and monuments" are human, and though they are wildly diverse in their humanity, they mostly fall into two categories: people whose resentments led them into the Communist party and people whose resentments didn't. When it is feasible, Kempton arranges his case studies in counterpoint. Thus, he examines together the careers of Lee Pressman, the clever government and C.I.O. lawyer who came closer, perhaps, than any other American to being an iron Bolshevik intellectual in the Lenin mold, and Gardner Jackson, the Boston newspaperman who organized the Sacco-Vanzetti defense thirty years ago, whose subsequent life (including a long period of services as an associate of, among others, Pressman in the C.I.O.) has been one loud protest after another, but who never succumbed to Communism. Paul Robeson, who succumbed, is paired with A. Philip Randolph, the president of the Brotherhood of Sleeping Car Porters, who did not. The chilling story of Elizabeth Bentley, the plain, meek, respectable Vassar girl who became the mistress and slavey of a Soviet spy, and the chilling story of Ann Moos Remington, the hard case from Bennington who made her Dartmouth boy friend, the late William Remington, promise that he would never, never be unfaithful to the Communist party, are told, along with that of Mary Heaton Vorse, a gay and venerable libertarian lady—never a Communist, though once fleetingly associated in matrimony with a man who later became one—of more deeply revolutionary instincts than either Miss Bentley or the former Mrs. Remington. Some of Kempton's exhibits are very rare birds indeed, incomparable in their plumage and altogether unique in their migratory habits, and these are dealt with separately. Such a one is Dr. J. B. Matthews, a son of the Bible Belt and former missionary to the Japanese who in the early thirties became the world's champion fellow traveler, joining Communist fronts as compulsively as a pie-eating champion eats pies, and who is still a titleholder, as the ranking heavyweight informer, the apostates' apostate, the dinner-jacketed tycoon of anti-Communism. Dr. Matthews is beyond compare, and for him Kempton abandons his counterpoint method.

The lives blighted by Communism are Kempton's "ruins," and the others are his "monuments." But it is no simple piety or modish sense of political rectitude that pervades his work. Some of the ruins are admirable and worth revisiting, while some of the monuments got to be monuments only because nature endowed them with an attribute of all statuary, lifelessness. Picking his way through the rubble, Kempton sees much that others have failed to see. Most Communists, he feels, were rebels whose rebelliousness was either defective or arrested, and this notion provides an illumination that no previous critic has offered. Where others, for example, have seen in the proper, fastidious, junior-executive comportment of Alger Hiss a devilishly clever masquerade, Kempton, in the study of the Hiss-Chambers case that opens his book, sees that comportment as the real thing. Hiss had a quarrel with the genteel side of his shabby-genteel upbringing, and he came out second best. He was a revolutionist *manqué*, a man in whom the doctrine's pull was strong but never as strong as the pull of his own past. The friendship with Chambers was the essence of Hiss's revolutionary experience—in fact, it was *the* experience, at least through the years it lasted. Hiss could be a Communist and pass documents and give a party organizer a beat-up Ford, but he could not be a revolutionist except vicariously, through the agency of Whitaker Chambers. This, of course, is a speculation on Kempton's part, but it is a compelling one. How human it would be, Kempton says, for Alger Hiss, granted his Marxism, granted his shabby-genteel background, granted a cozy bureaucratic success he could not reject, to find in Chambers exactly what he found wanting in himself. "Chambers must have sat in the Hiss apartment with all his scars upon him, a lowering symbol of power and experience . . . the image of dedication and adjustment to alienation . . . the image of absolute revolt and the breaking of the bands." As Hiss, in this subjective reconstruction, perceived in Chambers a means of redressing his grievances against himself, Chambers perceived, or imagined he perceived, in Hiss what he himself had lost through winning, years earlier, the argument with his own shabby-genteel environment. In the friendship with Hiss, Kempton thinks, Chambers was already straining toward the respectability and orderliness he now sets such store by. "Could Chambers have seen in Hiss the image of absolute security? . . . [He] seemed to reach out to the Hisses with some of that same passion for the ordinary and the normal which runs through his later odes to simple Americans. . . . [A] whole part of Whittaker Chambers must have come fleeing to Alger Hiss, and this apartment, poor in imagination though it was, must have been . . . as close to peace as this man pursued by the furies could ever get. For, if the Hisses had consciously rejected the sheltered life, they still lived within it."

It is a weakness of Kempton's method that Communism keeps getting reduced to a kind of do-it-yourself psychotherapy. He knows it is more than that, and now and then he says so, but he never really takes the full measure of the idea or the movement. Still, this approach unearths a few ironies, one of which is that so malevolent a conspiracy should have been staffed by men and women of such piddling malevolence, of what (by any rational analysis) would appear to be a strictly third-rate talent for evil. Their boldest dreams were not very far beyond their realities. To have been a Communist bureaucrat rather than a New Deal bureaucrat would, apparently, have been the height of romance for Alger Hiss. The most incendiary remark Chambers could recall Hiss making was "Joe Stalin certainly plays for keeps." A bit of appreciation—by untutored savages in the mission fields, by May Day paraders, or by a claque rounded up on Madison Avenue by George Sokolsky—seems to be all that Dr. Matthews has ever asked. Elizabeth Bentley faltered into Communism while seeking the company that misery craves. She might as easily have found it in the Y.W.C.A. Broadening her horizons, she sought domesticity and ended up a spy queen.

Kempton makes his points most vividly in his consideration of the Communist writers in Hollywood. Communism in Hollywood had no function and no consequences except those that could be bought, outside Hollywood, with the money the movie people kicked in. And this was never very much. By plodding through transcripts of Congressional hearings and by undertaking other research, Kempton has established that all the cash the Communists got from Hollywood would not have kept the *Daily Worker* solvent for six months, and that getting it was a terrible ordeal for the party. Like bankers beefing about their tax burdens, the fifteen-hundred-a-week Gorkis were forever beefing about the high cost of subversion, and in many cases they returned to Americanism heavily in arrears to un-Americanism. Kempton has also made a painfully close study of the output of the Gorkis when their revolutionary ardor was high—films like "Pride of the Marines," "Mama Runs Wild," "They Shall Have Music," "Sorority House," "The Kid from Kokomo," and "Radio City Revels." He found the contents fairly represented by the titles. It might be supposed that men who aspired to liberate humanity from the kingdom of necessity, to strike the shackles from all the slaves of capitalism, would be violently in revolt against a fate that compelled them (or did it? Who said they had to work in Hollywood?) to expend their talent on such stuff. They were in revolt, but not aggressively so. The Hollywood Communists, Kempton says, "sounded passionate in their protest against Hitler or Franco or Tom Girdler and countless other distant devils. But they ceased very soon to be passionate in their protest against Hollywood." When they learned that Budd Schulberg was saying nasty things about the industry in "What Makes Sammy Run?," their ideologues descended on him and tried to talk him out of allowing the book to be published, because they regarded it as an attack on a great folk art. Schulberg found this argument unconvincing and quit the party. The truth is that there were more affinities between Hollywood and Communism than were ever dreamed of by Congressional investigators. Both made the same demands on artists—"the presentation of an image of the common man so . . . hyperbolic and so contrived as to be totally removed from reality. . . . The slogans, the sweeping formulae, the superficial clangor of Communist culture had a certain fashion in Hollywood precisely because they were two-dimensional appeals to a two-dimensional community." In the end, the industry turned out to have the greater vitality. "The Hollywood Communists . . . were unable to corrupt them, and they got rich fabricating empty banalities to fit Hollywood's idea of life in America."

In the course of this survey, Kempton goes in some detail into the history of three trade unions: the National Maritime Union, the Brotherhood of Sleeping Car Porters, and the United Automobile Workers. His commentaries must be among the most readable and instructive ones ever written on American trade unionism, a subject that normally attracts only the most cloddish sort of researchers. Of these three organizations, only the National Maritime Union was ever controlled by Communists. The two others were given a good deal of trouble by them but were never captured. Many of the principal leaders of the N.M.U. had at one time been members of the party. When the moment came, however, for them to choose between their union and their party, the best of them, with hardly a trace of anguish, chose the union. Kempton makes the point that these labor men were almost the only American Communists whose quarrel with society was clearly distinguishable from their quarrel with themselves. Doubtless there were some Communists whose alienation had similar causes, who were in rebellion against the realities of life around them and not simply in flight from reality, but most American Communists, according to Kempton, had a strong sense of their own guilt and only a feeble awareness of any evil in the economic system. If his theory is sound, it is politically encouraging, for it suggests that those who become Communists out of hunger, actual or metaphorical, can easily put Communism aside. When the hunger of the Maritime leaders "was appeased and they were no longer alienated, they departed with only a backward glance." It has become fashionable lately to say that Communism is a malady of the spirit and will not be cured by Marshall Plans, Point Four programs, and military alliances. Our experience with Communists in this country is often cited in defense of this view. Kempton's investigation suggests that the meaningful kind of Communism, the kind that has real consequences in the real world, is a malady of society and can be socially dealt with.

✳ On Political Sophistication

1 9 6 1

POLITICS, Bismarck is said to have said, is the art of the possible. Nothing, on the one hand, could be more obvious; nothing, on the other, could be closer to the height of sophistication. There is, after all, no art of the impossible, and there are other disciplines—engineering, for example—in which the essential calculations are of feasibility. Still, Bismarck struck at the heart of the matter. The essence of political judgment is the appraisal of potentials. The true political sophisticate knows what the options are and how much of what is desirable is attainable. (If his gift is of the highest order, he knows how much of what is attainable is desirable.) He knows which tensions can be withstood and which are unendurable. He knows that the magnitude of commitments must be matched by the magnitude of available power.

In politics, sophistication has nothing to do with chic or refinement or the *haut monde*. It is not a finish or a façade; it is a supporting member, part of the foundation. It can be accompanied by coarseness of mind and manner. Up to a point, it is a morally and intellectually neutral quality. Up to a point, Joseph Stalin and Joseph McCarthy shared it with Mahatma Gandhi and Woodrow Wilson. It is not in all cases required for success, and success is not invariably the lot of those who possess it. Dwight Eisenhower lacked it and got along splendidly. Robert A. Taft had it in abundance and lost all the big games. In general, though, the memorable figures are the astute reckoners of the possibilities, and the most memorable are those who have made the boldest reckonings and been proved right—those, that is to say, who have seen and sought the outermost limits of the realm of the possible, Franklin D. Roosevelt was such a one. John F. Kennedy gives promise of being another. Our age has also been rich in men who have seen possibilities one wishes they had been blind to—Lenin at the Finland Station, Hitler in Munich, Mao Tse-tung in the marshes with the Eighth Route Army.

Conservatives are, by and large, fonder than liberals and radicals of Bismarck's dictum, and they habitually consign all idealists and apostles of change to the ranks of the unsophisticated. In this, they are gravely mistaken. There are sophisticated idealists, and there are naïve conservatives. The Reverend Martin Luther King is an example of the first, the Reverend Barry Goldwater of the second. The Alabama pastor had a large vision of what might be attainable through militant nonviolence, and he is today the effective leader and symbol of an exceedingly influential movement in American life. The Arizona pastor may get the Republican nomination in 1964, but only if at convention time the Republican party is resigned to a defeat of great magnitude; he is unlikely in any event to have a significant impact on our society, for he is an atrocious judge of the options of leadership in an industrial society in the twentieth century. Indeed, he will not so much as address himself to the problem. Connoisseurs of political naïveté would be hard put to pick up a choicer piece than this—from *Conscience of a Conservative:* "The principles on which the Conservative position is based have been established by a process that has nothing to do with the social, economic, and political landscape that changes from decade to decade and from century to century." A man can be both far out and sophisticated—but not far out of this world and this century.

The politician fearful of having sins of omission charged to his account will take refuge in the doctrine that politics is the art of the possible, which in folk wisdom may be translated as, "Don't bite off more than you can chew." The political sophisticate honors this injunction and knows of instances in which too large a bite or too few teeth has led to grief. The late John Foster Dulles was in many respects a great public servant, but he was in certain crucial ways a most unsophisticated diplomat. He confused preachment with power. He everlastingly proposed more than he was able to dispose. He talked of "liberation" of the captive nations as though it could be accomplished by the letting of rhetoric rather than by the letting of blood. He sought to form impregnable alliances in the Far East and in the Middle East, and he got the signatures of the head men on paper. Paper turned out to be what the alliances were made of. He was operating outside the realm of the possible; he had bitten off more than he could chew. But this is no greater a failing than its corollary, which is underestimation of masticatory and digestive capacity. The ranks of the forgotten and the dishonored are filled with those who have not seen far enough. The name of Neville Chamberlain would be celebrated today if he had had Winston Churchill's sense of how much was within the realm of the possible for the British people. The political sophisticate, having acknowledged the supreme unwisdom of biting off more than you can chew, would also point out that there can be folly and misery in biting off less than you can chew.

Power can serve good, bad, or indifferent ends, and most political men must now and then traffic in ideas and principles. Where ideas are involved, another and more traditional aspect of sophistication—taste, intellectual discrimination, cultivation— becomes relevant. The Messrs. Stalin and McCarthy can be described as political sophisticates only because principles did not compete with one another in their closed universes. The Russian accepted Marxist dogma as a completed science. The American was cheerfully free of any concern about the validity of ideas. There are many less lustrous figures of high sophistication who are simply beyond ideology. The United States Congress has many skillful, wily, and knowing men whose basic notions of justice, truth, and beauty are communicated to them directly from the grass roots toward which their ears are always bent. But most men recognize a conflict of principles, and most men wish to believe that there is a correspondence between their own ideology and virtue. In free societies, participants in the political process may shop for remedies in a market that contains a staggering variety of them—cunningly advertised, as a rule, and gaudily packaged. It seems to me that there are two equally sophisticated approaches to political ideas. One may be taken by the man who feels a call to have an early and direct impact

—a sitting President, let us say, or almost any serious officeholder or office seeker. The other may be taken by a man who, while aware that mere sermonizing is unlikely to deflect human evil, knows what power there can be in the repeated assertion and exemplification of principle. Both types must be concerned with what is within the realm of the possible, but the realm of the possible is within the realm of time, a dimension that alters perspectives. It was not Mr. Dulles' zeal for liberation of the satellites that revealed a lack of sophistication; the principle is noble and probably essential to the foreign policy of the Western powers. His naïveté was revealed by his effort to make it a programmatic aim of the American government in 1953 and 1954. Similarly, Senator Goldwater seems naïve not because his ideas lack dignity, moral worth, or even practicability, but because the energies he expends for their advancement are expended within the framework of operative power, which in his time will offer them no hospitality. Norman Thomas, the Socialist leader, has been vastly more sophisticated. He has spent a lifetime outside the framework of operative power, where reason, eloquence, and force of character have a chance, and his influence over the long run has probably been as great as that of Senators Styles Bridges and Everett McKinley Dirksen, in tandem.

The sophisticate, when he deals with political ideas, must do more than take moral soundings and measure the currents of power. There are ideas that positively ooze goodness and are altogether within the realm of the possible, yet are unacceptable on the grounds that their consequences would be awful. Unilateral nuclear disarmament, as a case in point, is surely an attainable goal. It has attracted some highly practical and sophisticated politicians in England, and the anxieties that have bred the clamor for it there are bound to mount on this side of the Atlantic. Its appeal is to the very best instincts. There are arguments in its favor plausible enough to commend themselves to Bertrand Russell, surely one of the most sophisticated men of our century. Its fatal programmatic weakness, which one supposes would have been spotted by a younger Lord Russell, is that it ignores the basic facts of power. Nations of either malign

or benign intent use superior power for whatever leverage they
can gain with it. The Soviet Union does it; we do it, when we
can. If Nation A were to disarm totally in advance of Nation B,
Nation B's power would be augmented by a factor of infinity.
To expect restraint and forbearance on the part of Nation B
would be to expect what all of human experience tells us we
have no right to expect. In considering such a proposition as
unilateral nuclear disarmament, the Westerner with a ripened
political mind would ask himself whether, if the shoe were on
the other foot and it were the Soviets who proposed to divest
themselves of power, the West would seek no gain whatever from
the absolute superiority it would thereby be accorded. Gullibility
may be an amiable failing in some departments of life. The
sucker may be afflicted by nothing but an excess of faith, hope,
and charity, and surely there are worse things than that. Political
gullibility has political consequences, which can be disastrous.
The specter that haunts several continents today—militant international communism, supported by intercontinental ballistic
missiles with atomic warheads—is to a large degree founded upon
the gullibility of men and women of irreproachable social morality and a high level of intellectual sophistication. The Soviet
Union may by now have schooled a bureaucracy of time-serving,
case-hardened bureaucrats, but among those who brought the
bureaucracy into being were many men of intelligence and of a
dedication that was not in itself despicable. Outside the Soviet
Union, in the decades since the Russian Revolution, communism
has advanced not by the efforts of the worst elements in society
but, more often than not, by those who have been close to the
best—if our measure of the best registers generosity of spirit and
an awareness of existing evils. Their weakness, which helped
to create a form of strength that imperils freedom, was generally
a weakness of the critical faculties. They would not give the
remedies that attracted them the same hard scrutiny they gave
to the ills they were eager to cure. They could not bring to their
own rebellion the detachment with which they viewed the institutions they judged to be oppressive. This seems always the tragedy
of political passion—that it is the enemy of a tempering sophisti-

cation. From the appearance of things at the moment, a similar tragedy is in the making where the nationalist fevers are running high in Latin America and in Africa.

It is a curious feature of politics that it corrodes sophistication even where passions are not deeply engaged. There is the case of Bertrand Russell, the greatest of modern skeptics and rationalists. There is the case of Jean-Paul Sartre, a living monument to shrewdness, who has propounded more childish nonsense about politics in the last decade than any other European except his close associate, Simone de Beauvoir, a great sophisticate in her own right, who has managed to misconstrue, in lengthy books, not only the problems of Europe, but those of the United States and China as well. And there is our own Ezra Pound, the most cosmopolitan of Americans, learned, tough-minded, and often breath-taking in his critical insights—but a patsy for Benito Mussolini and a great clutch of lesser scoundrels. Somehow an intimate knowledge of human folly and a study of its myriad manifestations through the ages is not enough to shield them from political folly and from what the late George Orwell liked to call the "smelly little orthodoxies" that have so often enlisted their sympathies and their talents.

Part of the difficulty, I think, is that politics, like love, appears to invite, even demand, involvement, passionate or otherwise. The sophisticated man can look upon the arts as something to be enjoyed, appraised, improved by, and indulged in if the consequences seem likely to be valuable to himself or anyone else. Politics calls for meddling as a ripe peach calls for eating—particularly, of course, in a free society, and most particularly in a time of crisis. In the twenties, Walter Lippmann could give the political sophisticate a simple credo that had detachment and observation at its core. "The mature man," he wrote, "would take the world as it comes and remain within himself quite unperturbed. And so, whether he saw the thing as comedy, or high tragedy, or plain farce, he would affirm that it is what it is, and that the wise man can enjoy it." Lippmann is the dean of sophisticates today, but the world of his seventies is a world too anguished and too imperiled for him to commend it as an entertaining spectacle. Yet there is, it seems to me, a saving value in

sophistication that can grow with detachment and should even
be able to survive involvement. An affair with a political idea or
a political leader may resemble a love affair, but there is no sound
reason why a man should play the game according to the same
rules. No doctrine must be embraced simply for being its own
dear self. There is nothing immoral or unfaithful in discarding
an idea that has lost its youthful charm. There is nothing fickle
in carrying on with several ideas at the same time. Ideas do not
demand to be adored; they demand to be studied and applied
when it is useful to apply them. Leaders have no claim upon our
loyalty or affection except as they earn it from day to day. It is
for them and not for their followers to remain constant. Politics
is the art of the possible, and the possible is always in flux.

Perhaps the greatest of all political sophisticates was the
Emperor Marcus Aurelius Antoninus, who reigned, according to
Gibbon, in "the period in the history of the world during which
the condition of the human race was most happy and prosperous.
. . . The vast extent of the Roman Empire was governed by
absolute power, under the guidance of virtue and wisdom. The
armies were restrained by four successive emperors, whose
characters and authority commanded involuntary respect . . .
who delighted in the image of liberty and were pleased with
considering themselves the accountable ministers of the law."
Marcus Aurelius "was severe to himself, indulgent to the
imperfections of others, just and beneficent to all mankind.
. . . War he detested as the disgrace and calamity of human
nature, but when the necessity of a just defense called upon him
to take up arms, he readily exposed his person to eight winter
campaigns on the frozen banks of the Danube, the severity of
which was at last fatal. . . ." In an army camp, he wrote his
great *Meditations,* which contains a sophisticate's credo that is
unlikely ever to call for revision:

Make for thyself a definition or description of the thing which is presented to thee, so as to see distinctly what kind of thing it is in its
substance, in its nudity, in its complete entirety, and tell thyself its
proper name, and the names of the things of which it has been compounded and into which it will be resolved. For nothing is so productive of elevation of mind as to be able to examine methodically and

truly every object which is presented to thee in life, and always to look at things so as to see at the same time what kind of universe this is, and what kind of use everything performs in it, and what value everything has with reference to the whole, and what with reference to man, who is a citizen of the highest city, of which all other cities are like families; what each thing is and of what it is composed, and how long it is the nature of this thing to endure which now makes an impression on me.